"The challenge for those writing a book on this topic is negotiating the question of breadth and depth. How broad should it be, and how deep can one go without risking a superficial overview or selective analysis? To the author's credit he dexterously steers through these challenges and provides us with a work that engages and interacts with the range and diversity of the living realities of the Christian faith in various regions of the world, opening up entryways to wonder at the global expressions of Christianity."

J. Jayakiran Sebastian, dean and H. George Anderson Professor of Mission and Cultures, Lutheran Theological Seminary at Philadelphia

"Derek Cooper's *Introduction to World Christian History* is a welcome contribution to the field. This accessible and informative historical narrative introduces the reader to the broad, diverse and far-reaching story of Christianity as it 'blows where it wills' from the first through the twenty-first century. In the end, the reader is left with little doubt that Christianity was and is a worldwide movement."

Jennifer Powell McNutt, associate professor of theology and history of Christianity, Wheaton College

"A welcome addition to the ever-expanding scholarship in the field of world Christianity studies, Derek Cooper's book helps to rewrite our traditional Western understanding of church history and course-correct away from North Atlantic–centrism. Cooper gently leads us away from our particular tendencies to see and tell only our own stories toward a broader canvas of the 'great cloud of witnesses' that came before us and has not had its time in the spotlight."

Allen Yeh, associate professor of intercultural studies and missiology, Cook School of Intercultural Studies, Biola University

"Derek Cooper's helpful volume reminds us that the global complexity of Christianity today is the fruit of a Christian past that is equally multifaceted and complex. His fresh rendering of that past emphasizes overlooked histories of Christians in Africa, Asia and other regions of the world, and downplays some familiar tales from the West that now seem quite parochial when viewed in global perspective. Cooper's kaleidoscopic account provides many different angles from which to view Christian similarities and differences, and readers will be enriched by the breadth and magnanimity of his presentation."

Douglas Jacobsen, author of *Global Gospel*

"It is widely known that today the majority of Christians live in Africa, Asia and Latin America. Less appreciated is Christianity's thriving presence in these locations for many centuries. In this book Cooper reintroduces us to the global story of Christianity— relocating the center of the Christian narrative to the Global South, joining an emerging chorus of scholars who are challenging the status quo of Christianity as a Western religion."

Todd M. Johnson, associate professor of global Christianity, Gordon-Conwell Theological Seminary

D1205904

Introduction to
World Christian
History

DEREK COOPER

IVP Academic
An imprint of InterVarsity Press
Downers Grove, Illinois

InterVarsity Press
P.O. Box 1400, Downers Grove, IL 60515-1426
ivpress.com
email@ivpress.com

InterVarsity Press® is the book-publishing division of InterVarsity Christian Fellowship/USA®, a movement of students and faculty active on campus at hundreds of universities, colleges and schools of nursing in the United States of America, and a member movement of the International Fellowship of Evangelical Students. For information about local and regional activities, visit intervarsity.org.

All Scripture quotations, unless otherwise indicated, are taken from THE HOLY BIBLE, NEW INTERNATIONAL VERSION®, NIV® Copyright © 1973, 1978, 1984, 2011 by Biblica, Inc.™ Used by permission. All rights reserved worldwide.

Cover design: Cindy Kiple
Interior design: Beth McGill
Images: canvas texture: rusm/iStockphoto
*   old map: katatonia82/iStockphoto*

ISBN 978-0-8308-4088-5 (print)
ISBN 978-0-8308-9906-7 (digital)

Printed in the United States of America ∞

Library of Congress Cataloging-in-Publication Data

Names: Cooper, Derek, 1978- author.
Title: Introduction to world Christian history / Derek Cooper.
Description: Downers Grove : InterVarsity Press, 2016. | Includes index.
Identifiers: LCCN 2016010690 (print) | LCCN 2016011630 (ebook) | ISBN
* 9780830840885 (pbk. : alk. paper) | ISBN 9780830899067 (eBook)*
Subjects: LCSH: Church history.
Classification: LCC BR145.3 .C66 2016 (print) | LCC BR145.3 (ebook) | DDC
* 270--dc23*
LC record available at http://lccn.loc.gov/2016010690

P	25	24	23	22	21	20	19	18	17	16	15	14	13	12	11	10	9	8	7	6	5	4	3	2	1
Y	38	37	36	35	34	33	32	31	30	29	28	27	26	25	24	23	22	21	20	19	18	17	16		

To our friends and hosts at 하늘 학교 (Haneul Hakyo) in South Korea.

Thanks for the wonderful memories.

CONTENTS

ACKNOWLEDGMENTS

There are many people who have contributed to this book. First, I would like to thank the wonderful staff at InterVarsity Press. Dan Reid was the first to believe in this project, and he offered excellent feedback in the early stages. David McNutt was instrumental in the last stages. He improved the focus of this work and did a great job overseeing its completion. Other staff at Inter-Varsity Press have also positively impacted this book.

Second, I would like to express my gratitude to the readers of this book in its various stages. This includes the anonymous readers provided by Inter-Varsity Press as well as many scholars who graciously took time out of their busy schedules to read portions of the manuscript. This includes Drs. David Grafton, Douglas Jacobsen, Frank James, Martin Lohrmann, Nelson Rivera, J. Jayakiran Sebastian, Joe Thomas and Amos Yong. Their comments were incisive, perceptive and greatly appreciated. You all made this book much better.

Third, I am grateful to the library staff at Biblical Theological Seminary. Denise Baum and Lydia Putnam processed countless Inter-Library Loans during the writing of this project. Thank you for all of your help.

Fourth, I would be remiss if I did not thank all of the students in my World Christian History courses over the years at Biblical Theological Seminary. Even though so much of the material we discussed each week was brand new, you were such good sports—even when I would occasionally use terms like *Oriental Orthodox, Miaphysite* and *One-Nature Christians* interchangeably in the same sentence!

Fifth, thanks go to my family's hosts in South Korea during the summer and fall of 2013: Dream Church and Haneul Hakyo under the guidance of Rev. Hyunjun Park. This church and school generously supported my family as my wife and I taught their eager students and our children gained new friends. The earliest stages of this book were undertaken on the school's campus, in a sleepy town near the border with North Korea.

Finally, my limitless gratitude goes to my wife, Barb, and our three children: Gabriela, Mia and Eli. You all make my life so much richer, and I am thankful for your love and support. We are co-laborers in this book. As I occasionally worked long nights and traveled the globe to visit some of the places discussed in this work, you were always with me in spirit. You all are the best!

CHRISTIANITY AS A WORLD RELIGION

In just over 100 years, the map of world Christianity has changed almost out of recognition. In 1900, it is estimated that 70 percent of all Christians were to be found in Europe . . . whereas . . . by 2025 Africa and Latin America will be vying with one another to claim the most Christians, having about a quarter each of the world's Christian population.

SEBASTIAN KIM AND KIRSTEEN KIM,
CHRISTIANITY AS A WORLD RELIGION

WE ARE NOT THE CENTER OF THE WORLD

When the culturally savvy Catholic missionary Matteo Ricci arrived in China in the late 1500s, he developed two main missionary strategies. The first, based on largely unsuccessful European interactions with the Chinese, deemphasized the missionary agenda. The learned Ricci perfected the Chinese language, mastered its literature and lauded Chinese culture. He even sported a flowing beard and donned the clothes of the educated elite. Ricci's second strategy sought to win the hearts of the Chinese by demonstrating skill in and knowledge about all things Western. He greatly impressed Chinese officials by teaching the up-and-coming subjects of mathematics and astronomy, the rudiments of which would launch European intellectuals like Galileo Galilei and Johannes Kepler toward scientific discovery in the next century. Ricci also illustrated his mapmaking skills, the results of which astonished the Chinese: Shockingly, it appeared, China was not the center of the world.[1]

Although I possess no mapmaking skills and am an inveterate failure in mathematics and science, it is my vocation to teach Christians that the world they live in is not the center of the universe. This is a consistently difficult task. Despite the fact that numerous studies in the past several decades have demonstrated that the West does not occupy the center stage of the Christian drama—nor will it likely in the immediate future—many Christians still brush aside non-Western forms of Christianity as peripheral to the main story of what God is doing in the world. We in the West have long assumed that we are the leading characters in the story of the church, and we are not at all disposed to begin taking on supporting roles. As one scholar notes, however, "it is becoming clearer that Christianity never was, and never will be, simply a Western faith."[2]

THE PURPOSE OF THIS BOOK

The purpose of this book is to provide an overview of *world* Christian history. The term *world* (or *global*) Christian history is a relatively new one.[3] It is meant to replace the archaic word *Christendom*, which many still associate with Western colonization and imperialism. As historian of China Daniel Bays explains, "From being 'Christendom,' the religion mainly of the North and West, Christianity has become a religion of the East and South."[4] To reflect the geographic shift from the North and West to the East and South, scholars have increasingly used the adjectives *world* or *global* to describe Christian history. I have mostly adopted such terminology in this book, though I will still use the words *world, global* and *church* history interchangeably for the sake of simplicity.

Who is instrumental in this field of research? Kenneth Latourette, Andrew Walls, Lamin Sanneh, Lesslie Newbigin, Philip Jenkins and Dana Robert, to name only a select group, are some of the leading scholars of

---

[1]Samuel Moffett, *A History of Christianity in Asia*, vol. 2, *1500–1900* (Maryknoll, NY: Orbis, 2005), 108.

[2]Dyron Daughrity, *The Changing World of Christianity: The Global History of a Borderless Religion* (New York: Peter Lang, 2010), 227.

[3]There is a debate whether the term *world* Christian history means the same thing as *global* Christian history, or if the latter is a démodé way to designate Western-influenced Christendom in non-Western regions. See Lamin Sanneh, *Whose Religion Is Christianity? The Gospel Beyond the West* (Grand Rapids: Eerdmans, 2003), 22-24.

[4]Daniel Bays, *A New History of Christianity in China* (Oxford: Wiley-Blackwell, 2011), 205.

world Christianity.[5] Despite a warm reception among scholars, many churches and theological schools are slow to embrace their findings— perhaps out of fear, perhaps out of ignorance. Whatever the reason, the phenomenon reminds me of the story of the Portuguese Jesuit Jerónimo Lobo, who arrived in Africa with other priests upon invitation from the Ethiopian king in 1625. Coming most recently from Goa in India, Lobo was keen to establish a Roman Catholic presence in Ethiopia. As he gazed upon the state of the Ethiopian Church, Lobo marveled at how the Ethiopian (Orthodox) Christians, though tracing their theological heritage all the way back to the first century, were "possessed with a strange notion that they [were] the only true Christians in the world."[6]

Lobo's observation does not apply only to Ethiopians of yesteryear or churches of today. It applies to Christians in various places, and especially in the West. Many in the church of the West assume that we are the only real Christians in the world. We sometimes base this assumption on the historically feeble premise that Christianity originated in the West and that Western missionaries doled out the Christian faith to the rest of the world. This assumption, though reflecting a glimmer of truth, does not satisfy the complete historical record. Nor does it do justice to the men and women outside of the West who have greatly contributed to Christian doctrine and practice. Despite its close connection to the West today, Christianity has always been a global and ethnically diverse religion. The time has come for the church to recognize that its history extends far beyond the Western hemisphere. The church was planted in Asia, nurtured in Africa and harvested worldwide.

How the Story Is Told

To reorient ourselves to the history of world Christianity, geography and chronology will be our guides. The United Nations geoscheme of nations, though not universally recognized and not without its limitations, will

---

[5]See, for instance, Andrew Walls, *The Missionary Movement in Christian History: Studies in the Transmission of Faith* (Maryknoll, NY: Orbis, 1996); Lamin Sanneh, *Translating the Message: The Missionary Impact on Culture* (Maryknoll, NY: Orbis, 1989); Lesslie Newbigin, *The Gospel in a Pluralist Society* (Grand Rapids: Eerdmans, 1989); Philip Jenkins, *The Next Christendom: The Coming of Global Christianity* (Oxford: Oxford University Press, 2002); and Dana Robert, *How Christianity Became a World Religion* (Oxford: Wiley-Blackwell, 2009).

[6]Jerónimo Lobo, *A Voyage to Abyssinia*, ed. Joel Gold (New Haven, CT: Yale University Press, 1985), 4.

provide parameters for each chapter. (These regions are defined in appendix one.) In each chapter I will focus on one of these geoscheme of nations before providing an overview of their subregions, followed by a more detailed examination of one or two locales from that subregion. Specific locales, when enough archaeological and documentary evidence exists, have been selected because they are either historically neglected or because they are especially influential in the development of world Christianity. Because we are following the UN geoscheme, this means that some regions that otherwise deserve more commentary from specific locales are required to share the spotlight with historically ignored areas.

Why use the United Nations geoscheme of nations, and why retell the history of Christianity based on geography? Tackling the second part of this question first, I must stress that geography is not the only consideration when narrating the history of Christianity in this book. Chronology is just as important. But to answer a question with a question, why not tell the history of the church from a geographic perspective? Why should chronology always take precedence over geography? After all, the emphasis on *when* things happened more than on *where* things happened has allowed many authors to gloss over whole regions of the worldwide church. As the celebrated church historian Robert Louis Wilken wrote in his survey of early global Christianity, "Geography gives the clearest picture."[7] I concur.

As far as the UN geoscheme is concerned, it provides an objective and, for the most part, theologically neutral way to describe *where* the church developed. As mentioned earlier, it's not a perfect schema but perhaps the only way we are going to break out of the mold of Eurocentric history writing is by leveling the playing field. Geographically sensitive writing will allow us to achieve this goal until (if ever) we find ourselves able to strike a balance among the regions of the world when it comes to telling the grand narrative of Christianity.

In addition to utilizing the UN geoscheme, I will frequently use current names of countries to describe past events. Thus, rather than referring to the large region in Western Europe as Gallia Lugdunensis (the ancient name the Romans gave to the province), I will typically refer to it as "modern France" or

---

[7]Robert Louis Wilken, *The First Thousand Years: A Global History of Christianity* (New Haven, CT: Yale University Press, 2012), 355.

"what is now France," since most of us are unfamiliar with such ancient designations of world regions. Although this strategy is historically inaccurate, it allows us to get a better sense of the scope of world Christianity. It is simply too cumbersome and too confusing to open the revolving door of historical terms that different people groups have used to refer to the same general location. In a similar way I will use the terms *Africa, Asia, Europe* and so on when referring to specific regions of the world in full awareness that such terms sometimes belie modern sensibilities. This strategy, too, is adopted for the benefit of the reader.

We will begin our study of world Christian history by tracing the spread of the Christian faith from what the United Nations schema calls "Western Asia." We will discover how the tiny religion of Christianity was catapulted into all directions of the world—eastward toward Iraq, southward toward Egypt, northward toward Turkey and westward toward Italy. We will learn that Europe was originally one piece of the Christian puzzle, and that its later dominance was perhaps more a matter of default than design. As historian Philip Jenkins provocatively writes:

> For most of its history, Christianity was a tricontinental religion, with powerful representation in Europe, Africa, and Asia, and this was true into the fourteenth century. Christianity became predominantly European not because this continent had any obvious affinity for that faith, but by default: Europe was the continent where [Christianity] was not destroyed. Matters could easily have developed differently.[8]

The Western church came to monopolize Christianity. Long accustomed to mixing politics with religion, Westerners mistook the mandate to evangelize the world for carte blanche to build a global empire with Western franchises. Despite ongoing challenges, however, indigenous Christianity in the East and in the South never completely died out. The brave Christians in these parts have eked out an existence for centuries, holding their breath under water until the arrival of the modern era.

Not only does this book differ from others by adopting the UN geoscheme of nations to demarcate geographic borders, but I also depart from

---

[8]Philip Jenkins, *The Lost History of Christianity: The Thousand-Year Golden Age of the Church in the Middle East, Africa, and Asia—and How It Died* (New York: HarperOne, 2008), 3.

most books in the way I periodize church history. In short, I divide Christian history into three fluid periods: (1) the first to the seventh centuries, (2) the eighth to the fourteenth centuries, and (3) the fifteenth to the twenty-first centuries. Countless scholars, past and present, have designated the fourth century as a watershed century in the history of Christianity. They have done so with good reason. Among many others, three significant events occurred in the fourth century: the Roman coemperors Constantine and Licinius legalized Christianity, Constantine converted to Christianity and the Council of Nicaea, the first gathering of the "worldwide" church, convened. Due to events like these, many scholars have divided histories of the church from the first to the fourth centuries.

I depart from this venerable tradition for four reasons. First, to state the obvious, Christianity never coexisted with the Roman Empire. According to Dana Robert, "the eastward spread of Christianity was so extensive that the fourth-century Persian empire contained as high a percentage of Christians as the Roman."[9] This is exactly as it should be. Christianity never aspired to such a limited sphere of influence as the Roman Empire. Christianity, from its earliest days, has nurtured a grander vision that encompasses all political empires and all people groups. It's true that Constantine put Christianity on a different trajectory, but let's not ascribe too much influence to Constantine. After all, he tolerated various forms of Christian Arianism—and was baptized by perhaps the most notorious Arian bishop alive—and his theology died with the death of his sons. Second, even after the Roman Empire formally recognized Christianity, it still persecuted many different sectors of the church, including East Syrians, Gnostics and West Syrians (see the glossary in appendix two for unfamiliar terms).

Second, the patronization of Christianity in the Roman Empire beginning in the fourth century negatively impacted Christians living under the Persian Empire since Persian rulers persecuted Christians under the notion that they were conspiring with the Romans. If anything, therefore, the legal recognition of Christianity in the Roman Empire made adherence to Christianity dangerous to non-Chalcedonians, that is, those who did not adopt the state-enforced theology of the East Roman Empire. Third, the

---

[9]Dana Robert, *Christian Mission: How Christianity Became a World Religion* (Oxford: Wiley-Blackwell, 2009), 8.

focus on Constantine's conversion to Christianity as a watershed event suggests that Constantine was the second Savior of the church. It also obfuscates the fact that Constantine's Arian sons marginalized orthodox Christianity and that Emperor Julian dedicated the entirety of his reign to reviving paganism and destabilizing Christianity. Finally, despite the significance of the Council of Nicaea in 325, this first of the "ecumenical councils" never represented the whole church. On the contrary, it reflected a patina of universality, as Christians from a variety of other ethnic and theological backgrounds were not invited or did not participate.

I have opted to extend the early history of Christianity beyond the fourth to the seventh century. This is not without some precedent. In the classic book *Mohammad and Charlemagne*, Belgian historian Henri Pirenne argued, in part, that classic civilization did not die out until around the seventh century. As he concluded in his posthumous classic, "The Germanic [or barbarian] invasions destroyed neither the Mediterranean unity of the ancient world, nor what may be regarded as the truly essential features of the Roman culture.... The cause of the break with the tradition of antiquity was the rapid and unexpected advance of Islam. The result of this advance was the final separation of East from West, and the end of the Mediterranean unity."[10] Although no shortage of subsequent scholars have intensely debated this thesis and offered numerous modifications,[11] there's no doubt that Islam completely changed the trajectory of Christianity in the regions where Islam spread. This change was gradual, of course, but it began in the seventh century. Although at this early time in its history Islam was a regional religio-political movement composed of Arabs for Arabs, Islam was on the ascendancy. In fact, argues historian of Arab antiquity Sydney Griffith, "perhaps 50 percent of the world's confessing Christians from the mid-seventh century [onward] . . . found themselves living under Muslim rule."[12] Recognizing how much Islam affected Christianity's development, how could this scarcely believable percentage not alter the way we think about

[10]Henri Pirenne, *Mohammad and Charlemagne* (London: Routledge, 1958), 284.
[11]See especially the following: Richard Hodges and David Whitehouse, *Mohammad, Charlemagne and the Origins of Europe: Archaeology and the Pirenne Thesis* (London: Gerald Duckworth & Co., 1983); and Emmet Scott, *Mohammad and Charlemagne Revisited: The History of a Controversy* (Nashville: New English Review, 2012).
[12]Sydney Griffith, *The Church in the Shadow of the Mosque: Christians and Muslims in the World of Islam* (Princeton, NJ: Princeton University Press, 2008), 11.

watershed periods in Christianity? Over the next several centuries Islam—in all of its ethnic, political and religious variety—came to completely transform the landscape of Africa, Asia and, to an extent, Europe. Unlike Buddhism, Hinduism, Judaism or any other major world religion, Islam has continued to wrestle with its cousin Christianity. Historically, it has not always been clear who has the upper hand, but there is no doubt that Islam's emergence in the seventh century began to seriously shift the plates of global Christianity. To be blunt, Muhammad is simply more important historically than Constantine. To be sure, it's not completely fair to boil down a complete era of periodization to one person, but if we must, I am inclined to concede Muhammad's significance over Constantine's, even when it comes to the history of Christianity.

Next, rather than dividing the latter history of Christianity from the sixteenth century onward, I have followed a model set in a recent three-volume global history of the church by allowing the fifteenth century to demarcate the next phase of worldwide Christianity.[13] As significant as the European Reformations of the sixteenth century were for the emergence of a new theological tradition, Protestantism did not impact the *global* church for hundreds of years. For quite a while, indeed for centuries, Protestantism was essentially an intramural affair among Europeans (and Northern Americans). Protestantism was in a zero-sum match with European Catholicism, but not really with non-Europeans. Protestant missions to Africa, Asia and Oceania, for instance, did not begin in full force until the nineteenth and twentieth centuries—hundreds of years after Catholic missions had already rounded the globe and evangelized much of the known world. Notwithstanding the European Reformations' importance over time, it was the explorations and discoveries of Portuguese and Spanish explorers such as Vasco de Gama, Ferdinand Magellan and Christopher Columbus that immediately, though in many ways negatively, affected global Christianity. The voyages that these *conquistadores católicos* (Catholic conquistadors) made in the late fifteenth century have arguably shaped the history of Christianity more than any other event in the second millennium. Likewise, from the East, the conquering of much of the Orthodox Christian world at the hands of Ottoman (Muslim) Turks completely reconfigured the religious makeup of parts of Asia and Europe. The

---

[13]The first in this volume is Dale Irvin and Scott Sunquist, *History of the World Christian Movement*, vol. 1, *Earliest Christianity to 1453* (Maryknoll, NY: Orbis, 2001).

official fall of Constantinople in 1453 is just one prominent example of this reality. All in all, such events underscore that the fifteenth century serves as an important period of transition in the history of global Christianity, not the sixteenth century.

(Not) Defining Christianity

In this book I do not attempt to arbitrate among rival articulations of what it means to be a Christian. Although it might be preferable to use something like the Apostles' or Nicene Creed to fence in Christian orthodoxy from heresy, this book allows those who claim to be Christians to run wild with their distinctive beliefs and practices. This is not necessarily a typical approach to church history, since many books seek to vindicate some particular branch of Christianity. But, arguably, a book purporting to retell the history of world Christianity is not worth its salt if it fails to acknowledge that Christianity has historically "been understood, expressed, and embodied in a dizzying variety of ways."[14] As a result, I adopt the method used by Philip Jenkins in *The Next Christendom*, in which he defines "a Christian [a]s someone who describes him- or herself as Christian."[15] Being inspired by Tertullian, a Christian author writing in what is now Tunisia in the year 200, I find hope in what he describes as a great diversity of believers at a very early stage of the church's past:

> For whom have the nations believed—Parthians, Medes, Elamites, and they who inhabit Mesopotamia, Armenia, Phrygia, Cappadocia, and they who dwell in Pontus, and Asia, and Pamphylia, tarriers in Egypt, and inhabiters of the region of Africa which is beyond Cyrene, Romans and sojourners, yes, and in Jerusalem Jews, and all other nations; as, for instance, by this time, the varied races of the Gaetulians, and manifold confines of the Moors, all the limits of the Spains, and the diverse nations of the Gauls, and the haunts of the Britons—inaccessible to the Romans, but subjugated to Christ, and of the Sarmatians, and Dacians, and Germans, and Scythians, and of many remote nations, and of provinces and islands many, to us unknown, and which we can scarce enumerate?[16]

---

[14]Peter Phan, "Introduction: Asian Christianity/Christianities," in *Christianities in Asia*, ed. Peter Phan (Oxford: Wiley-Blackwell, 2011), 1.

[15]Jenkins, *Next Christendom*, 102.

[16]Tertullian, *An Answer to the Jews* 7, in *The Ante-Nicene Fathers*, vol. 3, *Latin Christianity: Its Founder, Tertullian*, ed. Alexander Roberts and James Donaldson (Grand Rapids: Eerdmans, 1978), 157-58.

If Tertullian could not enumerate the variety of cultural, ethnic and linguistic groups who adopted Christianity by 200, we can scarcely define the varieties of Christianity existent after the year 2000.

TRAIL MARKERS AND CHAPTER OVERVIEWS

As is the case with any study of church history, and so much more so since our aim is to cover Christian history from every major world region, this book covers a great deal of material. Readers must take up a gauntlet of ideas, names, events, regions and stories. For this reason I have included several trail markers per chapter. Just as trail markers help trekkers make it to the clear path when they are lost in the forest, so these sidebars will help readers who have found themselves overwhelmed with new information. Similarly, I provide a chapter overview for each chapter in the book. These overviews are meant to orient the reader to the main contours of the story told per chapter. Also be sure to refer to the appendixes for aid when deciphering the division of world regions and when encountering terminology such as *West Syrian*, *metropolitan* or *autocephaly*.

FINAL THOUGHTS

The study of world Christianity is in its earliest stages, and this book is designed to offer only a broad introduction to a vast subject matter. There's no doubt that this book falls short of describing world Christian history in all its fullness and grandeur. In fact, such a history may still be decades in the making, a project held in check by unexcavated archaeological ruins, untranslated documents, cultural biases and as yet untold stories. As historians Samuel Noble and Alexander Treiger point out, for instance, "Close to 90 percent of the vast corpus of Arab Christian literature has not yet been edited or translated, let alone adequately studied."[17] It's no wonder that most church history books gloss over Arab Christianity, which, by the way, boasts one of the richest vestiges of Christianity in all of history, without batting an eyelash. Without accessible and sufficient primary artifacts, we historians are like builders without materials. How can we construct a suitable building when half of our

---

[17]Samuel Noble and Alexander Treiger, introduction to *The Orthodox Church in the Arab World, 700–1700: An Anthology of Sources*, ed. Samuel Noble and Alexander Treiger (DeKalb: Northern Illinois University Press, 2014), 4.

materials have been lost, destroyed or delayed? We will do our best with that afforded us, but our product is only as good our materials are.

Although it is not possible to recount the entire history of world Christianity, the history we uncover will remind us (and occasionally shame us) of the frailty of humanity, even Spirit-filled humans. We will discover heart-shattering and almost-better-left-forgotten tragedies just as we will encounter heart-warming moments in the ever-expanding global story of Christianity. We proceed with the hope that Jesus dwells with the church today in its entire regional splendor just as the early Christian scholar Jerome wrote that Jesus did with the forefathers of the Christian faith:

> Jesus dwelt in places; with Thomas in India, with Peter in Rome, with Paul in Illyricum, with Titus in Crete, with Andrew in Achaia, with each apostolic man in each and all countries.[18]

---

[18]Jerome, "Letter 59," in *Nicene and Post-Nicene Fathers*, vol. 6, *St. Jerome: Letters and Select Works*, ed. Philip Schaff and Henry Wace (Grand Rapids: Eerdmans, 1952). Scholars contest whether Jerome wrote this letter or whether another author did. See Evariste Regis Huc, *Christianity in China, Tartary and Thibet*, vol. 1, *From the Apostleship of St. Thomas to the Discovery of the Cape of Good Hope* (Boston: D&J Sadlier, 1857).

PART ONE

Christianity from the First to the Seventh Centuries

This first section of the book narrates the exciting history of the church in the three major world zones where Christianity took root in the first seven centuries: Asia, Africa and Europe. Although we neatly distinguish these continents from one another today, the Roman Empire ruled over parts of each of them. And where the Roman Empire ruled, it bestowed a common language, culture and worldview. As mentioned in the introduction, however, Christianity has never been bound by the borders of the Roman Empire. Indeed, there's good reason to believe that some Christians were living outside of the Roman Empire as early as the first century, such as in Iran or India. As we will see, Christian communities were blanketed across parts of Asia, Africa and Europe. Though sharing many similarities, Christian communities did not often see eye to eye. Like a seed scattered across various lands, some fertile and others barren, Christianity developed in relation to the cultural and political climate in which it was embedded. The unique traits that formed among one group were just as often demonized as they were accepted by other Christian groups.

Briefly, and speaking in general terms, Christianity in each of the three continents discussed in this section held to a different form of Christianity. In Asia, one of the most dominant groups was East Syrian Christians. Recent historians have settled on referring to the church these Christians were part of as the Church of the East. More often than not, East Syrian Christians lived outside of the Roman Empire, partly due to preference and partly to the fact that such

Christians were not tolerated among the dominant Christians living in that empire. Who was that dominant group? They were the Christians living in Europe, who were divided among Catholic Christians (in the West) or Eastern Orthodox or Byzantine Christians (in the East). Although not exactly correct, it has been common to say that Europe was divided in the fourth century into western and eastern halves, that is, the West Roman and the East Roman (or simply Byzantine) Empires. Over time this division became more pronounced. Though there were Catholics and Orthodox living in Africa, the dominant groups of Christians in this region were West Syrian Christians. Scholars regard such Christians as part of the Oriental Orthodox Church, which includes those Christians who were located principally in Egypt, Ethiopia, Sudan, Armenia and the western parts of Syria.

Each of the major forms of Christianity in these regions often emphasized their differences more so than their similarities, which led to ongoing friction, fragmentation and even violence. The litmus test of orthodoxy for these Christians was how they interpreted the relation between Christ's humanity and divinity. Though each group affirmed that Christ was both human and divine, they disagreed vigorously when it came to fleshing out this mystery. In short, Catholic and Byzantine Christians believed that one could not be a Christian unless he or she affirmed that Christ consisted of fully human and divine (two) natures that existed side by side yet not mixed in the (one) person of Christ; East Syrian Christians believed that it was essential to affirm the complete humanity and divinity of Christ within two loosely related natures and one personhood; while West Syrian Christians believed that Christ the Word was fully human and fully divine yet had only one nature, which is why they are called miaphysites (see table 0.1).

Although such stark divisions often get lost on modern readers, they were the stuff of early worldwide Christianity. Failure to affirm belief in one group's definition of orthodoxy meant not only that such a person was in serious theological peril but was not even a Christian. The third and fourth ecumenical councils, held in 431 and 451 in what is now Turkey and under the authority of Byzantine Christians, led to the permanent division among these different groups that lasts to this day. In addition to these four major Christian traditions scattered across Asia, Africa and Europe, there were also minor Christian groups such as Arians, Donatists, Gnostics, Manichaeans,

Marcionites, Montanists and Novatianists. These Christian groups had their heydays. But unlike the East and West Syrian traditions, however, which were also condemned by the Byzantine and Catholic Churches, the churches from these traditions all but vanished from the historical record.

Table 0.1. Division of major Christian groups according to theological traditions

Theological Tradition (Other Designations)	Understanding of Christ (on the Relation Between His Humanity and Divinity)	Churches (Geographic Regions)
Byzantine **(Chalcedonian, Melkite, Imperial, Eastern Orthodox)**	Two (human and divine) natures of Christ that come together in one hypostatic union without confusion, change, division or separation; "Two natures in the incarnate Jesus, and one hypostasis"	Eastern Orthodox Church (Turkey, Palestine, Israel, Syria and Jordan) Church of Cyprus (Cyprus) Maronite Church (Lebanon) Georgian Apostolic Church (Georgia and Jerusalem)
Catholic **(Catholic Church, Imperial Church)**	Affirms same definition as given in the Byzantine tradition	Catholic Church (Western and Southern Europe)
East Syrian **(Assyrian, Diophysite, Church of the East, Nestorian, Persian Church)**	Two natures of Christ: a human one (from Mary) and a divine one (from God) that are united without being mixed; "Two natures in the incarnate Jesus with their two Qnomi and one Parsopa"	(Assyrian) Church of the East (Syria, Iraq, Iran, India, China and Central Asia)
West Syrian **(Jacobite, Miaphysite, Monophysite, Oriental Orthodox Church)**	One nature of Christ whose humanity and divinity were united after the incarnation; "One nature of the incarnate Word of God after the union and one hypostasis"*	Armenian Apostolic Church (Armenia and Jerusalem) Syrian Orthodox Church (Syria/Turkey) Coptic Orthodox Church (Egypt) Ethiopian Orthodox Tewahedo Church (Ethiopia)

*The phrases in quotations for each section come from Suha Rassam, *Christianity in Iraq: Its Origins and Development to the Present Day* (Leominster, UK: Gracewing, 2005), xxviii-xxix.

one

ASIA

Christianity is Asian in origin and character.
Jesus was Asian.

DALE JOHNSON, *JESUS ON THE SILK ROAD*

ASIA, THE CRADLE OF THE CHRISTIAN FAITH

Asia is the birthplace of Christianity, the largest religion on the planet. Two thousand years ago a woodworker from a village in Western Asia gathered a hodgepodge of followers, traveled around the countryside teaching and performing miracles, and disputed with religious and political leaders who later crucified him for sedition and blasphemy. Three days later he was reported to have risen from the dead. Many have called the story of this man's life, death and resurrection the greatest story ever told, but few have associated the story with Asia, the only continent where this world Savior walked, taught and died.

The story of Jesus of Nazareth spread rapidly across the known world. Not only did people groups in what are now Armenia, Iraq, Iran, Israel, Jordan, Lebanon, Palestine, Syria and Turkey become followers of Jesus the Messiah, but people in what are now Afghanistan, India, Saudi Arabia, Uzbekistan, Turkmenistan and Yemen also adopted the new Asian religion he inspired. By the seventh century even the emperor of China was promoting Christianity. According to a decree issued by Emperor Taizong in 638, Christianity was to be proclaimed "everywhere for the salvation of the people."[1]

---

[1]Martin Palmer, *The Jesus Sutras: Rediscovering the Lost Scrolls of Taoist Christianity* (New York: Ballantine Wellspring, 2001), 227.

Despite its rapid growth, the Christian religion experienced great challenges in the continent where it was born. Baha'i, Bon, Buddhism, Confucianism, Daoism, Hinduism, Islam, Jainism, Judaism, Manichaeism, Sikhism,
Shamanism, Shintoism and Zoroastrianism would all sprout from the same
Asian soil, and it should come as no surprise that they did not always get along.
At times the competition among these Asian religions was fierce. In Iran the
thought and practices of Christianity clashed with Zoroastrianism, just as they
did with Shintoism in Japan. And it was not just other religions that the
Christian religion contended with—Christians also frequently fought among
themselves. Such intramural squabbling likely contributed just as much as any
other outside religious factor to its decline after centuries of expansion and
growth in Asia.

CHAPTER OVERVIEW

In this chapter we will discover that Christianity was originally an Asian religion. This is a helpful fact to keep in mind as we begin our study of the history
of world Christianity. Some of us will be surprised to discover that Christianity was thriving in what is now Iraq and Syria centuries before it existed in
many parts of Europe and the Americas. In fact, Christianity was not only
widespread on the Asian continent during the earliest years of the church but
it was also extremely diverse, which was also regrettably the cause of many
controversies and church schisms. Although we will discuss some of these
issues later, our survey of Asian Christianity during this time period aims to
provide a general overview rather than a detailed outline. As you read through
this chapter, be mindful of the vast extent of early Asian Christianity, and try
to imagine living in a world where the church in Asia was the most populous
and most vibrant of any global region. That was the reality for Christians
during the earliest centuries of the church.

WESTERN ASIA

We will start our overview of early Asian Christianity in Western Asia, the place
where the church was born and nurtured during its earliest years. The origins
of Christianity can be traced back to the Jewish festival of Pentecost around AD
30 in the Western Asian city of Jerusalem. According to Acts, the Spirit of God
overpowered Jesus' disciples, and "about three thousand" (Acts 2:41) accepted

the message of salvation that disciples like Peter proclaimed. At long last, it seemed, the prophecy that the law would "go out from Zion, the word of the LORD from Jerusalem" (Is 2:3) was being fulfilled, as people from all over the world accepted the message that Christ rose from the grave, who then spread it to their respective families and tribes. Commenting on Pentecost, New Testament historian Richard Bauckham notes that the location names and peoples in Acts 2:9-11 corresponded to the four points of a compass, "beginning in the east and moving counterclockwise."[2] With Jerusalem at the center, the message radiated out into all cardinal directions: to the East in what is now Iran and Iraq; to the North in what is now Turkey; to the West in Northern Africa and parts of Italy and Greece; and to the South in what are now parts of the Middle East and the Arabian Peninsula (see table 1.1).

Table 1.1. Hypothetical expansion of Christianity based on Acts 2:9-11

Region	Verse(s)	Locations or Peoples	Corresponding Modern Nation(s)	From Judea
East	9	Parthians, Medes, Elamites and Mesopotamians	Iran and Iraq	→
North	9-10	Cappadocia, Pontus, Asia, Phrygia and Pamphylia	Turkey	↑
West	10-11	Egypt, Libya, Cyrene, Rome and Cretans	Egypt, Libya, Italy and Crete	←
South	11	Arabs	Syria, Jordan and the Arabian Peninsula	↓

There are three things to gather from Acts 2:9-11. First, regardless of where Asian Christians spread the Christian religion in the first centuries, it was almost always adopted first among the Jewish people before spreading among Gentiles. In this way the so-called Jewish dispersion laid the groundwork for the establishment of Christianity across the ancient world. Second, this list is more suggestive than definitive. Jews were living well beyond the regions these verses indicate, whether in what is now Afghanistan, Armenia, Germany or Spain. Third, although the people groups and regions listed in Acts are foreign to us today, they signify that Christianity was introduced at a very early date to areas now populated by only a small percentage of Christians. When we think of the Middle East today, for instance, we immediately link this region with its dominant religion—Islam. Yet centuries before Arabs were worshiping Allah,

---

[2]Richard Bauckham, "James and the Early Church," in *The Book of Acts in Its Palestinian Setting*, ed. Richard Bauckham (Grand Rapids: Eerdmans, 1995), 4:420.

from Syria to Saudi Arabia, Asian Christians were worshiping Jesus Christ, from Turkey to Tibet. Shedding its Semitic skin, Christianity found itself well able to adapt to cultures from seemingly all walks of life.

Turkey. Beginning with Christianization north of Jerusalem, in what Acts 2 refers to as "Cappadocia, Pontus and Asia, Phrygia and Pamphylia," we will discover that what is now Turkey proved a fertile region for Christianity to grow for well more than a thousand years. According to the New Testament, the apostles Peter and Paul evangelized current-day Turkey in the early first century and used the cosmopolitan city of Antioch as their missionary base. By the second century, this rich soil had produced an impressive crop of Christian communities. Contemporary documents reveal the growth of Christianity throughout Asia Minor. Consider the Roman emperor Trajan's reply to the governor of Bithynia's letter about how to deal with Christians in the early second century:

> [These Christians] are not to be sought ought; if they are informed against, and the charge is proved, they are to be punished, with this reservation—that if any one denies that he is a Christian, and actually proves it, that is by worshipping our gods, he shall be pardoned as a result of his recantation, however suspect he may have been with respect to the past.[3]

Contrary to Hollywood movies and outdated books that have inspired imagination, there were likely no large persecutions of Christians in the first couple of centuries after Christ. As historian of antiquity Kevin Madigan writes, "there was no Roman law specifically outlawing the practice of Christianity."[4] Despite some localized cases, including the well-known martyrdom of Bishop Polycarp of Smyrna in the late second century, many Christians worshiped relatively freely and were otherwise unfettered by the state in what is now Turkey until the middle of the third century. This lack of state regulation allowed for a great diversity of Christian groups and practices to emerge. In the late second century, for instance, a Christian named Montanus launched a movement called "the New Prophecy" (or simply Montanism), which emphasized charismatic gifts, female leadership alongside male leadership and rigorous spiritual practices.

---

[3]Trajan, cited in *Documents of the Christian Church*, ed. Henry Bettenson, 4th ed. (Oxford: Oxford University Press, 2011), 5.

[4]Kevin Madigan, *Medieval Christianity: A New History* (New Haven, CT: Yale University Press, 2015), 15.

And many other fringe groups emerged as well. Christianity was so successful in the Roman Empire, in fact, due in part to the great diversity that unregulated worship afforded, that it eventually became the state religion—and henceforth much more regulated and mainstream. In 313, Roman co-emperor Constantine promulgated an Edict of Milan, providing a legal status to Christianity for the first time in the Roman Empire. (This need not imply that Christianity itself was outlawed beforehand, unless we are talking about the Roman law against unauthorized assemblies.) Whether Constantine was truly converted by the famous vision purported to have come to him in 312 or whether he simply decided to serve as a patron of Christianity for political reasons (or a combination thereof), Constantine showered the church with gifts and money, and even underwent baptism on his deathbed in 337. (It was a common practice then to delay baptism until later in life since baptism erased former, but not future, sins.) In 325, the year after he became sole emperor, Constantine convened the first of the so-called Seven Ecumenical Councils and also began construction of a new capital of the Roman Empire.

As a military leader caught up in the ancient political game of expansion and preservation, Constantine sought a new capital where he could control both land and sea routes between the continents of Asia and Europe and where he could keep a close eye on Rome's inveterate enemy, the Iranians (or Persians). He settled on the ancient city of Byzantium, an impressive site straddling the Euro-Asian border that provides panoramic views of some of the most beautiful real estate anywhere in the world. To mark this momentous change from Old Rome to "New Rome," otherwise known as Constantinople (and now Istanbul), historians call the East Roman Empire (330–1453) "the Byzantine Empire," and therefore everything associated with this empire is labeled "Byzantine."

The image of a building is an apt one when referring to all things Byzantine. Not only did the Byzantine Empire construct some of the most splendid buildings in all of Christendom—most stunning is Hagia Sophia (or Holy Wisdom), the largest church in the world for almost a thousand years and a building still inspiring awe today among visitors in the heart of Muslim Istanbul—it also constructed the core of Christian doctrine and practice. The Seven Ecumenical Councils refer to seven worldwide meetings that took place intermittently in modern Turkey from 325 to 787. Though aspiring to a global status, these councils were almost exclusively attended by Greek-speaking bishops, often under the pressure of emperors who demanded a unified church that corresponded with an imagined unified empire. Politics aside, the theology hammered out at these councils was wide ranging, though Christology, the study of Christ, dominated discussions.

If viewed solely from the perspective of Christology, we could summarize the seven councils as follows. The Council of Nicaea (325) condemned the view that Christ was not equal in substance with God the Father, a position labeled Arianism after a priest named Arius (see chap. 2), and authored a creed explaining who Christ was—and was not. At this first council, the Greek term *homoousios*, meaning "same substance," was chosen to indicate the relationship between God the Father and God the Son. Years after the council, Bishop Athanasius of Alexandria was the most stalwart defender of this term against Arian Christians. Despite being exiled from his diocese on five separate occasions by emperors, he held steadfast to the conciliar belief that Christ was of the same substance with God the Father. The Council of Constantinople (381), responding to an insurgence of Arianism in the empire, affirmed and expanded the creed that emerged out of Nicaea called the Nicene Creed, and confirmed that Christ, though fully a human, was also equal in substance with God the Father—and with God the Spirit. The conclusions drawn about the Holy Spirit at the Council of Constantinople had been greatly influenced by the theologically adept writings of the so-called Cappadocian Fathers, three bishops from the central part of Turkey who affirmed the full deity of the Holy Spirit: Basil of Caesarea, Gregory of Nyssa and Gregory of Nazianzus. The Council of Ephesus (431) rejected the idea that Christ consisted of two separate persons, sometimes inaccurately referred to as Nestorianism.[5] The Council of Chalcedon (451) argued that Christ's humanity and divinity are not mixed together but inseparably united in one person. The next two councils, both at Constantinople (553 and 681), affirmed previous conciliar decisions in rejecting the recent conception that Christ had two wills (corresponding to his two natures—one human and one divine). Finally, the Second Council of Nicaea (787) ruled that Christ can be pictured and that icons can be venerated. Although this decision had been made by the council, it took an entire century before it was fully enforced and accepted.

---

[5]For more about whether Nestorius was a Nestorian, see Sebastian Brock, *Fire from Heaven: Studies in Syriac Theology and Liturgy* (Aldershot: Ashgate, 2006), 1-14.

TRAIL MARKER
The Nicene Creed

The Nicene Creed, a document confessed at churches throughout the world, has a contested history. The original creed at Nicea (325) was written based on existing creeds in the church. But because of inadequacies that became more apparent in the years to come, it was expanded and edited at the Council of Constantinople in 381. Two centuries later, however, the Spanish (Catholic) Christians made a change to it at the Third Council of Toledo (589), maintaining that the Holy Spirit proceeds from the Father *and the Son* (the words in italics not being part of the original—*filioque* in Latin). This change, known as the Filioque clause, became the official teaching of Western (Catholic) churches. In the West today, when we recite the Nicene Creed, we are referring to the creed from 381 that later underwent change in 589 and was spread in the eighth and ninth centuries. Orthodox Christians, however, only recite the 381 version, asserting that the Western addition, only one word in Latin, is heretical.

Despite the span of five centuries in a political empire whose borders constantly fluctuated, the seven councils shared many commonalities. First, the councils included more than theological formulas. The first council, for instance, produced twenty canons of guidelines for ministerial practice, though many Christians only focus on the creed that the council produced. Second, it is crucial to recognize that the emperor convened the councils, and that the theological pronouncements determined became the law of the land. Thus, when a bishop, as the representative of a certain segment of Christians, fell outside of the theological parameters that a particular council drew, Byzantine authorities could banish, imprison or otherwise punish that bishop or group of Christians. Third, the Greek language and Greek philosophical thought was the medium in which these councils were conducted. This partly explains the linguistic and theological clashes Byzantine Christians experienced with, for instance, the Latin Church in the West, the Coptic Church in the South and the Syriac Church in the East. Fourth, despite its namesake, the Seven Ecumenical Councils never represented the *oikoumenē*, "the whole inhabited world." For instance, Christians from Armenia, Egypt, China, Georgia, Lebanon, India and Iran never received adequate representation, let alone fringe Christian groups like Montanists and Marcionites (see chap. 3). Fifth, politics, pride and personality often drove the agendas. The "Gangster Synod" of 449, though later rejected as one of the ecumenical councils, was not the only church synod of questionable motives.[6] Finally, in its attempt to preserve the mysteries of the church and protect it against perceived threats, the seven councils seriously divided much of Christianity. In this way, the overall effect of the councils brought about precisely what it sought to prevent: the fragmentation of the worldwide church.

TRAIL MARKER
The Byzantine Empire

The Byzantine Empire is the name given to the eastern part of the Roman Empire from the year 330 to 1453. (The western part of that empire, as we'll discover in chapter three, had a completely different history.) Constantine, arguably the first Christian emperor of Rome, was the first of a chain of emperors who married the Christian religion with the state, ensuring Christianity's survival and wealth, but also stifling Christian diversity and all but forcing bishops to play politics just as much as tending to their flocks.

Although the Byzantine Empire experienced periodic revivals in the centuries to come, it entered a steady period of decline around the seventh century. Justinian, who ruled from 527 to 565, was one of the strongest and most successful emperors of the Byzantine Empire before this time. He, along with his almost invincible general Belisarius, kept the empire intact.

---

[6]See Philip Jenkins, *The Jesus Wars: How Four Patriarchs, Three Queens, and Two Emperors Decided What Christians Would Believe for the Next 1,500 Years* (New York: HarperCollins, 2010). Jenkins uses the term Gangster Synod for what is traditionally known as the Robber Council.

But this could not be sustained over time. Plagued by ongoing battles with Persia and with persistent theological disputes among rival Christian groups, the empire was too fragmented to offer sustained resistance to the Arab Muslim conquest, provoking what Byzantine scholar Judith Herrin labels "the first major turning point in Byzantine history."[7] This turning point shook the empire to the core and ultimately brought it to its knees. Over the course of the next several centuries various kingdoms simultaneously chipped away at the Byzantine Empire until there was nothing left but an empty shell. With the end of the empire went the presence of the Christian faith.

Arabia. In consideration of one other locale in Western Asia, let us turn to Arabia, a rather fluid geographic term encompassing many arid regions in the Middle East.[8] This region, always on the fringe of the Byzantine Empire, was to be a thorn in Byzantium's side even after many in Arabia adopted Christianity. The Nabataeans, one group living in Arabia around the time of Christ, spoke a dialect of Aramaic and worshiped various gods. After centuries of Nabataean rule, Emperor Trajan annexed Arabia as a Roman province in 106. In the eyes of Rome, Arabia's importance lay in its trading capabilities since its capital, Petra, was "situated at the crossroads of two major trade routes."[9] After joining with two other provinces, Arabia included parts of the Arabian Peninsula, Jordan, Israel, Lebanon, Palestine and Syria.

Due to its location, Arabia served as a buffer zone between the quarreling Romans and Parthians in the first centuries after Christ and, later, between the Byzantine and Sassanid Empires. There is good reason to believe that Christianity existed in Arabia in the early part of the first century. Historian J. Spencer Trimingham went so far as to say that "Jesus must have been in close contact with Arabs," as he carried out his ministry in the multiethnic and multireligious context of Galilee.[10] And two decades after Jesus, the apostle Paul made two references to Arabia (Gal 1:16-17; 4:25). Although the extent of this region is difficult to determine precisely since the borders of ancient kingdoms were

---

[7]Judith Herrin, *Byzantium: The Surprising Life of a Medieval Empire* (Princeton, NJ: Princeton University Press, 2007), xviii.

[8]See J. Spencer Trimingham, *Christianity Among the Arabs in Pre-Islamic Times* (New York: Longman, 1979), 1-2.

[9]Eckhard Schnabel, *Early Christian Mission*, vol. 2, *Paul and the Early Church* (Downers Grove, IL: InterVarsity Press, 2004), 1034.

[10]Trimingham, *Christianity Among the Arabs*, 41.

always in flux, it is likely that Paul was referring to the Nabataean kingdom located in Jordan. It is not unreasonable to conclude that Paul lived in the Nabataean kingdom because there was already "a nucleus of Jesus-followers there,"[11] and it's also possible that Paul evangelized Gentile cities while there over the course of several months.[12]

From the second century onward, we have several reports of different Christian groups in Arabia. Bishop Eusebius of Caesarea, the first real church historian, gave reports of a Christian named Elkasai who was active from between 100 and 120. His followers, the Elkasites, rejected "parts of every book of the Bible, though they [made] use of passages from every Old Testament book and every gospel." According to Eusebius, Elkasai exercised the gift of prophecy, wrote a theological book and claimed direct messages from angels in Aramaic, the language of Jesus. More recently, Anglican bishop and scholar Kenneth Cragg has argued that the Elkasites prayed facing Jerusalem (as Muhammad's followers did centuries later before redirecting their posture toward Mecca), practiced circumcision and water baptism, observed the sabbath, used bread and salt as a sacrament and centered on the remission of sins.[13] Eusebius also conjectured that Philip, born in Arabia in 204, not only extended sympathies toward Christians but was also a Christian himself, making him the first Christian emperor of Rome, more than a century before the same claim has been made about Constantine.[14]

By the fourth century, Christianity was thriving among the various tribal groups living in Arabia. Such Arab tribes included the Ghassanids in Yemen, the Lahkmids in Southern Iraq, the Salihids in the Arabian Peninsula and the Tanukhids in Syria.[15] As for the Tanukhids, it is likely that a Christian queen named Mawiyya began ruling the tribe after her husband died in 373, and she requested an Eastern Orthodox Arab bishop for her people at a time when the Roman

---

[11]Ibid., 42.

[12]Schnabel, *Early Christian Mission*, 2:1038.

[13]Kenneth Cragg, *The Arab Christian: A History in the Middle East* (Louisville, KY: Westminster John Knox, 1991), 37-38.

[14]Eusebius, *The History of the Church* 6.34, trans. G. A. Williamson (London: Penguin, 1989), 206. While scholars accept the former interpretation, no evidence corroborates that Philip the Arab was a Christian.

[15]David Thomas, "Arab Christianity," in *The Blackwell Companion to Eastern Christianity*, ed. Ken Parry (Oxford: Wiley-Blackwell, 2010), 2.

Empire was ruled by Arians.[16] Some scholars have even claimed, somewhat controversially, that Arab Christians invented the Arabic script.[17] Although no firm evidence has corroborated this hypothesis, it's possible that Christian martyrdoms suggest the existence of an Arabic liturgy among Arab Christians: "If Christianity possessed their soul," Arabic scholar Irfan Shahid reasons, "it is quite likely that it also touched their literary sensibilities."[18] Indeed, it appears that Arab liturgies and an Arab Bible could have been crafted early in the history of Arab Christianity, perhaps around the same time the Qur'an was being written.[19]

TRAIL MARKER
Early Arab Christians and the Qur'an

There is much heated debate regarding when the Qur'an was written in its current format. Needless to say, that discussion will not be immediately resolved. What is important to keep in mind is that there were Arab Christians in existence well before the Qur'an was written, and it is possible that Arab-speaking Christians had created their own liturgies in Arabic before the rise of Islam in the seventh century.

Theologically, many Arab Christians subscribed to different theologies than did the Byzantine Christians, who generally represented a more unified and dominant branch of Christianity. Among later Arab Muslim writers, Arab Christians were called Nestorians, Jacobites and Melkites. Each has a specific historical meaning—and each was a slur. In terms of theology, to be called a Nestorian was to be identified with that school of thought that regarded Christ as consisting of two natures and, often incorrectly, two persons.

---

[16]David Grafton, "'The Arabs' in the Ecclesiastical Historians of the 4th/5th Centuries: Effects on Contemporary Christian-Muslim Relations," *Hervormde Teologiese Studies* 64, no. 1 (2008): 177-92.

[17]Cragg, *Arab Christian*, 45.

[18]Irfan Shahid, *Byzantium and the Arabs in the Fifth Century* (Washington, DC: Dumbarton Oaks, 1989), 456-57.

[19]Thomas, "Arab Christianity," 5; and Sydney Griffith, *The Church in the Shadow of the Mosque: Christians and Muslims in the World of Islam* (Princeton, NJ: Princeton University Press, 2008), 9.

Such Christians are grouped with the Church of the East. Jacobites, by contrast, were those Christians who believed that Christ, though fully human and divine, had only one nature.[20] They are linked with the Oriental Orthodox Church. Finally, the term Melkite referred to Christians living outside of the borders of the Byzantine Empire who were nonetheless affiliated theologically with the Byzantines, meaning that they held to the belief that Christ had two fully human and divine natures but still was only one person. They are part of what we call the Eastern Orthodox Church. How did the Arab Christians refer to themselves? They probably called themselves Nazarenes, a common way to refer to Semitic-based Christians to this day—that is, those speaking Arabic or Syriac.

By the fifth and sixth centuries, the "whole Province of Arabia became eventually studded with church buildings."[21] The earliest known Arab church, built in Jordan, dates to 345, but has remains of more than fifteen church buildings of different time periods.[22] Countless other houses of prayers dotted the Arabian landscape, including one consecrated as a Christian church in 515.[23] This church, now called the Basilica of St. George in Syria, contains the following Greek inscription on the front of the building, testifying to its use as a pre-Christian religious site before being turned into a church:

> From being the abode of gods ["demons"], it has become the House of God. Where darkness cast its veil, now shines the light of salvation; where sacrifices to idols were offered, now are heard choirs of angels; where the wrath of God was evoked, now all is peace.[24]

Christianity had achieved so much success in Arabia by the sixth century that one of the last Himyarite kings, Dhu Nuwas, a recent convert to Judaism, attacked the Christian town of Najran (in what is now southwestern Saudi Arabia) and massacred those who would not renounce Jesus as God, almost

---

[20]Although identical in spelling, the term *Jacobite* here refers to miaphysite Christians of the Oriental Orthodox Church, not to Roman Catholic supporters of James II in Britain.

[21]Trimingham, *Christianity Among the Arabs*, 75.

[22]Ibid., 76; it is debatable whether the famous church found in Dura-Europos, dating to around 256, was Arab or not. For the range of meaning of the term *Arab*, see Marshall Hodgson, *The Venture of Islam*, vol. 1, *The Classical Age of Islam* (Chicago: The University of Chicago Press, 1974), 62-63.

[23]Irfan Shahid, *Byzantium and the Arabs in the Sixth Century* (Washington, DC: Dumbarton Oaks, 2009), 2:1, 148-56.

[24]Trimingham, *Christianity Among the Arabs*, 77.

five thousand in number, including men, women and children.[25] Dhu Nuwas forced the Christians to confess that "Christ is a man and not God" on pain of death. Because none apostatized, he gathered all the Christians in a church, locked the door and burned it to the ground.[26] Dhu Nuwas's heinous actions raised the ire of the Christian kingdom of Ethiopia, which had officially adopted Christianity in the fourth century. A zealous Ethiopian Christian viceroy named Abraha destroyed Dhu Nuwas's army and "made Christianity the state religion of southern Arabia for 40 years."[27]

Abraha resided in Sana'a, the current capital of Yemen, where he constructed many churches, including the Cathedral of Sana'a. The Christian Abraha soon set his sights on Mecca, the future birthplace of Muhammad, and although Abraha won his first skirmish against the Meccans in 552, Muhammad's grandfather later destroyed his army.[28] The Qur'an, delivered to the prophet Muhammad from 610 until his death in 632, memorializes Allah's protection of Arabs against the Christian leader Abraha in surah 105: "Do you [Prophet] not see how your Lord dealt with the army of the elephant? Did He not utterly confound their plans? He sent flocks of birds against them, pelting them with pellets of hard-baked clay: He made them [like] cropped stubble."[29]

We can only surmise how world history would have developed differently had Mecca come under the full authority of Ethiopia and thus the Christian religion. Saudi Arabia was poised to adopt Christianity before this time, and it has been argued that members of Muhammad's clan may have embraced Christianity.[30] Muhammad himself may have attended Christian services at the cathedral in Sana'a and wrote about sermons he heard Bishop Quss ibn Sa'ida expound.[31] However and whatever Muhammad learned about Christianity, the Qur'an leveled a thorough critique of the Christian religion, though it also required Muslim leaders to protect Christians under their jurisdiction.

---

[25]Thomas, "Arab Christianity," 3.

[26]Robert Louis Wilken, *The First Thousand Years: A Global History of Christianity* (New Haven, CT: Yale University Press, 2012), 218.

[27]Christoph Baumer, *The Church of the East: An Illustrated History of Assyrian Christianity* (London: I. B. Tauris, 2006), 142.

[28]Ibid., 142; Keith August Burton, *The Blessing of Africa: The Bible and African Christianity* (Downers Grove, IL: InterVarsity Press, 2007), 142.

[29]*The Qur'an*, trans. M. A. S. Abdel Haleem (Oxford: Oxford University Press, 2010), 437.

[30]Irfan Shahid, "Arab Christianity Before the Rise of Islam," in *Christianity: A History in the Middle East*, ed. Habib Badr (Beirut, Lebanon: Middle East Council of Churches, 2004), 447.

[31]Burton, *The Blessing of Africa*, 142.

CENTRAL AND EASTERN ASIA

Around the same time that Muhammad was uniting the Arab world under the name of Allah, an envoy of Christian monks was traveling thousands of miles by foot along the famed Silk Road from Iran to China in order to spread the Christian faith. The Silk Road was a long and busy trading route and religious thoroughfare, giving way to caravans of camels carrying exotic spices, traders looking for profit and Asian missionaries seeking converts. The Church of the East, the most evangelistic of any tradition in the early and medieval church, made extensive use of the Silk Road. Ishoyahb II, a *catholicos* of the Church of the East during the seventh century, sent out missionaries and established leading dioceses in places like Herat, Afghanistan and Samarkand, Uzbekistan, building on the success of Christian communities already formed in the modern Central Asian nations of what is now Kazakhstan, Kyrgyzstan and Tajikistan.[32] "By the mid-seventh century," historian of Muslim antiquity Robert Hoyland writes, "there were twenty dioceses east of the river Oxus, including Samarkand and Kasghar."[33] Nonetheless, the study of early Christianity in these regions is still in its infancy.

China. Perhaps Ishoyahb II's most famous missionary enterprise was sending a group of Christians, headed by a Syrian bishop named Aloben, to the great Chinese Empire in the seventh century. The timing was providential. The Tang Dynasty, founded less than twenty years earlier, was openly tolerant, welcoming religious groups from all over the known world. Aloben's retinue arrived in 635 in the capital of the Tang Dynasty—in Chang'an (now Xian), at that time the largest city in the world. Aloben's entourage was sporting white tunics and carrying Christian paraphernalia such as holy books, crosses and statues. It must have been quite a sight to behold.

Was this the first time Christians had traveled to China? Not at all. Asian Christians had certainly traveled through China before this time,[34] but not enough evidence exists to reconstruct what the state of the church may have looked like (if there was an organized body there at all). The so-called Nestorian Stele or Monument Sutra—engraved in the year 781 but only

---

[32]Wilhelm Baum and Dietmar Winkler, *The Church of the East* (New York: RoutledgeCurzon, 2003), 41, 73.

[33]Robert Hoyland, *In God's Path: The Arab Conquests and the Creation of an Islamic Empire* (Oxford: Oxford University Press, 2015), 15.

[34]Baum and Winkler, *Church of the East*, 47; Daniel Hays, *A New History of Christianity in China* (Oxford: Wiley-Blackwell, 2012), 5.

discovered in the 1620s—documents the first 150 years of Christianity's existence in China. The limestone stele, constructed with dragons at the top and a tortoise at the base, was written in ornate Chinese characters.

TRAIL MARKER
The Titles of Church Leaders

The titles of different church leaders can be a great source of confusion. Here are a few aids when reading this book.

- A *pope* is the leading bishop of the Coptic Orthodox Church and of the Roman Catholic Church. Example: the bishops of Alexandria in Egypt and of Rome are popes. Who had the title first? Probably the pope in Alexandria, not the one in Rome!

- A *catholicos* is the leading bishop of the Church of the East and of the Armenian Orthodox Church. Example: the bishop of Etchmiadzin in Armenia is a catholicos.

- A *patriarch* is the bishop of a historically important diocese or bishopric (in this case, technically a patriarchate) in the East. Example: the bishop of Antioch in Syria is a patriarch. (Today, for reasons that will become clear in part three, there are five patriarchs of Antioch!)

- A *metropolitan* is the bishop of a historically important diocese or bishopric (in this case, technically a metropolitanate) in the East. Example: the bishop of Moscow in Russia is a metropolitan.

- An *abuna* was the leading bishop of the Ethiopian Orthodox Tewahedo Church in what is now Ethiopia when it was under the ecclesial authority of the Coptic Orthodox Church and its pope. Today, the term is used more generally for bishops and priests.

Regardless of the title, what is important to keep in mind is that authority was extremely important in the early church. Each of these titles was (and is) a specific title for bishops of great authority and prestige.

Three years after the group of Christians had arrived, the Chinese emperor commissioned the building of churches in the provincial capitals and issued an edict in support of Christianity:

> The way [Christianity] does not have a common name and the sacred does not have a common form. Alouben, the man of great virtue from the Da Qin [Western] Empire, came from a far land. . . . His message is mysterious and wonderful beyond our understanding. The message is lucid and clear; the teachings will benefit all; and they shall be practiced throughout the land.[35]

Lest we think that Christianity monopolized the religious marketplace at this time, we must interpret this decree in the context of the religiously tolerant Tang Dynasty, which gave patronage to many foreign religions. Despite the grand language, it's unlikely that the emperor would have welcomed Chinese conversions to Christianity.

Nonetheless, the Christianity that emerged in China expressed itself using ideas and language prevalent within the cultural and religious thought of the day, including well-known Buddhist and Daoist concepts and language. Evidently, the Chinese backdrop inspired Syriac Christians to imagine anew what it meant to be a Christian. The life of Jesus, a story so familiar to Westerners that it is almost banal, was told in a unique way:

> In the beginning was the natural constant, the true stillness of the Origin, and the primordial void of the Most High. Then, the spirit of the void emerged as the Most High Lord, moving in mysterious ways to enlighten the holy ones. He is Joshua, my True Lord of the Void, who embodies the three subtle and wondrous bodies, and who was condemned to the cross so that the people of the four directions can be saved. . . . He set afloat the raft of salvation and compassion so that we can use it to ascend to the palace of light and be united with the spirit.[36]

Although concepts such as "subtle and wondrous bodies" and the "raft of salvation" sound foreign to Western ears, this was common Buddhist language. The description of Christianity in this way illustrates what Christianity was able to look like within the vastly different cultural and religious landscape of Eastern Asia.

---

[35]Martin Palmer, *The Jesus Sutras: Rediscovering the Lost Scrolls of Taoist Christianity* (New York: Ballantine, 2001), 43.
[36]Ibid., 225-26.

In the past century archaeological discoveries in China have confirmed that Christianity spread beyond the imperial capital. Literary documents, gravestones and paintings reveal how Christianity contextualized in Chinese society. Despite its successes, however, China's first experiment with Christianity ultimately failed. Historian of Asia Samuel Moffett writes that a Christian monk in Baghdad may have been right when he said in 987, "There is not a single Christian left in China."[37] Because of its attachment to the dynastic court, Christianity disappeared during the transition from the Tang to the Sung Dynasties. By this time, however, "more than 500 writings, including the entire New Testament and a few books of the Old Testament, had been translated from Syriac into Chinese."[38] With the door closed in China, the Church of the East apparently set its sights elsewhere, making strides into nearby places such as Tibet, Korea, Japan and possibly into Southeastern Asia.

SOUTHERN ASIA

In contrast to the great length of the time it took for Christianity to be established in China, we have very early traditions claiming that the apostle Thomas preached the gospel in India within a couple of decades of Jesus' death. There are actually two major sources making this claim, one Indian and the other Syrian. The Indian and Syrian sources differ in a number of ways, but their larger storylines are the same: Thomas traveled to India, planted churches, performed wonders and died as a martyr. Although it's not possible to determine with certainty that Thomas traveled to India, it is clear that an Indian Christian tradition developed very early, one that was incorporated into the Syriac tradition—the Church of the East—by at least the fourth century. By this time there were two competing Christian traditions in India—one claiming descent from the apostle Thomas in the first century and the other claiming descent from a certain Thomas of Cana, who immigrated to India with Christian families from the Middle East in the fourth century. Whatever the exact origins of the church in India, we have reports of the existence of Christian believers in nearby Sri Lanka, a Buddhist stronghold for centuries. But even before Christianity was established in

---

[37]Samuel Moffett, *A History of Christianity in Asia*, vol. 1, *Beginnings to 1500*, 2nd ed. (Maryknoll, NY: Orbis, 1998), 314.
[38]Baum and Winkler, *Church of the East*, 49.

India, it is likely that Christianity had passed through various parts of Southern Asia by the second century, such as Afghanistan and Pakistan.

Iran. When Christianity emerged in the first century, Iran was under the governance of the Parthian (or Arsacid) Empire, a long-time rival to the Roman Empire. In the year 224, however, the Parthians were ousted by the Sassanians, a powerful dynasty that took control of what we often refer to as the Persian Empire (now including Greater Iran and also Iraq). According to Acts 2:9, "Parthians, Medes and Elamites"—all tribes from modern Iran—were present during Pentecost. Yet three decades prior, the Gospel of Matthew (2:1-12) recounts that magi, possibly from Iran, were the first to give homage to Christ. Although a strong Christian community was taking shape in Iran by the second century, the Christian faithful soon faced threats. Due to the reestablishment of the Zoroastrian religion under the Sassanians, the fourth-century shah, Shapur II, issued the following decree based on his perception of the differences between the native Zoroastrian religion and the foreign religion of Christianity:

> The Christians destroy our holy teachings, and teach men to serve one God, and not to honor the sun or fire. They teach them, too, to defile water by their ablutions, to refrain from marriage and the procreation of children, and to refuse to go out to war with the king of kings [or "the shah of shahs," the leader of the Sassanians]. They have no scruple about the slaughter and eating of animals, they bury the corpses of men in the earth, and attribute the origin of snakes and creeping things to a good God. They despise many servants of the king, and teach witchcraft.[39]

Besides the perception that Christianity contradicted Zoroastrian thought and practice, the Sassanians believed that Persian Christians were fraternizing with their enemies, the Romans, since the Roman Empire was becoming increasingly supportive of the Christian religion. As the shah pointedly stated, "These Nazarenes inhabit our country and share the sentiments of our enemy Caesar."[40] Byzantine emperor Constantine did not help matters when he

---

[39]Shapur II, quoted in Richard Foltz, *Religions of the Silk Road: Premodern Patterns of Globalization*, 2nd ed. (New York: Palgrave Macmillan, 2010), 63-64; and William Young, *Patriarch, Shah and Caliph: A Study of the Relationships of the East with the Sassanid Empire and the Early Caliphates up to 820 A.D.* (Rawalpindi, Pakistan: Christian Study Centre, 1974), 6.

[40]Shapur II, quoted in Mark Bradley, *Iran and Christianity: Historical Identity and Present Relevance* (London: Continuum, 2008), 138-39.

wrote to the Persian shah, commending the existence of Christians in Iran: "I am delighted to learn that the finest districts in Persia also are adorned with the presence of Christians."[41]

Although Western historians have highlighted the persecution of Christians in the Roman Empire, Sassanian persecution of Christians exceeded in number and in intensity those in Rome. Some scholars put the number of Christian martyrs in Iran at 200,000. Ancient martyrologies document their stories in detail.[42] In one story, on Good Friday 344, Shapur II ordered the destruction of all churches and the death of clergy who refused to worship the sun. In one grim act the Sassanian authorities forced the bishop of Seleucia-Ctesiphon (the ecclesial capital of the Church of the East outside of modern Baghdad) to watch as soldiers beheaded more than one hundred of his bishops and priests before then killing him.[43]

By the end of the fourth century Sassanian aggression against Christians began to diminish. This respite came upon the accession to the throne of the new shah, Yazdgird I, who sought peace with Rome. Yazdgird I released Christian captives in his empire and allowed them to rebuild churches. Like Constantine in the East Roman/Byzantine Empire, Yazdgird convened a council for the majority Christians under his direction—in his case, the Church of the East. At the Synod of Isaac in 410, the Church of the East adopted the Nicene Creed.[44] It also declared itself autocephalous ("self-headed" in Greek), meaning that it was independent of other churches such as those existing in the Byzantine Empire (and thus Eastern Orthodoxy). Subsequent church councils in Persia followed the same path set by the Synod of Isaac.

In terms of theology, a great matter of contention in the early church, the Church of the East emphasized the distinction between the divinity and humanity of Christ—going so far as to say that Mary was the mother of Christ the man, but not Christ the God. (The word used at the time was that the Virgin Mary was *Christotokos* or "mother of Christ" in Greek, rather than *Theotokos* or "mother of God.") The fact that the Church of the East developed outside of the Byzantine Empire and conducted its liturgy and constructed its

---

[41]Constantine, quoted in Lamin Sanneh, *Disciples of All Nations: Pillars of World Christianity* (Oxford: Oxford University Press, 2008), 32.

[42]Moffett, *History of Christianity in Asia*, 1:145.

[43]Bradley, *Iran and Christianity*, 138-39.

[44]Baum and Winkler, *Church of the East*, 16.

theology in Syriac contributed to misunderstandings between it and church traditions in the West. Despite the significance of later councils in the Byzantine Empire, the Church of the East neither attended the Seven Ecumenical Councils nor condemned them. Instead, as mentioned earlier, the Church of the East looked to the east and south, establishing churches in Arabia, Central Asia, Mongolia, China and India, and possibly even into Southeast Asia.

THE EXTENT AND SIGNIFICANCE OF THE ASIAN CHURCH

Although it has been commonplace in the past to link early Christianity with Europe and the Roman Empire more so than with Asia and the Persian and Chinese Empires, the early worldwide church was largest and most widespread on the Asian continent. This should not come as a surprise given that Christianity was born in Asia and was embraced by many Asian communities. From present-day Saudi Arabia to Turkmenistan to China and India, the church in Asia included people from many cultural and linguistic backgrounds that were united in their belief that Jesus was God's Messiah and Savior of the world, although they differed vigorously with each other in other important matters. In fact, employing the geoschematic designations in use today by the United Nations, Christianity was practiced in all but one of the regions of Asia at the time Islam emerged in the seventh century: Eastern, Central, Southern and Western Asia.

Far from being faded dots on a map from a bygone era, the churches that developed in Asia have left an indelible mark on the subsequent history of Christianity. Among many other accomplishments, Christians living in these lands preserved and transmitted the first Christian writings, translated the Bible into local languages (creating an almost unbroken bond between the Bible and the language of the people), established schools and monasteries, safeguarded ancient practices, mourned and celebrated thousands of martyrs, codified Christian doctrine, built the earliest churches and led the way in international missions, including into neighboring Africa, a region that shared much in common with Western Asian Christianity.

two

AFRICA

*There are communities in Africa
that could claim an involvement in the
Jesus movement from its inception.*

Ogbu Kalu,
"African Christianity: An Overview"

The Deep Roots of the African Church

Although Christianity originated in Asia, it likely spread to Africa by the second half of the first century. The extent of the early African church was remarkable. From Egypt in the north to Morocco in the west and Sudan and Ethiopia in the south and the east, early African Christians were worshiping Jesus Christ in a variety of languages across large cities and sparsely populated villages in Eastern and Northern Africa. Not only was the church pervasive, it was also prolific. Some of the most influential persons in the entire history of world Christianity have arisen from Africa, and they have produced deeply influential writings and theological doctrines.

Yet Africa's religious significance goes deeper still. The continent of Africa was not only the home of the Hebrews for hundreds of years before the exodus, but Africa served as a refuge for the infant Jesus during Herod's final, furious moments of kingship. And during the last hours of Jesus' life, a man from Africa, Simon of Cyrene, came to his rescue, bearing the Savior's cross when he could not bear it alone. Though Israel and Palestine were the geographic backdrops to Jesus' ministry, Africa was Jesus' safe place. During Jesus' most vulnerable moments on earth, while a helpless infant and an abandoned Messiah, Mother Africa came to the rescue.[1]

CHAPTER OVERVIEW

In this chapter I will provide a broad overview of the early church in Africa. As was the case with Asia, despite the state of the church in this area today, Christianity was widespread and very active in Northern and Eastern Africa in the earliest centuries after Christ. In fact, many doctrines and institutions taken for granted by churchgoers today were codified by Christians in Africa more than a millennium ago. As you read about the early history of Christianity in Africa, try to imagine what it would have been like to be a contemporary of some of the greatest theologians in all of the church's past. Such was life for early Christians living in Africa.

NORTHERN AFRICA

Eight of the most influential Christian theologians of any time are products of the early Northern African church. Beginning in the Maghreb (an Arab Muslim term referring to northwestern Africa), Tertullian, Cyprian and Augustine were the architects of Catholic theology and Western doctrine. Tertullian coined words like *Trinity* and the *Old and New Testaments*. Cyprian famously declared that "You cannot have God as Father without the Church as Mother,"[2] and Augustine crafted the doctrines of original sin, justification and amillennialism. Tertullian and Cyprian were born in what is now Tunisia while Augustine was born and lived most of his life in Algeria. In neighboring Libya, the Christian priest Arius, though soundly condemned at the First Ecumenical Council, deeply influenced theology, especially after the Germanic tribes in Europe adopted Arian Christianity in the fourth century.

East of the Maghreb, in Egypt, lay the land of pyramids, wheat fields and the Nile River. In its leading city, Alexandria, Origen shaped Eastern theology for centuries to come despite the fact that later church councils condemned many of his teachings. Two subsequent bishops of Alexandria also played important roles in the church's development: Athanasius doggedly maintained

---

[1]See especially Aziz Atiya, *History of Eastern Christianity* (Notre Dame, IN: University of Notre Dame Press, 1967), 20, 22-24.
[2]Cyprian, *The Unity of the Church* 6.

the divinity of Christ during one of the church's earliest and most widespread controversies while Cyril gave voice and direction to the one-nature theology of the Coptic Church. Around the same time period, Saint Antony fled to the Egyptian desert, inaugurating one of the most significant movements in all of world Christianity: monasticism. Meanwhile, the discovery of the Nag Hammadi library in 1945 has shed light on early Gnostic Christianity, leading us to expand our scope of the church in Northern Africa. Early Christianity, it turns out, was much more diverse than we ever imagined.

Less known but just as ancient were the stories of Nubian Christianity, taking place in what is now Sudan. It has been argued that Christianity entered Sudan in the first century, particularly if we suppose, as some scholars have, that the "Ethiopian eunuch" in Acts 8 was referring to a treasurer of the queen of the Nubian Kingdom in Sudan rather than to the queen in Ethiopia.[3] Even if we doubt this hypothesis, it was likely the presence of Egyptian and Ethiopian monks that led to the growth of Nubian Christianity from the fourth century onward. When the Ethiopians invaded Nubia, the biblical kingdom of Cush—also called Meroe or the Meroitic Kingdom—collapsed. On the ruins of the kingdoms of Cush and Meroe, three small kingdoms emerged from among the Nubian people: Nobatia in the north, with its capital in Faras; Makuria in the central part, with its capital in (Old) Dongola; and Alodia (or Alwa) was in the south, with its capital at Soba (near the present-day capital of the Sudan, Khartoum) on the Blue Nile. Each of these kingdoms adopted Christianity as their state religions by the sixth century, and they produced beautiful art in their churches, including distinct representations of common biblical characters, events and doctrines, such as a representation of the Trinity with three human faces and veneration of local saints and martyrs.[4] Like the Egyptians (or Copts), the Nubian Christians adopted that form of Christianity arguing for the one human-divine nature of Christ—miaphysitism (or one-natured theology).

---

[3]Abraham Buruk Woldegaber and Mario Alexis Portella, *Abyssinian Christianity: The First Christian Nation? The History and the Identity of the Ethiopian and Eritrean Christians* (Pismo Beach, CA: BP Editing, 2012), 23; and Hassan Abdelwahab, *Influence (Supremacy) of Religion on Sudan's Foreign Policy Decision-Making* (Bloomington, IN: Author House, 2012), 44.

[4]Gawdat Gabra, "The Eastern Churches and Their Heritage (5th-8th Century): Churches in the Coptic Tradition. II. The Nubians," in *Christianity: A History in the Middle East*, ed. Habib Badr (Beirut, Lebanon: Middle East Council of Churches, 2004), 341-44.

> ## TRAIL MARKER
> ### The Copts
>
> According to Egyptian historian of Christianity Aziz Atiya, "The
> words Copt and Egyptian are identical in meaning, and both are
> derivatives from Greek 'aigyptos,' which the [Greeks] used for both
> Egypt and the Nile. . . . Ethnically, the Copts are neither Semitic nor
> Hamitic, but rather Mediterranean. They have been described as
> direct descendants of the ancient Egyptians."[a] Common tradition
> asserts that Mark, the author of the Gospel of Mark, evangelized
> what is now Egypt in the first century and served as the first head
> of the Coptic Orthodox Church, whose people are believed to be
> the descendants of the ancient Egyptians and not Arabs like the
> majority Arab Muslim population there today.
>
> ---
> [a]Aziz Atiya, *History of Eastern Christianity* (Notre Dame, IN: University of Notre
> Dame Press, 1967), 16.

Algeria and Tunisia. The Roman/Byzantine Empire ruled over Northern
Africa during the first six centuries after Christ. Besides Romans, the region
consisted of the original inhabitants of the land, the Berbers, as well as Punic-
speaking communities descending from the seafaring Phoenicians. As Christianity developed, Latin-speaking Romans clashed with indigenous Berbers,
which some scholars believe made Christianity susceptible to Islam in the
subsequent centuries.[5] In fact, theological controversy, division and persecution characterized Northern African churches from their earliest years.

Near the capital of what is now Tunisia (in Tunis), the ancient city of Carthage served as a center of early Christianity in Northern Africa. In the first
century, at which time Christianity plausibly entered, this largely Latin-
speaking city numbered around one hundred thousand people.[6] The earliest
accounts of Christianity in Carthage give witness to imperial persecutions that

---

[5]W. H. C. Frend provides the classic articulation of this theory in his influential book *The Donatist Church: A Movement of Protest in Roman North Africa* (Oxford: Oxford University Press, 2003).
[6]François Decret, *Early Christianity in North Africa*, trans. Edward Smither (Eugene, OR: Cascade Books, 2009), 11.

the church endured. The first of these, in the year 180 and called the *Acts of the Scillitan Martyrs*, offers a spartan description of the arrest and martyrdom of seven men and five women. Rather than postponing their decision to die for Christ as the Roman proconsul advised, the Scilli martyrs boldly declared: "Today we are martyrs in heaven. Thanks be to God."[7]

One of the more well-known series of persecutions in Northern Africa occurred at the turn of the third century. In 203, Roman authorities killed several Christians, including a young Roman noblewoman named Perpetua along with her slave girl Felicitas and other Christian catechumens (those undergoing catechesis in anticipation of baptism and thus membership into the Catholic Church). The account of their martyrdoms, *The Martyrdom of Perpetua and Felicitas and Their Companions*, comes from the journal that Perpetua kept. The gripping account of Perpetua's prison testimony still has the power to connect with readers today. While still nursing an infant, Perpetua was haunted by the thought of leaving her child motherless, just as her father, a non-Christian Roman, was terrified of watching his daughter be torn into pieces by wild animals as a result of joining a new religious sect. As she reported in one of her journal entries written from her prison cell:

> While I was still with the police authorities . . . my father out of love for me tried to dissuade me from my resolution [to die a martyr]: "Father," I said, "do you see here, for example, this vase, or pitcher, or whatever it is?" "I see it," he said. "Can it be named anything else than what it really is?," I asked, and he said, "No." "So I also cannot be called anything else than what I am, a Christian." Enraged by my words, my father came at me as though to tear out my eyes.[8]

Persecution of Christians in northwestern Africa led to a struggle for survival, which soon gave way to schism. The contemporary theologian Tertullian wrote prolifically about these matters from the city of Carthage. In the middle of the third century, Emperor Decius required citizens to publicly sacrifice to the Roman gods in an effort to unite the empire amidst disintegration. Officials gave certificates to those who made sacrifices, censuring those who refused. Because of their belief that sacrificing to Roman gods was idolatrous,

---

[7]Elizabeth Isichei, *A History of Christianity in Africa: From Antiquity to the Present* (Grand Rapids: Eerdmans, 1995), 34.
[8]Perpetua, "Martyrdom of Perpetua (203)," in *In Her Words: Women's Writings in the History of Christian Thought*, ed. Amy Oden (Nashville: Abingdon Press, 1994), 26.

certain Christians refused to offer these sacrifices, subsequently experiencing banishment, imprisonment, torture and even death. Included among this list of confessors (those who confessed Christ but did not die directly as a result of their confession) and martyrs were the bishops of Alexandria, Antioch, Jerusalem and Rome, as well as the famous scholar Origen.

Northern African Christians responded to the imperial mandate to make sacrifices to the Roman gods in any number of ways. Some, such as the well-known bishop of Carthage, Cyprian, fled. To the delight of the authorities, many sacrificed. Some bribed authorities for a certificate without sacrificing or forged their own, while others refused to sacrifice in the name of Christ. When persecution ceased, the church was deeply divided. On the one side were the *confessors*, those who refused to sacrifice to the Roman gods and experienced persecution as a result; on the other side were the *lapsed*, those who sacrificed, swore an oath or offered incense but who returned to the church once persecution ceased. Because of their faithfulness under persecution, confessors were enshrined in the early church, and they carried with them religious gravitas. Some even believed that confessors, who were often laypeople, possessed the power to forgive the sins of the lapsed (a right only reserved for those properly ordained), as if their confession of faith against the authorities imbued them with religious authority. In Rome the confessors consecrated a rival pope named Novatius on account of the perceived impurity of the Catholic Church. These Novatianists endured for centuries and considered themselves the pure church in distinction to the impure Catholic Church. It was not long at all before Novatianist churches popped up across North Africa.

In northwestern Africa a council convened from among the leading bishops to resolve this widespread pastoral concern. In contrast to the Novatianists, the Northern African bishops ruled moderately: Those who sacrificed could, through penance, return to the church on their deathbeds (or on confessing Christ during a future persecution), while those who bribed authorities for certificates could be reconciled earlier through a prescribed manner of penance. Those who sacrificed but did not repent could never be readmitted into the church. Finally, only bishops, and not confessors, could forgive sins and receive the lapsed back into the fellowship of the church.

Despite the ruling, this Catholic-Novatianist controversy hung over the church like a dark shadow due to continued persecution. As if in its death throes in the West, the Roman Empire once again required its citizens to sacrifice to the Roman gods—this time during the so-called Diocletian Persecution. The Romans targeted Christian leaders. As before, Christians responded to the persecutions in different ways. Although the same pastoral concerns regarding how, or if, to readmit the lapsed back into the church remained, the schism intensified. A related issue surfaced about what to do with the "traitors," that is, clergy who did not sacrifice to Roman gods but handed over Scriptures to the authorities (to destroy). Before long a rival church emerged out of Catholicism called the Donatist Church.

TRAIL MARKER
Division in North Africa

The early church in Northern Africa was rampant with division. Some of the names associated with this division—such as Donatism and Novatianism—may be unfamiliar terms, but it's important to keep in mind that different Christian groups splintered from others on the basis of a very practical concern: How should Christians treat those who backslid? There were a variety of responses to this question, and each Christian group believed that it was right and the others were wrong on this matter.[a]

[a]For more, see Derek Cooper, *Twenty Questions That Shaped World Christian History* (Minneapolis: Fortress Press, 2015), 35-50.

The year 311 marks the formal appearance of the Donatist Church. A rigorous contention of Catholic Christians had regarded the consecration of the new bishop of Carthage, Caecelian, as illegitimate since many considered one of the fellow ordaining bishops a traitor during Christian persecution. Consequently, this rigorous group elected a rival bishop of Carthage named Majorinus. When Majorinus died, the confessors consecrated a new bishop named Donatus, who gave name to the movement. The Donatist Church maintained that Christian clergy who complied with the Roman authorities during the persecution lost the purity of their office and thereby administered invalid sacraments—the sacraments, of course, being the lifeblood of the church.[9] Such a view hinged on the Donatist belief that sacraments received their efficacy from the righteousness of the cleric. The opponents of Donatism, most notably Augustine, argued that the sacraments were efficacious based on God's righteousness alone, not on the priest's. Augustine, a deeply influential bishop from what is now Algeria, considered the Donatists schismatics (rather than heretics) with a feeble understanding of ecclesiology. His opposition to the Donatists, as well to many of Augustine's theological views in general, shaped the development of the Western Christian tradition, with its heavy hand against those who sowed schism in the church.

Toward the end of his life Augustine witnessed the decline of the Western Roman Empire. The Arian Vandals' destruction of Hippo (and Carthage) in the fifth century prefigured the disruption of Christianity in the Maghreb after the Arab conquest in the centuries to come. In a twist of fate, the Arian Vandals, first under King Genseric and then under his son Huneric, launched a legislative campaign against the Donatist-persecuting Catholics. These Vandal kings exiled Catholic clergy, confiscated property, refused to allow and recognize Catholic sacraments, and demanded the conversion of Catholics to Arian Christianity. Huneric summoned a council of bishops and ordered conversion to Arianism or exile.[10]

Although the Arianization of the church continued for some time, the Catholic Church experienced relief during the reigns of the subsequent Vandal kings Gunthamund, Thrasmund and Hilderic in the late fifth and early sixth centuries. Byzantine armies, opponents to Arian Christianity under the aegis of Emperor Justinian that were eager to expand their influence in Northern Africa, eventually reclaimed northwestern Africa from the Vandals in 533 and reestablished Byzantine Christianity. Justinian, one of the greatest of the Byzantine emperors who financed extensive building projects across his empire, even ordered the construction of new, elaborate churches to adorn Northern African cities. Yet this was in vain. In a little more than a century, the Arabs

---

[9]There were also ethnic and economic factors involved in this dispute. See Ogbu Kalu, "African Christianity: An Overview," in *African Christianity: An African Story*, ed. Ogbu Kalu (Trenton, NJ, and Asmara, Eritrea: Africa World Press, 2007), 26.

[10]Anna Leone, "Christianity and Paganism, IV: North Africa," in *The Cambridge History of Christianity*, vol. 2, *Constantine to c. 600*, ed. Augustine Casiday and Frederick Norris (Cambridge: Cambridge University Press, 2007), 240.

would take control of the land, and we would begin to witness the gradual erosion of Christianity in the Maghreb. At this time, some of the Christian Berbers fled to what is now Niger and into the Sahara while Latin Catholics moved to Europe. According to some scholars the controversies and divisions of the Northern African churches made them susceptible to conversion to Islam, or it's simply possible that inhabitants of northwestern Africa found Islam more compelling than Christianity.[11] Whatever the case, Christianity was not only deeply divided in Northern Africa, it was disappearing.

EASTERN AFRICA

In addition to the churches in Northern Africa, Christianity developed very early in Eastern Africa. The story of how Christianity came to be practiced in Eastern Africa is rooted in the history of Israel, when the kingdom of Israel was just uniting under the reign of King Solomon in the tenth century BC. According to the fourteenth-century Ethiopian document *The Glory of the Kings*, a literary product of Christian origins with connections to the Christian Aksumite Empire of centuries past, King Solomon had intercourse with the queen of Sheba, whose child, Menelik I, became the first king in an unbroken line of royal succession of the Ethiopian throne.[12] As reported by *The Glory of the Kings*, Menelik later traveled to Israel to meet his father, Solomon, who entrusted his Ethiopian son with the Ark of the Covenant, an artifact that allegedly resides in the Church of Our Lady Mary of Zion in the ancient city of Aksum (Axum), Ethiopia. Today, this church still exists, and a priest guards the ark twenty-four hours a day from the public.

Ethiopia. The Aksumite Empire was a powerful kingdom in the ancient world. At its pinnacle, it included parts of what are now Ethiopia, Eritrea, Djibouti, Saudi Arabia, Somalia, Sudan and Yemen. Although believers possibly lived in Ethiopia before Christianity was established as the state religion of the Aksumite Kingdom in the fourth century, the most reliable reports we have link the introduction of Christianity to Ethiopia with brothers from current-day Tyre, Lebanon: Frumentius and Edesius. According to ancient reports, these two boys were traveling on a boat in the Red Sea with their tutor when

---

[11]David Grafton, "Northern Africa," in *The Atlas of Global Christianity* (Edinburgh: Edinburgh University Press, 2009), 122-24.

[12]This comes from chapter thirty of *The Kebra Nagast* (New York: Cosimo Classics, 2004), 34.

pirates confiscated their ship in Adulis, Eritrea. As slaves, Frumentius became the tutor of the young Aksumite prince, Ezana, while Edesius became the king's cupbearer. The brothers introduced Christianity to the royal house and, upon their release, Edesius returned home while Frumentius was ordained by Athanasius of Alexandria as bishop of Ethiopia. The time frame was likely in the 340s, and this event solidified the millennia-long jurisdiction of the Coptic Church over the Ethiopian Church.

TRAIL MARKER
The Miaphysites

The Coptic and Ethiopian Churches are called *Miaphysites* (part of the so-called Oriental Orthodox Church), meaning Christians who believed that Christ had one human and divine nature. From the fifth century onward, this theology put many of those living in current-day Egypt and Ethiopia out of favor with the Eastern Orthodox Church, which was the state church of the Byzantine Empire.

Ezana, deeply influenced by his teacher Frumentius while a prince, had grown into a powerful ruler by the time he made Christianity the state religion of the Aksumite Empire. With the king's approval, Frumentius established churches and schools across the empire even though the general populace did not immediately convert to Christianity. To signify the unbroken bond now linking his kingdom with the Christian religion, King Ezana minted the first known coins with Christian symbolism. These coins, minted in the middle of the fourth century, depicted a cross with the accompanying words, "May this cross please the country." A Greek inscription from the king discovered in the twentieth century declared, "In the faith of God and the power of the Father, and the Son and the Holy Spirit who have saved my kingdom. I believe in Your Son, Jesus Christ who has helped me who will help me always. I Aezanas [*sic*] king of Axum . . ."[13]

---

[13]Woldegaber and Portella, *Abyssinian Christianity*, 17.

After Frumentius's and Ezana's death, Christianity began to spread across the Aksumite Empire from beyond the royal court. In the later part of the fifth century, nine saints, originally from Syria, played an important role in the establishment of monasticism in Ethiopia. These saints also evangelized unreached parts of the empire and translated the Bible into the ancient language of Ge'ez. As world historian Lamin Sanneh has persuasively argued, the translation of Bibles into the native languages of Africa (and elsewhere) led to the growth and vitality of indigenous Christianity. Over time, the Ge'ez-speaking church came to be called the Ethiopian Tewahedo Orthodox Church. The Ge'ez word *Tewahedo*, which means "oneness" or "unified," refers to the church's belief in the one, united human-divine nature of Christ, and it also reveals the closeness between its theology with the Muslim doctrine of *tawhid*, or oneness of Allah.

Although Ethiopian Christians shared much in common theologically with Armenian and Egyptian (or Coptic) Christians, they were distinct in other ways. To begin with, the Ethiopian Church lays claim to the largest biblical canon of any church tradition. In its fullest form, there are forty-six Old Testament books and thirty-five New Testament ones, several of which are unique to Ethiopian Christianity. Second, Christianity in Ethiopia fused with existing Jewish practices based on the Israel-Ethiopia connection of generations past. Quite distinctly, Ethiopian Christians came to practice two sabbaths, circumcise male infants on the eighth day, observe Jewish ritual cleanness and dietary regulations (including the restriction of eating pork) and make replicas of the Holy of Holies and Ark of the Covenant in their churches. Even today, such practices distinguish Ethiopian Christianity from that in other world regions.

Despite its promising growth, Islamic conquests halted expansion of the Ethiopian Church. But unlike what other regions experienced, Arab Muslims did not attack Ethiopia or enjoin conversion to Islam due to the refuge that the Aksumite Kingdom provided to Muhammad's earliest disciples. Nonetheless, the Muslims took control of the Red Sea and the kingdoms surrounding Ethiopia. As global church historians Dale Irvin and Scott Sunquist explain, "The Red Sea became an Arabian lake, and the trade routes to India were entirely controlled by Muslims after the seventh century."[14] The Ethiopian Church

---

[14]Dale Irvin and Scott Sunquist, *History of the World Christian Movement*, vol. 1, *Earliest Christianity to 1453* (Maryknoll, NY: Orbis, 2011), 294.

moved increasingly into the highlands and away from the sea, leading to the isolation of the Ethiopian Church from most of Asia (and even much of Africa) for centuries to come.

THE EFFECTS OF PERSECUTION AND DIVISION

Although often overlooked, Christianity has deep roots in African soil. In the words of historian Thomas Oden, "no century has lacked some form of baptism and Christian testimony in Africa."[15] According to the rich literature of the Coptic Church of Egypt, John Mark, the author of the Gospel of Mark, introduced Christianity to Alexandria in the first decades after Christ's death and resurrection. By the second century a prestigious Christian school had developed in Alexandria, and Christianity was spreading rapidly to the south and to the west. In fact, the Egyptian desert was becoming an international destination for Christians seeking a life of rigorous prayer and devotion, just as other individuals and institutions in Africa were playing leading roles in early world Christianity.

Although the seed of Christianity initially took root in African soil, it would die out in many areas in the centuries to come. There were perhaps two forces at work. First, persecution against the church was intermittent during the first Christian millennium throughout Africa. These persecutions came in many shapes and in many sizes. Yet, whereas such persecutions strengthened the church in Europe, they seemed to sow division in Africa. Second, and in a related way, theological controversy and division marked the Christian communities in Africa from their earliest days. Perhaps Christianity's success among such varied people groups and diverse theological traditions caused an inevitable distrust among alternate expressions of Christianity, or perhaps there were other factors at play. Whatever the case, despite its early growth and promise in the first several centuries, the church in Africa eventually declined in all areas where it existed, particularly as Islam emerged as the dominant religious system in the region.

---

[15]Thomas Oden, *Early Libyan Christianity: Uncovering a North African Tradition* (Downers Grove, IL: InterVarsity Press, 2011), 73.

three

EUROPE

Christianity did not start out as a
European religious movement.

RODNEY STARK,
THE TRIUMPH OF CHRISTIANITY

THE RECENT HISTORY OF THE EUROPEAN CHURCH

Although there have been pockets of Christians living in Europe since the first century, early Christianity was largely confined to Asia and Africa. As historian Jonathan Wright puts it, "Christianity was a decidedly un-European affair."[1] It must be repeated that Christianity was born in Asia, and missionaries of the Christian religion had ably transported their faith across much of the Asian continent by the time Islam emerged in the seventh century. As for Africa, Christians living on this continent were regarded as some of the most creative and prolific of any region. When we look back at the history of early Christianity, therefore, we see the foundational role that Asian and African Christians played.

At the same time, we must not undervalue European Christianity in the places where it did exist—and flourish—from the earliest centuries of the Christian era. Christianity eventually prevailed among the various kingdoms of Europe, but the transition from paganism to Christianity was not immediate. As historian Peter Brown states, "Christianity did not come to Europe

---

[1]Jonathan Wright, *Heretics: The Creation of Christianity from the Gnostics to the Modern Church* (New York: Houghton Mifflin Harcourt, 2011), 69.

in a single, neatly wrapped package, with a crisp structure of popes, bishops, priests, and laity."[2] Christianity, like a living organism, grew and matured where it was planted. But it was not indigenous to European soil.

The history of Europe during the first centuries after Christ was one of transition and intense theological debate and controversy. In the west, within and around the borders of the languishing Roman Empire, Germanic peoples from the north began settling in what are now Austria, Belgium, France, Spain and Switzerland. In their new surroundings these Germanic peoples, who were formerly polytheists, came to adopt a form of Christianity called Arianism, which, in contrast to Catholic or Orthodox Christianity, did not regard Christ as fully God. Although Arian Christianity largely died out in medieval Europe, the well-preserved, sixth century Basilica of Sant'Appollinare Nuovo in Ravenna, Italy, serves is a reminder of the powerful Arian Christian kingdoms once scattered throughout Europe. In the eastern parts of Europe it was the expansion of the East Roman (or Byzantine) Empire, on the one hand, and the migration of the Slavs, on the other, that led to the ascendancy of the Catholic or Orthodox Churches. Gradually, however, from perhaps the fifth and sixth centuries onward, we get our first glimpses of a mounting division between the so-called Catholic and Orthodox Churches—a division that would become more apparent during the Middle Ages. Before that time, however, there was a whole host of Christian churches vying for legitimacy and believing themselves to be the true heirs of Christianity. And in the first several centuries, before what we may call imperial Christianity emerged, it was not at all clear which Christian groups would survive and which ones would perish.

CHAPTER OVERVIEW

In this chapter we will discuss the early history of Christianity in Europe. Although it is tempting to think that Christianity is really a European religion and that it was always deeply connected to the peoples of Europe, Christianity was an Asian religion that was foreign to Europeans. In the first several centuries after Christ the church in Europe was like a toddler taking its first uneasy steps. There were many falls. There were also a lot of sibling rivalries forming, and it took centuries before the two oldest brothers (the

---

[2]Peter Brown, *The Rise of Western Christendom: Triumph and Diversity, A.D. 200–1000*, rev. ed. (Oxford: Wiley-Blackwell, 2013), xxxv.

Catholic and Orthodox Churches) prevailed. As you read about early Christianity in Europe, try to imagine living amid a constantly changing population whose religious traditions were melding very slowly with a foreign religion from the East (Christianity), for such was the reality for many Europeans in the early church.

EASTERN EUROPE

Some ancient sources suggest that the apostle Paul preached to people groups in what is now Eastern Europe in the course of his extensive missionary travels, but it was more likely Paul's disciples, or even potentially other apostles such as Andrew, who first took the Christian message to this region. And even though churches existed in modern Bulgaria and Romania by the second century, Eastern Europe was highly unstable due to ongoing population transfers. In the fourth century, tribes of nomadic Avars and Huns invaded what are now Belarus and Ukraine, causing the migration of the Slavic peoples southward into Eastern Europe and across the Danube River. The different Slavic tribes settled in Eastern and Southern Europe, where they later adopted Christianity under the influence of the Roman Empire, split at this time into a Western (increasingly Germanic) and Eastern (or Byzantine) division.

Romania. According to ancient Christian sources, the apostle Andrew evangelized Dacia (in modern Romania) in the first century. Although possible, it is more plausible that Roman soldiers took Christianity there at the turn of the second century, at which time the Roman emperor Trajan defeated the Dacian king Decebalus and incorporated much of Romania into the Roman Empire. The Romans called the inhabitants of this land *Dacians*, a name they also gave to the province. And even though the Romans left Romania as early as 271, they intermarried with the Dacians, forming a Daco-Roman population that would eventually adopt Christianity. Rather than among kings and the nobility, Christianity spread in Romania at the popular level among poor villagers, enabling Christianity to take "deep roots throughout the whole country."[3] Lamentably, many of those who embraced Christianity faced great peril during the so-called Diocletian Persecution of the early fourth century. And even though many lost

---

[3]Romita Iucu, "Religion and Religious Education," in *Values and Education in Romania Today*, ed. Marin Calin and Magdalena Dumitrana (Washington, DC: Council for Research in Values and Philosophy, 2001), 52.

their lives for their faith, archaeologists have discovered artifacts confirming Christianity's survival in the midst of persecution.[4]

One of the most influential Christians coming from what is now Romania was the fourth-century Gothic missionary Ulfilas. Ulfilas grew up in the Gothic Church before being ordained as bishop to the Goths around 340 by the well-known Arian bishop Eusebius of Nicomedia, who had baptized Emperor Constantine only a few years earlier. Like certain other Christian bishops at the time, Ulfilas was a Homoean, meaning that he considered Christ to be "like" (*homoios* in Greek) God the Father rather than "of the same substance" (*homoousios* in Greek) as the Father. This Christian faction opposed the Council of Nicaea's use of the word *substance* (*ousia* in Greek), and although his Arian views were held in suspicion at the time, Ulfilas evangelized the Goths under the full sanction of Constantius II, an emperor sympathetic to the Arian cause.

Ulfilas served the Christian Gothic community in Dacia for several years before an antagonistic ruler persecuted the Christians in the late 340s. Such persecution caused Ulfilas and a group of Christian Goths to settle south of the Danube River in modern Bulgaria, allowing Ulfilas to then spread the Christian faith among the Goths living there. In what would become a consistent practice among Christian missionaries, Ulfilas decided that creating a local alphabet and translating the Bible into that language would be the most effective way to evangelize the people. Yet knowing the inherent limitations of translation from one language to another, Ulfilas reassured the Gothic people that the Bible had only one meaning:

> [In] relation to what is contained inside the [Bible], in case it should seem to the reader that in the translated version one thing is signified in the Greek language and something else in Latin or Gothic, he should take note that if the text displays a discrepancy arising from the rules of the language, it does nevertheless concur in a single meaning. So, no-one should on these grounds be in any doubt that the true sense of the original text has been determined by careful consideration in accordance with the meaning of the translated language, taking into account differences in the sense of (individual) words.[5]

---

[4]Mircea Pacurariu, "Romanian Christianity," in *The Blackwell Companion to Eastern Christianity*, ed. Ken Parry (Oxford: Wiley-Blackwell, 2010), 188.

[5]Ulfilas, quoted in Peter Heather and John Matthews, *The Goths in the Fourth Century* (Liverpool: Liverpool University Press, 1991), 171.

Ulfilas's missionary work among the Goths bore much fruit, as many Goths adopted the Christian faith under his leadership.

By the late seventh century Germanic tribes such as the Goths were beginning to transform the (West) Roman Empire. And although many of the Germanic tribes would later unite or conquer one another, for now they migrated across Europe, where they eventually adopted Byzantine-Roman customs, institutions, languages and what came to be the orthodox practice of Christianity, namely, Catholic or (Eastern) Orthodox. As one historian described the church in Romania, it was "connected to Rome by language and to Constantinople by faith and organization."[6] The subsequent arrival of the Slavs would tilt the Romanian church in an Eastern Orthodox direction, and thus toward Constantinople, even though that church would retain its Roman-influenced language—forming a distinct church identity that continues to this day.

TRAIL MARKER
Contested Land

The early Christian history of Eastern Europe, particularly in the southern parts, can be very confusing. But try to remember this: the region was the cultural setting for a tug-of-war match between the Germanic tribes in the West (who were transforming the Roman Empire) and the Greek-based Byzantine (or East Roman) Empire in the East. While the West eventually became Catholic and the East eventually became Orthodox, it was not at all clear which way the countries in the southern portion of Eastern Europe would go. In fact, some, such as Romania, went both ways.

NORTHERN EUROPE

While the church was gradually taking shape in what is now Romania, Christianity on the opposite side of Europe was following a similar course. Although Christianity could have theoretically reached the British Isles as early as the

[6]Pacurariu, "Romanian Christianity," 188.

first century, it is much more likely that it entered England, Ireland and Scotland by means of Roman merchants, missionaries and soldiers in the third and fourth centuries. In Roman Britannia, what is now England, Christianity first appeared in urban centers like Lincoln, London and York. The church in England aligned with the bishop of Rome, or the pope, who sent Bishop Augustine of Canterbury to revitalize the church there at the end of the sixth century. At this time in England's history numerous petty kingdoms scattered across the island were gradually adopting Christianity. The king in Kent, for instance, was baptized in 597 while the king of Northumbria passed through the baptismal waters in 627. In Scotland a Briton named Saint Ninian had formerly evangelized the Picts and erected a church in the southwestern part of Scotland in the year 400. Irish missionaries soon followed, leading to the evangelization of communities across what is now Scotland.

Although Bible production was not limited to the British Isles, some of our most splendid copies of the medieval Bible originated in what are now England and Ireland. Before Johannes Guttenberg printed the first Bible using mechanical moveable type in 1455, all books were copied by hand. During the early and medieval periods, most Bibles were incomplete, only containing, for instance, the Gospels, Epistles, Psalter or Pentateuch. Dating from around the year 700, we have four decorative Bibles with origins at famous monasteries in England and Ireland. These include the oldest surviving complete Bible in Latin, the Codex Amiatinus, as well as three complete copies of the Gospels, the Lindisfarne Gospels, the Book of Durrow and the Book of Kells (likely produced a century after the others). These carefully illuminated books reveal that medieval Bible reading was just as visually stimulating as it was spiritually.

Ireland. A patchwork of Celtic tribes inhabited ancient Hibernia at the time the earliest Christians entered there in the fourth century. The official establishment of Irish Christianity is traced to Pope Celestine's ordination of the first bishop to Ireland, Palladius, in 431; yet among early Irish Christianity the figure of St. Patrick has always loomed large and overshadowed those figures living before him. At the age of sixteen Patrick, a boy from northwestern England who grew up as a Christian, was captured and enslaved by an Irish raiding party. He was put to work as a shepherd in the north of Ireland among the Ulaid for six years.[7] There, as a slave and exile, Patrick turned his attention toward God, spending his days and nights in contemplation and prayer. As he later wrote about this time in his life:

> But after I had come to Ireland, it was then that I was made to shepherd the flocks day after day, so, as I did so, I would pray all the time, right through the day. More and more the love of God and fear of him grew strong within me. And as my faith grew, so the Spirit became more and more active, so that in a single day I would say as many as a hundred prayers, and at night only slightly less. Although I might be staying in a forest or out on a mountainside, it would be the same; even before dawn broke, I would be aroused to pray. In snow, in frost, in rain, I would hardly notice any discomfort, and I was never slack but always full of energy. It is clear to me now, that this was due to the fervor of the Spirit in me.[8]

After escaping with divine aid, Patrick eventually returned to Ireland as a missionary and, quite possibly, as a self-appointed bishop. Despite persecution, he established many Irish churches and monasteries in areas probably not previously Christianized. As was common at the time in Europe and elsewhere, Patrick evangelized in a top-down fashion, zoning in on tribal or clan leaders whose conversion to Christianity guaranteed the conversion of their entire tribe or clan. Later Irish Christians continued his pioneering work and successfully adapted Christianity to the tribal-like Celtic society at large.

After the death of Patrick around the year 461, sixth- and seventh-century missionary-minded Irish monks such as Columba, Columbanus (no relation) and Aidan began transplanting Christianity to other regions in Europe. Columba founded monasteries in Derry and Durrow before leaving Ireland and forming a Celtic community off the Scottish coast in Iona, which Celtic monks used as a launching pad for the Christianization of England and Scotland. In the year 585 the Irish abbot Columbanus landed in Brittany, or northwestern France, accompanied by twelve monks. One historian describes the scene: "[The Celtic monks] wore long white habits, nothing else, carried curved staffs and their liturgical books packed in waterproof leather bags; and around their necks they had water-bottles and pouches containing holy relics and consecrated wafers."[9]

---

[7]Oliver Davies and Thomas O'Loughlin, *Celtic Spirituality* (Mahwah, NJ: Paulist Press, 1999), 16.
[8]Patrick, *The Confession of Saint Patrick and Letter to Coroticus*, trans. John Skinner (New York: Image, 1998), viii-ix.
[9]Paul Johnson, *A History of Christianity* (New York: Simon & Schuster, 1976), 144.

Columbanus's "wandering for Christ" embodied the lifelong commitment to self-exile for the sake of Jesus that many Celtic missionaries practiced.[10] Columbanus established Christian communities on Continental Europe in areas that are now Austria, France, Italy and Switzerland. The Irish monk Aidan remained closer to Ireland but still exemplified the missionary impulse of Irish monasticism. He evangelized Northumbria and founded the monastic community on the Scottish island of Lindisfarne.

The Christian communities that these Irish missionaries formed became incubators of spirituality, education, evangelism and cultural preservation. Unlike the Goths and Slavs, who received translations of the Bible in their own languages (Gothic and Slavonic), Irish Christians adopted the foreign tongue of Latin and copied countless Christian works into that language during the Middle Ages. Regrettably, however, many monks lost their lives—and monasteries lost their religious treasures such as Bibles and relics—due to Viking invasions beginning at the end of the eighth century. And although these invasions deeply disrupted the Irish church, Irish monks used their enslavement among the pagan Scandinavians to share their faith and serve as the first wave of Christian missionaries to that people. Back home, Irish Christians also made developments in the system of penance. Whereas formerly penitence for Christians was public and reserved for heinous sins, the Irish developed the practice of private penitence, whereby a Christian could repeat any number of penitential acts under the supervision of a confessor. This practice soon caught on and became a hallmark of Catholic Christianity all over Europe (and later, beyond).

SOUTHERN EUROPE

Of all the regions of Europe, Christianity emerged earliest in Southern Europe. The apostles Peter and Paul reportedly preached and died in Italy, and Paul evangelized inhabitants of Greece and Malta, and possibly of Albania and Macedonia.[11] And as early as the second century we have several reports of Paul preaching in Spain, a dream seed that was planted in the book

---

[10]Davies and O'Loughlin, *Celtic Spirituality*, 19.
[11]Edwin Jacques, *The Albanians: An Ethnic History from Prehistory to the Present* (Jefferson, NC: McFarland, 1995), 138-39; and Jim Forest, *The Resurrection of the Church in Albania: Voices of Orthodox Christians* (Geneva: WCC Publications, 2002), 19.

> ### TRAIL MARKER
> ### Bible Production in the Middle Ages
>
> Who produced Bibles during the early and medieval periods? Although we can rightly envision monks painstakingly copying pages of the Bible by hand in scriptoria, the production of Bibles also included laymen and women. For most people owning Bibles was cost prohibitive. It is estimated, for instance, that five hundred sheep were needed to produce parchment (a writing material made of animal skin) for the Codex Amiatinus.

of Romans. As alluded to previously, there were three church traditions taking shape in Southern Europe during the earliest centuries of Christianity: Arian, Byzantine and Catholic Christianity. Although distinctions between so-called Byzantine (East Roman) and Catholic (West Roman) Christians were minimal at first, over time these groups evolved into separate yet loosely affiliated traditions. Theodosius I, a pious Christian from the Roman province of Hispania, was the last emperor to rule over both the eastern and western portions of the Roman Empire. From 395 onward, at which time Theodosius's two sons divided the empire into East (centered in Constantinople) and West (centered in Milan and then Ravenna), a religious fault line—most evident in the Balkan Peninsula—began to run through Eastern and Southern Europe. As one historian of the Balkans explains:

> This line became a permanent feature on the cultural map of Europe, separating Byzantium from Rome, the Greek from the Roman cultural heritage, the Eastern Orthodox from the Roman Catholic Church and the users of the Cyrillic script [used in Orthodox Slav churches] from those of Latin [the prescribed liturgical language of the Catholic churches].[12]

On the western side of the line in Southern Europe, the Italian and Iberian Peninsulas eventually became bastions of Catholicism (though southern Italy

---

[12]Fred Singleton, *A Short History of the Yugoslav Peoples* (Cambridge: Cambridge University Press, 1995), 11.

and Sicily faced a potpourri of religious and political overlords). Before that time, however, great ethnic and theological diversity characterized the region. The West Goths, or Visigoths, sacked Rome in 410 before expelling rival Germanic tribes and establishing an Arian Christian empire in modern Portugal and Spain. A related Germanic tribe, the East Goths, or Ostrogoths, also ransacked Rome. The Ostrogoths's most capable king, Theodoric, ruled from Ravenna a generation before Byzantine Emperor Justinian rose to prominence. The Lombards, meanwhile, eventually settled in the northern part of Italy after the migrations of the Germanic peoples from Northern Europe. In northern Italy, the Lombards were a thorn in the side of Italian Catholics in part because the Lombards were Arian Christians.

TRAIL MARKER
The Forging of an Identity

So many names and so many locations! Let's get ourselves out of the woods by keeping two things in mind. First, Christianity in Southern Europe was like a soup in its early stages at this point. It had not all mixed, and some ingredients were either on their way out or yet to be added. Second, what we today call the Balkans, a location that has experienced great unrest in the past century, has a rich yet complex past.

On the eastern side of the fault line, in an area we now call the Balkans, Christians were spread across the Roman provinces of Dalmatia, Illyria, Moesia and Pannonia by the second century. The reference in 2 Timothy 4:10 to Paul's disciple Titus in Dalmatia—a Roman province incorporating parts of what is now Albania, Bosnia-Herzegovina, Croatia, Montenegro and Serbia—suggests the existence of churches in that region at an early date.[13] Perhaps due to its early establishment there, the church in the Balkans produced many prominent Christians. The biblical commentator Victorinus, for

---

[13]Noel Malcolm, *Bosnia: A Short History* (New York: New York University Press, 1996), 2-3.

instance, was born and martyred in modern Slovenia, where he served as bishop in Pettau in around the year 303. Two generations later, the famous translator of the Latin Bible, Jerome, was also possibly born in what is Slovenia. By the time the Slavs began settling in the region in the sixth and seventh centuries, however, Christianity had died out in many parts of the Balkans, and the local culture had mostly reverted to paganism.

Italy. The first Christians to the Italian Peninsula likely entered from Western Asia in the first half of the first century. As elsewhere, Christianity spread among the Jewish diaspora before becoming predominantly Gentile in orientation. We do not know the origins of the Italian church, but Paul's New Testament letter to the Romans, written in Greek rather than in Latin, suggests a vibrant multiethnic community. From its earliest days the Roman church appears to have reflected Roman society at large, containing a large percentage of immigrants and slaves. It also contained its fair share of early martyrs. According to tradition, the apostles Peter and Paul both immigrated to Rome and became martyrs there toward the end of Emperor Nero's reign, along with hundreds of other Christians. Despite the trauma of losing two of its earliest shepherds, a strong church leadership structure developed by the end of the first century. In all likelihood the fourth bishop of Rome was a man named Clement, who wrote an influential Christian letter (First Clement) to the church in Corinth at the end of the first century, which many early Christian traditions included as part of their biblical canons.

In the early Roman church there was widespread diversity. Although the authority wielded by people like Clement came to embody mainstream Christianity, there were just as many individuals and groups on the other end of the Christian spectrum whose views were eventually condemned. One of the most renowned yet maligned figures in the early Roman church was Marcion, originally from what is now Turkey. He was living in Rome around the same time period another notorious Christian leader was active, a man named Valentinus, whose teachings sparked an independent movement that endured for centuries to come. The son of a bishop, Marcion had immigrated to Rome in the 140s and joined the church there before being expelled on account of his belief in two Gods (the Old Testament God and Jesus' God) and his firm rejection of the material world. The community that Marcion established, called the Marcionite church, lingered much longer than church leaders in the

Roman Empire wanted, and these leaders endeavored to differentiate their form of Christianity from Marcion's. One of the most enduring controversies that erupted between the Marcionites and the Catholics had to do with determining how to distinguish between Christian documents associated with the apostles and a growing number of Christian "Acts," "Apocalypses" and "Gospels" used by various churches in different capacities.

One of the more famous of these questionable books, the *Acts of Peter*, was written in the second century. (The Gnostic Christian library unearthed in Egypt in 1945 has many other such books from this time period.)[14] According to the document, Peter moved to Rome, where officials soon forced him to flee for his life after teaching several women of high status that they should not have sexual intercourse with their husbands but remain celibate. Yet as he exited the Eternal City, Peter saw Jesus entering it:

> And as he was leaving the city, [Peter] saw the Lord entering Rome. And when he saw him, he said: "Lord, where are you going?" And the Lord said to him: "I am going into Rome to be crucified." And Peter said: "Lord, are you being crucified again?" He said: "Yes, Peter, I am being crucified again." And Peter came to himself. And having seen the Lord ascend into heaven, he returned to Rome.[15]

After his brief conversation with the risen Lord, Peter understood that he was to return to Rome to die as a martyr on a Roman cross just as his Lord had done in Jerusalem a generation earlier. Peter thus returned to Rome and requested his executioners to crucify him upside down.

On the site of the reputed conversation between Jesus and Peter in Rome stands a small church nicknamed the Church of Domine Quo Vadis (Latin for "Lord, where are you going?" the words Peter uttered to Jesus). Not far from this spot lay the catacombs of the early Christians, scattered across Rome's ancient city in underground tunnels. In use from the second to the fifth centuries, the catacombs of Rome attest to the vitality of the early Italian church. Christians used these underground chambers to bury their dead (and later to

---

[14]See Marvin Meyer, ed., *The Nag Hammadi Scriptures: The International Edition* (New York: HarperOne, 2007).

[15]*Acts of Peter* 36, in *The Apocryphal New Testament: A Collection of Apocryphal Christian Literature in an English Translation Based on M.R. James*, ed. J. K. Elliot (Oxford: Oxford University Press, 1993), 423.

venerate them), but not necessarily to hide from Roman authorities. In all, more than forty catacombs exist—the catacomb of San Callixtus standing out as one of the most prominent of the catacombs, given its illustrious examples of early Christian art. In these earliest known depictions of Christ, Christians depicted Jesus as a beardless good shepherd who lays down his life for his sheep.

In addition to art, several descriptions of early Christianity in Rome have come to us in the form of literary documents. The Palestinian-born Justin Martyr immigrated to Rome in the middle of the second century. Once there, Justin started a Christian school. In order to convince authorities and educated Romans of the loyalty and value of the Christian religion on the one hand, and to dispel common myths that Christians practiced atheism and sorcery on the other, Justin led the way in writing Christian *apologies* (Greek, "speaking in defense"). In one section of his *First Apology*, Justin sought to disprove the myth that Christians practiced cannibalism (a common accusation among Romans) by explaining how Christians ate "the flesh and blood of . . . Jesus" by means of bread and wine mixed with water:

> This food we call Eucharist, of which no one is allowed to partake except one who believes that the things which we teach are true, and has received the washing for forgiveness of sins and for rebirth, and who lives as Christ handed down to us. For we do not receive these as common bread or common drink; but as Jesus Christ our Savior being incarnate by God's word took flesh and blood for our salvation, so also we have been taught that the food consecrated by the word of prayer which comes from him, from which our flesh and blood are nourished by transformation, is the flesh and blood of that incarnate Jesus.[16]

Around the year 165, Roman authorities arrested Justin and forced him to offer sacrifice to the Roman gods. Upon his refusal the authorities beheaded him.

Although the Roman emperors to whom Justin wrote his apologies likely never read them, residents in the Italian Peninsula slowly warmed to the Christian religion. The bishops of Rome, who seemed to be filling a power vacuum after the capital of the empire had moved east to Constantinople, had been gradually consolidating their influence across the peninsula. We may attribute this ascendancy of power to various factors, including Rome's strategic location in the historic heart

---

[16]Justin, *First Apology 66*, in *Readings in Christian Thought*, ed. Hugh Kerr, 2nd ed. (Nashville: Abingdon Press, 1990), 23.

of the Western Roman Empire, its association with the apostles Peter and Paul, New Testament passages linking transferable authority from Jesus to Peter via apostolic succession, political patronage after Constantine legalized Christianity, the honorary status the church gave to Rome at the Council of Nicaea as "first among equals," the papacy's increasing wealth and its oversight of cathedrals and the sites of holy martyrs and saints, and the need for an authority figure to address the Germanic and Hunnic invasions. Collectively, these forces led to an impressive increase in power that with each passing century expanded the papacy's base across the Italian Peninsula and beyond by means of alliances with kingdoms, fresh converts to Catholicism, popular support, church tradition and the consolidating power of the Latin language.

Lest we think that the papacy equals early Italian Christianity however, it is important to also recognize Christianity's presence outside of the Eternal City. There were many other Italian centers of the church, including Milan, where Ambrose, a bishop in the fourth century, baptized Augustine and popularized the cult of the martyrs. Christianity was growing across Italy, and there were two major factors for this. First, especially after the fourth century, the building of great churches in Italy proliferated. These churches were almost always connected to the relics of martyrs and saints, and their construction outside of city walls (where tombs of saints and martyrs formerly existed) led to the geographic expansion of Christianity outside of cities. The bishops who oversaw the various construction of churches associated with relics became powerful. As inheritors of the ancient Roman system of *patronage*—which imposed certain obligations on the patron and his clients—bishops sponsored massive building projects and offered the relics of martyrs and saints for public veneration.

Second, the spread of monasticism fueled early Italian Christianity just as in many other parts of the world. Although born in Egypt and Western Asia in the third century, monasticism came to flourish in Europe. In around the year 500, Saint Benedict of Nursia abandoned his academic studies and city life in order to embrace God and solitude. It took him many years of living in the Italian countryside in different places before coming to the realization that communal living provided a better model of the Christian life. After founding twelve Italian monastic houses, Benedict settled on Monte Cassino. On this rocky mountain more than eighty miles southeast of Rome, Benedict not only established a monastery and served as its abbot but also penned one of the most enduring books of Christian history. Though brief, Benedict's *Rule* provided a rhythmic beauty and flexible structure to communal living that has radiated out beyond the mountains of Italy. It has profoundly shaped the global history of Christianity. His *Rule* still calls out today:

> Listen, my son, and with your heart hear the principles of your Master. Readily accept and faithfully follow the advice of a loving Father, so that through the labor of obedience you may return to Him from whom you have withdrawn because of the laziness of disobedience. My words are meant for you, whoever you are, who laying aside your own will, take up the all-powerful and righteous arms of obedience to fight under the true King, the Lord Jesus Christ.[17]

The earliest biographer of Saint Benedict was one of the few others in Italy who rivaled his stature as a Christian leader: Pope Gregory, who was head of the Catholic Church from 590 to 604. By this time in European Christian history, many of the bishops came from the aristocracy. Gregory was one such bishop, and he was probably the wealthiest citizen of Rome when he became pope. In his *Dialogues*, which he wrote about many Italian Christian monks and saints such as Saint Benedict, Pope Gregory used a literary genre scholars today call *hagiography* (based on the Greek words for "holy writing"). In this type of literature, mundane and miraculous events were intermingled in order to inspire believers. (Like Gregory's hagiography of Saint Benedict, Athanasius of Alexandria had previously written one of Saint Anthony, the father of monasticism.) Pope Gregory lived at a crucial juncture in the history of Italian Christianity. Because a plague had killed about a third of the Roman population a few decades before, many poverty-stricken immigrants relied on the Roman church for food and for protection. In addition to providing food for refugees out of his own fortune, Gregory is celebrated for reigniting missions to Western and Northern Europe, reforming the liturgy, standardizing church music and writing many books on Christian doctrine and practice. Many also regard Gregory as a transitional figure from the ancient to the medieval world since his life coincides with one of the most shaping events in Western civilization: the migration of the Germanic peoples from around the late 300s to the 700s.

---

[17]Benedict of Nursia, *The Rule of Saint Benedict*, trans. and intro. Anthony C. Meisel and M. L. del Mastro (New York: Doubleday, 1975), 43.

WESTERN EUROPE

Although Christianity is often linked with Italy, given its later development as the capital of the Catholic world, it took centuries for the entire region to fully embrace the Christian faith. Even then, many forms of Christianity existed across the peninsula—including Arianism in the north, Catholicism in the center and Orthodoxy in the south and in Sicily. One of the most influential of the groups in the Italian Peninsula was the Germanic groups that adopted Arianism. Germanic tribes (not exactly direct descendants of Germans today), originally from the north of Europe, had blanketed Western Europe by the sixth century. Their migration into Roman territory was not belligerent but grew out of their desire for land and safety; it would prove momentous in European history. The union of Germanic and Roman ethnic, economic, political and religious cultures distinctly shaped Western medieval Christianity.

The Germanic language-based peoples consisted of various tribes and clans that worshiped gods associated with nature. Due to the missionary efforts of Ulfilas, several Germanic tribes abandoned their former religious practices in exchange for Arian Christianity. The Germanic tribes were a federated people generally given permission to reside in the Roman Empire, although the Romans did not always know how to handle such a mass of "barbarians"—that is, foreigners from beyond the empire. Using the (somewhat artificial) language the Romans devised when classifying the different Germanic groups, by the fifth and sixth centuries the following tribes had settled in much of Western Europe: Burgundians in southeastern France and Switzerland; Franks in modern Belgium, France, western Germany and Luxembourg; Frisians in the Netherlands; Lombards in Italy and Liechtenstein; Ostrogoths in Austria and Monaco; and Visigoths in southern France and Spain.

France. Of all the Germanic groups who traveled across Europe, the Franks would leave the greatest footprint in world Christian history. They even gave their namesake to the modern country of France, then called Francia, a region where Christianity has existed in some form since at least the second century. (Later, after a division emerging during the fourth and fifth centuries, the East Franks were instrumental in the development of what is now Germany while the West Franks were instrumental in the emergence of what is now France.) As in the Maghreb, our earliest reports of Christianity in modern France indicate a church swept up in persecution. According to one report, in the summer of 177 a group of Christians was being tortured for their faith by wild animals in a Roman amphitheater in the ancient city of Lyons. The leading exhibit that day was the torture and death of Lyons' first Christian bishop, Pothinus, whose martyrdom was regarded as the highest form of Christian piety. As that bishop's North African contemporary Tertullian later wrote, "The blood of the martyrs is the seed [of the church]."[18]

During the same time period that Lyons's first bishop was killed for his faith, we learn about one of the most prominent early leaders of the church in Gaul. Irenaeus became the second bishop of Lyons. Although born in Smyrna (now Izmir, Turkey), where, as a child, he reportedly listened to the teachings of Polycarp, a man who, as if part of a link in a chain, is said to have learned from the apostle John, Irenaeus moved to Lyons in the second century and was on business in Rome when his bishop and mentor was killed in 177.

As with other early orthodox Christian leaders, religious pedigree was crucial for Irenaeus. In his defense of orthodox churches against what he perceived as highly suspect groups such as Gnostic Christians, Irenaeus developed the doctrine of apostolic succession, which held that only churches under bishops that traced their heritages back to the apostles were genuine. As he wrote in his book *Against Heresies* in the 180s:

> Therefore we ought to obey only those presbyters who are in the church, who have their succession from the apostles, as we have shown; who with their succession in the episcopate have received the sure gift of the truth according to the pleasure of the Father. The rest, who stand aloof from the primitive succession, and assemble in any place whatever, we must regard with suspicion, either as heretics and evil-minded; or as schismatics, puffed up and complacent; or again as hypocrites, acting thus for the sake of gain and ambition. All these have fallen from the truth.[19]

Arguments such as these proved very attractive to early Christian leaders since they allowed bishops and priests to distinguish apostolic (and hence legitimate) churches from nonapostolic (and hence schismatic and heterodox) ones.

---

[18]Tertullian, *Apology* 50.14.
[19]Irenaeus, *Against Heresies* 4.26.2

> ## TRAIL MARKER
> ### Differing Interpretations
>
> Why didn't early Christians simply demonstrate from the Bible who were true Christians and who were false ones? What was the need to appeal to what has been called "apostolic succession"? Though amply obtainable today, the Bible was simply not available to most Christians in the early and medieval history of the church, and even if it was, most Christians could not read. And those few who were literate often disagreed with one another. As the fifth-century French monk Vincent of Lérins wrote about the Bible, there are "as many interpretations as there are interpreters."[a] For the early Christians theological accuracy was about pedigree—that is, about tracing one's theological heritage to the ancient fathers and disciples of Christ. The consensus from those who demonstrated adequate pedigree is the early tradition of the church, which was used to interpret the Bible among the elite who could read.
>
> ---
>
> [a]Vincent of Lérins, quoted in Thomas Guarino, *Vincent of Lérins and the Development of Christian Doctrine* (Grand Rapids: Baker, 2013), 5.

While Irenaeus was active in Lyons, Christianity was expanding across what is now France and developing in unique ways. As was the case throughout the ancient world (including, of course, Asia and Africa), the veneration of saints was a major cause of the spread and growth of Christianity in France. It was a common belief that saints, and the religious objects connected to them (including their corpses), both embodied and channeled divine power. The deaths ("birthdays") of the martyrs were carefully annotated (becoming feast days and forming the earliest stages of the church calendar), as were the dates associated with saints so that they would be venerated. Churches were increasingly built on the physical remains of martyrs and deceased saints, and Christians attributed countless miracles to the supernatural power radiating from their blood-stained and anointed bones. In the early and medieval church (and still today in different traditions), there was a full expectation that martyrs and saints could perform miracles for those who curried their favor.

A soldier named Martin brings together many of the themes associated with monasticism, miracles, relics and saints. He also serves as a transitional figure from the cult of martyrs (venerating those who died for their faith) to the cult of monks and saints (venerating holy Christian men and women and the objects connected to them). Born in the modern country of Hungary around the time the Roman Empire gave Christianity a legal status, Martin moved to the northeastern French town of Tours later in life. There he studied under the tutelage of Bishop Hilary of Poitiers, eventually establishing a nearby monastery and becoming bishop of Tours in 371. While bishop, Martin gained an international reputation as a miracle worker, and his evangelistic techniques among the *pagani* (or country dwellers) led to countless conversions. Bishop Gregory of Tours, a distant successor to Martin, constructed the former church of Tours over Saint Martin's bones, since they were reported to transmit God's power on earth to those who humbly petitioned him. As his grave marker states: "Here lies Martin the bishop, of holy memory, whose soul is in the hand of God; but he is fully here, present and made plain in miracles of every kind."[20]

Of the countless men and women who paid homage to the God of Saint Martin was the newly baptized king of the Franks. Born to the Frankish king Childeric I, Clovis came to power while living among a hodgepodge of Germanic tribes in Western Europe, including in the extreme north of what is now France. Clovis was an ambitious ruler, simultaneously absorbing and repelling different Germanic tribes inhabiting the region. Clovis, realizing that Catholic Christianity provided the best religious and political alliances available, married a Burgundian Christian queen and converted from paganism to Catholicism between 496 and 506. Bishop Gregory of Tours, writing in the sixth century, described the day Clovis and his soldiers converted to Catholicism as follows:

> The public squares were draped with colored cloths, the church was adorned with white hangings, the baptistery was prepared, incense gave off clouds of

---

[20]Peter Brown, *The Cult of the Saints: Its Rise and Function in Latin Christianity* (Chicago: University of Chicago Press, 1981), 4.

perfume, sweet-smelling candelabra gleamed bright, and the holy place was filled with divine fragrances . . . [all those present] imagined themselves transported to some perfumed paradise.[21]

TRAIL MARKER
Relics and the Growth of the Church

As in many parts of the world the growth and expansion of the church in France occurred in tandem with the spread of monasticism and the cult of the saints (not that these emerged only in France). Monastic houses were established all across France, and churches were almost always connected to the relics of saints and holy men and women. As one historian put it, "Of all religions, Christianity is the one most concerned with dead bodies."[a] The miracles emanating from the dead bodies of saints were very effective evangelistic tools—and early church leaders, such as bishops, knew that.

[a]Robert Bartlett, *Why Can the Dead Do Such Great Things: Saints and Worshippers from the Martyrs to the Reformation* (Princeton, NJ: Princeton University Press, 2013), 3.

The so-called Merovingian Dynasty that Clovis inaugurated ruled over parts of modern France (and also of Germany) for two centuries, and by the time Clovis died in 511, he had united the Franks and prepared the way for the expansion of the dynasty in the coming centuries. The Merovingian adoption and eager propagation of Catholic Christianity in the sixth century accelerated the growth of the Christian religion not only in urban centers but also in the countryside and among rival pagan tribes. In fact, writes historian Kevin Madigan, it is likely that "the Catholic Church could not have survived the political and military calamities of the sixth and seventh centuries" had not the Merovingian Dynasty adopted Catholicism.[22] In addition to having strong

---

[21]Gregory of Tours, *History* 2.31, in Brown, *Rise of Western Christendom*, 138.
[22]Kevin Madigan, *Medieval Christianity: A New History* (New Haven, CT: Yale University Press, 2015), 41.

bishops and a cultic focus on saints and relics, Frankish Christianity experienced a surge in monasticism. By the turn of the seventh century more than 220 convents and monasteries dotted the French urban and suburban sprawl,[23] and vibrant Christian communities were found in Arles, Auxerre, Lyons, Lérins, Marseilles, Paris, Poitiers, Tours and Reims.

THE GRADUAL DOMINANCE OF EUROPEAN CHRISTIANITY

Although Christianity was initially more of an African and Asian affair than a European one, a momentous shift was taking place in the sixth, seventh and eighth centuries.[24] Due, in part, to monasticism, miracles connected to saints and the conversion of the Germanic tribes, European Christianity began to blossom in places like modern Ireland, France and Italy, just as it would in the Balkans after the arrival of the Slavs. The two major events that shifted the balance of Christianity toward Europe and away from Africa and Asia were the rise and expansion of various Arab empires in Africa and Asia on the one hand and the rise and expansion of Christian empires in Europe on the other.

On the frontier of Western Asia in the colorful city of Constantinople, the well-known Byzantine emperor Justinian died just five years before one of the most influential people in world history—whose birth symbolized the eventual end of Byzantine rule in Asia and Africa—was born in the arid lands of Arabia: the prophet Muhammad. The expanding empire that Justinian oversaw would eventually experience a centuries-long entrenchment in Western Asia and Northern Africa. Meanwhile, back in the western regions of Europe, the impressive federation of Germanic tribes brought together by Clovis in the early sixth century was poised for sustained development in the heartland of Europe. Hence Christianity was entering a period of Christian growth and fortification across Europe just as its political and religious influence was waning across Africa and Asia.

---

[23]Brown, *Rise of Western Christendom*, 221.
[24]Ibid., 2.

PART TWO

Christianity from the Eighth to the Fourteenth Centuries

The eighth to the fourteenth centuries were a time of great upheaval for Christians living in Asia and Africa. In many parts of these continents, as elsewhere in the ancient world, there was a revolving door of empires, petty kingdoms and ambitious rulers. This time period witnessed not only the decline but the disappearance of Christian communities in many parts of Africa and Asia. This is even true of Armenia and Georgia, where rugged terrain discouraged Islamic expansion and where the fusion of national identity with Christianity kept it intact. In what is now Turkey, where the Byzantine Empire was headquartered, Christianity floundered until it numbered less than a hundred thousand in the 1400s, by which time the Ottoman Empire was fully poised to strike a death blow.

What was the cause of the decline? I will save the full response to this question for later chapters, but I might say that Islam starved out Christianity across Africa and many parts of Asia. In Eastern Asia, by contrast, where Islam never gained a real foothold, Buddhist, Confucian and shamanistic religions proved unfavorable to the establishment of a Christian realm. Even Buddhism, which is part and parcel of Eastern Asia today, was a foreign religion like Christianity, but one that eventually took root in a way that Christianity could not.

Who were the various Christian groups active in Asia and Africa from the eighth to the fourteenth centuries? There were many groups. The Church of the East was the most widespread branch of Christianity in Asia. There were dioceses of the Church of the East from Syria to China and from Azerbaijan to India. Syriac was the liturgical language. The Christians comprising what we call the Church of the East were mostly found in Eastern, Central and Southern Asia. The Church of the East was never really the state religion in any place it existed, though it sometimes wielded great influence on the royal court. The Oriental Orthodox Church and the Eastern Orthodox Church spread across many parts of Africa and in Western Asia. A person from the Oriental Orthodox branch of Christianity was persona non grata in the Byzantine Empire. Oriental Orthodox Christians were active in the southern parts of the Arabian Peninsula and certain parts of the Middle East. Oriental Orthodoxy was the state religion of Armenia, the oldest country in continuous existence to have made Christianity its official religion—all the way back in 301. It was also the official religion in what are now Egypt, Ethiopia and the Sudan.

The Eastern Orthodox Church was in the western part of Western Asia and was scattered across Asia. In what is now Lebanon, for instance, the Maronite community communed in fellowship with the patriarch of Constantinople, the head of the Eastern Orthodox Church. The same is true for Christians in Georgia, a mountainous region that enjoyed a degree of autonomy when it was not pressured by either the Byzantine Empire or the various Islamic ones. Inside the Byzantine Empire, Eastern Orthodoxy was the state religion. The Christians there were simply regarded as orthodox; outside the Byzantine Empire they were branded as Melkites, roughly translated as "the king's men," an obvious slur. Outside of protected monasteries and united communities, Melkites would have found it much easier to live in the Byzantine Empire rather than outside of it during this time period since the Islamic empires perceived Christians faithful to the Byzantine Empire as a threat to their rule.

What about Europe? Unlike the situation in Africa and Asia, Europe exploded with Christian growth from the eighth to the fourteenth centuries. With the church languishing in Africa and Asia, it grew lopsided in Europe. Slowly but consistently Christianity became the official religion of Europeans due to a marriage alliance between monarchs and the church. The major Christian tradition in Europe, particularly in the west, was the Catholic Church. Headquartered in Rome, the Catholic Church had inherited the structural and political edifice of the Roman Empire, down to the city districts (or dioceses) and the clothing worn by those governing these districts, the bishops. In addition to Catholicism, there were of course many fringe Christian groups. The Waldensians, who favored voluntary poverty and were critical of authority, originated in France but clashed with the luxury and hierarchy of Rome. (They still exist to this day.) Another fringe Christian group was the Cathars. Catharism was dualist in outlook, believing that the physical was evil and that Christ could not have taken the form of a body. Like many other fringe groups who formed in the Middle Ages in Europe, the Catholic Church deemed the Cathars heretical and sought to prosecute its leading practitioners.

four

ASIA

*If a faith as vigorous and pervasive as . . . Asian Christianity
could have fallen into such oblivion, no religion is safe.*

PHILIP JENKINS,
THE LOST HISTORY OF CHRISTIANITY

THE ECLIPSE OF CHRISTIANITY IN ASIA

The church in Asia faced great challenges during the Middle Ages. This is especially evident between the years 1200 and 1500, during which time it has been estimated that the number of Christians in Asia declined from twenty-one million to less than four million.[1] Although it is not accurate to state that Christianity died in Asia at this time, it certainly diminished—and fairly rapidly and extensively so. What accounts for this sharp decline? Collectively, there were four major factors contributing to Christianity's diminishment in the land where it was born and grew into adolescence.

To begin, the Asian church was completely divided. Christians living in different regions of Asia were isolated from one another, and they never united around a mission or a common identity. In fact, distrust of Christian rule led some persecuted Christian groups to welcome Muslim rule, though such rule inevitably proved harmful to Christian expansion and witness. The Crusades, infamous for Christian violence against Muslims, also led to bitterness between European and Asian Christians, causing the latter to be further marginalized by

---

[1]Philip Jenkins, *The Lost History of Christianity: The Thousand-Year Golden Age of the Church in the Middle East, Africa, and Asia—and How It Died* (New York: HarperOne, 2008), 24.

Islamic governments once the Catholic Christian kingdoms in Western Asia were dismantled in the twelfth and thirteenth centuries.

Second, although Islamic empires in Southern and Western Asia allowed Christians to freely worship, they did not allow Christians to publicly evangelize, convert non-Christians, repair churches or build new ones. Out of sheer necessity, therefore, Asian churches under Islamic rule became inward-looking, marginalized and relegated to maintaining their ground rather than looking outward, engaging new groups and expanding.

Third, the Black Death, the spread of which was made possible by the vast and interlocking empire of the Mongols, wiped out countless millions of Asian Christians in the first half of the fourteenth century. From China to Turkey and from India to Central Asia this plague killed everyone in its path.

Finally, the fourteenth-century Mongol khan Tamerlane, a claimed descendant of Genghis Khan, resurrected his forefather's empire across Asia, killing millions in the process. Tamerlane was an equal-opportunity offender. He murdered just as many Muslims as he did Christians (or Jews). In terms of the Asian church, his destructive reign was the culmination of centuries of devastation and diminishment, and the clerical offices of the Church of the East had to become hereditary in order to survive.

CHAPTER OVERVIEW

In this chapter we will discuss the eclipse of the Asian church. As asserted in chapter one, the church began in Asia. There it grew rapidly and spread out across the Asian continent. Over time, however, the church found itself incapable of sustaining its growth. As you read about the diminishment of the Asian church in this chapter, try to imagine the ramifications of centuries of foreign political and religious rule on the church, and how economic and other social incentives for those who converted to the dominant religion influenced countless Christians to abandon the faith of their forebears. Such was the reality for many Christians in Asia at this time.

CENTRAL AND EASTERN ASIA

Christianity was widely practiced across Central and Eastern Asia in the first millennium of the Christian era. The Silk Road enabled merchants and missionaries to spread the Christian faith across thousands of miles, and we have extensive archaeological and literary remains confirming Christianity's presence in this region of Asia, ranging from Christian tombstones in Kazakhstan to crosses and statues in South Korea. In Central Asia—across Kyrgyzstan, Turkmenistan and Uzbekistan—several Turko-Mongolian clans such as the Kerait and Uyghur people adopted Christianity under the evangelistic efforts of the Church of the East. Writing in the year 781, Timothy I, who probably oversaw more Christians than any patriarch of any Christian tradition before or during his time, wrote of a Turkic people living in Central Asia: "The king of the Turks abandoned idol worship and, together with nearly his entire people, became Christian. He asked us to create a metropolitan see, and this we have done."[2] Writing ten to fifteen years later, Timothy I not only indicated success among the Turkic peoples but also expressed hope in reaching Tibet: "The Holy Spirit has in these days consecrated a metropolitan for the Turks, and we are preparing for the consecration of another metropolitan for the land of the Tibetans."[3]

In China, Christianity's introduction in the year 635 led to imperial patronage of the religion during the Tang Dynasty, and recent archaeological discoveries of murals on churches and literary documents from formerly sealed caves have confirmed how extensive Christianity was in China. But Christianity's success was short-lived. Although we do have vague reports of Christians living in China after the year 1000, the Sung Dynasty did not have any formal ties to the Christian religion. Hence Christianity, in whatever formed it existed, was without imperial patronage until the emergence of the Yuan Dynasty in the thirteenth and fourteenth centuries.

China. The reintroduction of Christianity to Eastern and Central Asia was a byproduct of the so-called Mongol Empire, a loosely overlapping and affiliated series of kingdoms in Central, Eastern and Western Asia. Born in the second half of the twelfth century, Temujin, otherwise known as Genghis Khan, was the architect of this massive empire—one of the largest empires in all of world history. Although Mongols such as Tamerlane later turned to violence against Christians, many early Mongol leaders not only tolerated but even embraced the Christian religion. Genghis Khan took Christian princesses for himself and for two of his sons from a tribe called the Keraits, whom the

---

[2]Timothy I, quoted in Christoph Baumer, *The Church of the East: An Illustrated History of Assyrian Christianity* (London: I. B. Tauris, 2006), 169.
[3]Ibid., 174.

Church of the East had evangelized in 1007. In fact, two of the most influential of Genghis's many grandsons, Kublai Khan and Hulagu, were the sons of an extraordinary Christian princess named Sorqaqtani, who raised two of the most powerful men in history. The thirteenth-century bishop, Bar Hebraeus, wrote of her as follows:

> This queen raised her sons so well that all the princes marveled at her power of administration. She was a Christian, sincere and true like Helena [Constantine's mother]. A certain poet said, *if I were to see a second woman like her, I should say that the race of women was far superior to that of men.*[4]

Although Sorqaqtani's baptized sons did not practice Christianity to the exclusion of competing religions, they controlled lands where Asian Christianity had existed for a millennium and were relatively friendly to the religion.

While Hulagu moved westward and controlled large parts of Central and Western Asia in an empire called the Ilkhanate, Kublai Khan established the Yuan Dynasty in China and moved the capital to Dadu (now Beijing). The Yuan Dynasty ruled over China from 1271 to 1368. Kublai Khan and his successors generally supported Christianity, and representatives from a variety of ethnically and theologically different churches played a role in the development of Christianity in China. Among the largest group of Christians the Church of the East, perhaps the most important to serve the Yuan Dynasty was an astronomer and physician named Jesus, or Ai Xieh. Kublai Khan appointed Jesus as the head of the office for Western astronomy and medicine, then the head of the office for Christian religion and finally to state minister. Kublai Khan also sent Jesus to Pope Honorius to discuss a possible alliance against the Mamluks, an Islamic empire in the Middle East hostile to Western Christians.

Although nothing tangible came from the talks between the court of Kublai Khan and that of Pope Honorius, negotiations between popes and Mongolian rulers were commonplace. The impetus of much of the European-Mongolian discussions about an alliance stemmed from the presence of the Mamluks in the Holy Land, with whom both the Mongols and Catholic Europeans clashed. In the 1240s, Pope Innocent IV commissioned two separate Franciscan "diplomatic-religious missions" to those in central and eastern Asia.[5]

---

[4]Bar Hebraeus, quoted in Baumer, *Church of the East*, 217.
[5]Daniel Bays, *A New History of Christianity in China* (Oxford: Wiley-Blackwell, 2011), 12.

```
                    ┌─────────────────────────────────────────┐
                    │                                         │
                    │            TRAIL MARKER                 │
                    │            The Mongols                  │
                    │                                         │
```

TRAIL MARKER
The Mongols

Although the Mongol Empires were initially receptive to Christianity and sought alliances with (Catholic) Europe against rival empires in Asia, most of the Mongol leaders gradually converted to Islam. As they did so, churches in Asia found themselves in more precarious positions and lost their patronage.

Among Catholic priests and missionaries sent by the pope at this time period, John of Montecorvino was the most prominent. An Italian in the newly created Franciscan order, John served as a missionary in India the year before arriving in modern Beijing in 1294, just after the famous Venetian explorer Marco Polo's service in the court of Kublai Khan from 1275 to 1291 had ended. John succeeded as a Catholic missionary. After about ten years of work in China, John had likely converted about ten thousand people to Catholicism, although, as a point of contention, most converts hailed from existing Christian traditions.[6] John achieved so much success that the Catholic Church sent more Latin missionaries to the Yuan Dynasty and consecrated John as archbishop of Khanbaliq (in what is now Beijing) in 1313.

It did not take long before the Catholic Church's successes in China raised the ire of the Church of the East.[7] In the second of three letters to the pope, John wrote the following about the Church of the East, which he and many former scholars called Nestorians:

> The Nestorians call themselves Christians, but behave in a very unchristian manner. [They] have grown so strong in these parts that they did not allow any Christian of another rite to have any place of worship, however small, nor preach any doctrine but their own. For these lands have never been reached by any apostle or disciple of the apostles and so the aforesaid Nestorians both directly and by the bribery of others have brought most grievous persecutions

---

[6]Richard Foltz, *Religions of the Silk Road: Premodern Patterns of Globalization*, 2nd ed. (New York, NY: Palgrave Macmillan, 2010), 125.
[7]Bays, *New History of Christianity in China*, 13.

upon me, declaring that I was not sent by the Lord Pope, but that I was a spy, a magician and a deceiver of men.[8]

Unfortunately, these East-West Christian conflicts were to be repeated on a regular basis across Asia. Christians found it very difficult to get along and share the imperial spotlight with other Christian groups. In fact, when the first person born in China to reach the continent of Europe—Rabban Bar Sauma, who happened to be a Christian—presented himself to the cardinal of bishops in Rome in the 1280s, he was almost immediately questioned by the cardinals and held in suspicion on account of his theology.

Back in China this intramural dispute came to an abrupt end once the Ming Dynasty supplanted the Yuan Dynasty in 1368. The Ming, not foreign Mongolians but coming from Chinese extract, ordered the expulsion of nonnative monks and the destruction of churches. It appears that, just as was the case during the Tang Dynasty, Christianity's collusion with dynastic leaders meant that it essentially disappeared once new rulers arrived in town. Internal church politics and confusion over the church's role in a non-Mongol empire also played a role in Christianity's decline and virtual disappearance in the new Chinese regime. Moreover, the Black Death that ravaged Europe in the middle of the fourteenth century ended the European mission to China at this time. Thus the third wave of Christian missions in China would have to wait for the Catholic Jesuits, whom the pope would not send until the sixteenth century. For several centuries Christianity in China was nothing more than a faint dream.

SOUTHERN AND WESTERN ASIA

During the Middle Ages, the histories of major parts of Southern and Western Asia were deeply intertwined. Although there were pockets of Christians in Afghanistan, India and Pakistan, as well as a stable community of faith in places such as Armenia, Georgia and Turkey, much of what is today called the Middle East was ruled by various Islamic empires. Like the Christian Church, the Muslim ummah, or the community of faithful Muslims, was deeply divided. Whether Sunni or Shia, Arab or Turkic or Christian or Zoroastrian converts, there were just as many differences among Muslims as there were similarities. After the collapse of the (Arab Muslim) Umayyad Dynasty, headquartered in

---

[8]Foltz, *Religions of the Silk Road*, 124.

Damascus, in 750, a series of Islamic dynasties emerged in the Middle East—some lasting a few decades, others for centuries. Among the larger Islamic empires that formed across Southern and Western Asia during the Middle Ages, there were prominent Arabs, Kurds, Turkic-Mongolians and Iranians in leadership. These empires did not get along.

TRAIL MARKER
The Crusades

The Crusades were a Christian failure in many ways. In 1097, heavily armored Christian "Franks" entered the edges of Western Asia and proceeded to fight against the Muslim Turks, both groups being regarded as interlopers by locals. Scholars call the battles that raged for two centuries the Crusades (1095–1291). They represent one of the most embarrassingly romantic episodes of Christian history among Westerners and one of the most contemptible among Easterners. Far from uniting the church against Islam, one of the original aims, the Crusades had the effect of causing greater disintegration of the church in Asia and placing Asian Christians in a more precarious position with their Muslim overlords once the Latin Christians left the Holy Land.

According to Islamic law Christians were protected under a system of dhimmitude (dhimmis were the "people of the book" mentioned in the Qur'an). The dhimmis, such as Christians, often lived in their own neighborhoods (called millets) and were relatively free to practice their faith as long as they paid their taxes and did not violate any laws. Yet there was also widespread social discrimination as well as occasional bursts of violence. As a general rule of thumb, Christianity and Islam clashed the closer one was to the West, where the Christian religion was now thriving and without the kinds of political and religious threats existing in the East. When combined with other factors, the rivalry between Christians in the West (not in the East) and Muslims sparked the Crusades, which led to further resentment and misunderstanding, as well as division among the Christian communities remaining in the Middle East. From roughly 1095 to 1291, Western Christians, indiscriminately called Franks, fought against various Islamic empires in the Middle East for control over the Holy Land, particularly of Jerusalem. Islam won. After centuries of decline and diminishment, compounded by the Fourth Crusade in the year 1204 when Western Christians sacked Constantinople, the Byzantine Empire collapsed in 1453. The Ottoman Turks then became the dominant regional empire in Western Asia just as the Mongol Empire was on its last leg in parts of Central, Eastern and Southern Asia.

Iraq and Iran. The Abbasid Dynasty was one of the most culturally rich, powerful and prosperous of the Islamic empires during the Middle Ages. The newly founded city of Baghdad served as the primary capital from 762 to 1258, but the dynasty expanded well beyond the borders of what is now Iraq. When the Abbasid Dynasty overtook the Umayyad Dynasty in the year 750, the Church of the East was the largest Christian body in that region. In order to remain closer to the central authority, the Church of the East moved its headquarters from Seleucia-Ctesiphon to nearby Baghdad in 775. The church's new headquarters in Baghdad allowed officials of the Church of the East to stay in close contact with the Muslim caliph or ruler. Over time the Abbasid Dynasty came to regard the catholicos of the Church of the East as the head of the Christian Church in all of Asia, as we can see from the decree of Caliph Muktafi II concerning Catholicos Abdisho III in 1138:

> The charter of the highest imamate of Islam is hereby granted to you to be the Catholicos of the Nestorian Christians inhabiting the City of Peace [Baghdad] and all the lands of the countries of Islam. You are empowered to act as their head and the head also of the Greeks [Byzantines], Jacobites [Miaphysites] and Melkites [Byzantines]. If any of the above-mentioned clerics treads in the path of revolt against your orders or refuses to accept your decisions, he will be prosecuted and punished. Your life and property, as well as that of your people, will be protected, likewise your churches and monasteries.[9]

Probably the most prominent catholicos of the Church of the East during the Abbasid Dynasty was Timothy I. Born in what is now northern Iraq, Timothy oversaw nineteen metropolitans and eighty-five bishops in a Christian

---

[9]Baumer, *Church of the East*, 148.

stronghold stretching thousands of miles. Although we are not used to thinking of Christianity in these regions, Timothy had oversight of churches in Western Asian regions like Syria, Qatar, Bahrain and Iraq, throughout India and Iran in Southern Asia, and Turkestan in Central Asia, all the way to Tibet, Mongolia and China in Eastern Asia.[10] Timothy was a contemporary of several well-known caliphs, and famously dialogued with Caliph al-Mahdi about Christianity. Having commissioned more than one hundred missionaries into unreached regions in Asia, he is one of the most important leaders in the first millennium of Christianity. Catholicos Timothy's pride in Eastern Christianity bubbles up in a letter he wrote to the bishop of Nineveh (now near Mosul, Iraq) in 785.

> If Rome is accorded the first and highest rank because of the Apostle Peter, how much more should Seleucia and Ctesiphon on account of Peter's Lord [Jesus]. If the first rank and position is due to the people who confessed on Christ before all others, and believed in him, then we Eastern[er]s were the ones to do so. We showed our faith openly in the person of our Twelve Envoys [the Magi], who were guided by a star, and in the gifts which they offered to Christ— gold, as to the King of all kings and the Lord of all lords; frankincense, as to the One who is God over all; and myrrh, to signify the passion of his humanity for our sake. . . . Thirty years before all others we Eastern[er]s confessed Christ's kingdom, and adored his divinity.[11]

The Abbasid Dynasty brought blessings and curses to the Christian community. Due to their lack of schools and need of administrators, physicians, scribes, teachers and translators, the early (Arab) Abbasid Dynasty turned to educated Christians to assist in their governmental transition. The Christian scholar Hunayn ibn-Ishaq, for instance, oversaw an important Muslim school and library. He also served as the chief physician of the caliph. Other Christians were leaders in mathematics, medicine, philosophy, science and in the translation of classic (Greek) Western texts into Arabic.

Despite some favor, the church experienced its fair share of setbacks, particularly after the Turks took control of the Abbasid Dynasty in the eleventh century. To begin with, the Abbasids never considered the

---

[10]Jenkins, *Lost History of Christianity*, 11.

[11]Timothy I, quoted in William Young, *Patriarch, Shah and Caliph: A Study of the Relationship of the East with the Sassanid Empire and the Early Caliphate up to 820 A.D.* (Rawalpindi, Pakistan: Christian Study Centre, 1974), 3.

Christian community equal to the Muslims. Christians lived in their own neighborhoods and were theoretically free to live as they chose, but they also experienced periodic bursts of hostility and sustained discrimination. Christian conversions to Islam likewise proceeded in stages, often on account of economic and social incentives rather than through forced conversion. According to the eleventh-century catholicos John VI, "Christians were compelled to wear distinctive dress and a number deserted the faith on account of the trials, woes, and injuries that befell them."[12]

Under the so-called millet system, Muslim rulers appointed Christian bishops to collect taxes from their parishioners since Christians were excluded from the armed forces and thus were unable to provide for the government through military service.[13] Although many churches were turned into mosques during the Middle Ages, it was illegal for Muslims to convert to Christianity. Christian martyrdom, though it existed, largely occurred when Muslims converted to Christianity rather than Christians being killed for the sake of being Christians. The following set of rules applying to dhimmis is traced to the eighth century, but was recorded in the tenth century by the jurist al-Mawardi of the Shafi'i school of Muslim thought.

1. They (i.e., the dhimmis) must not denigrate or misquote the book of Allah.

2. May not accuse the messenger of Allah of lying or speak of him despairingly.

3. Must not mention Islam with slander or calumny.

4. Must not approach a Muslim woman to commit adultery with her or with view to marriage.

5. Must not undermine a Muslim's faith or cause harm to his wealth or religion.

6. Must not help the enemies of, or spies on, Islam.[14]

Although some Christian communities were relatively autonomous under early Arab rule, Muslim laws increasingly restricted the rights and privileges of Christians. In the middle of the ninth century, persecution erupted against Christians and Caliph Mutawakkil, "who was one of the first 'Abbasid caliphs

[12]John VI, quoted in Christian Van Gorder, *Christianity in Persia and the Status of Non-Muslims in Iran* (Plymouth, UK: Lexington Books, 2010), 53.
[13]Thomas Walker Arnold, *The Preaching of Islam: A History of the Propagation of the Muslim Faith* (New York: Charles Scribner's, 1913), 55.
[14]Suha Rassam, *Christianity in Iraq* (Leominster, UK: Gracewing, 2006), 78-79.

systematically to promote specifically anti-Christian policies throughout the caliphate," deposed and imprisoned Catholicos Theodosius.[15] The twelfth-century Syriac historian Mari describes this event:

> Al-Mutawakkil was angry and commanded [Theodosius] to be deposed, and a month after his appointment sent to Baghdad and put him in prison, and proceeded to destroy the churches and monasteries.... And he prevented the Christians from riding on horses, and he commanded them to wear dyed garments and to put a patch upon their shirts, and that none of them should be seen in the market on Friday, and that the graves of their dead should be destroyed, and that their children should be brought to the mosque, and that the wooden images of devils should be erected on their gages, and a sound summoning them to prayer should not be heard, and place should not be set apart for the liturgy.[16]

Even though it was not state policy to physically harm Christians, such harm did occur, whether intentional or not, contributing to the general malaise of the church. Over the course of several centuries it comes as no surprise that the church gradually diminished in Iraq and Iran during the Abbasid Dynasty.

TRAIL MARKER
Dhimmitude

Officially, Christians were to be protected by the Islamic government (under the system of dhimmitude) and were under the authority of a Christian bishop. But Christians were increasingly under social strains, leading many to convert to Islam over the centuries.

The change of political and religious rule from the Abbasids to the Mongols in the thirteenth century gave the church a respite, though it could not revive it. Hulagu, the first khan in the (Mongolian) Ilkhanate, headquartered in Iran,

---

[15]Sidney Griffith, *The Church in the Shadow of the Mosque* (Princeton, NJ: Princeton University Press, 2010), 147.

[16]Mari, cited in Samuel Moffett, *A History of Christianity in Asia*, vol. 1, *Beginnings to 1500*, 2nd ed. (Maryknoll, NY: Orbis, 1998), 358.

surrounded himself with Christians. Both his primary wife, Doquz-Khatun, and his most trusted general, Kitbuqa, were Christians of the Syriac tradition. In fact, when Hulagu sacked Baghdad in 1258 and slaughtered thousands of Muslims, he spared the Christians in deference to his wife. The next year Hulagu even gave the royal place in Baghdad to the catholicos of the Church of the East, Makkikha II, and Hulagu also ordered the construction of a cathedral to be built for that church body.[17]

After overthrowing the Abbasid Dynasty, Hulagu and his Christian general Kitbuqa turned their eyes west. Kitbuqa took control of Aleppo and Damascus in Syria, and freed the Christians from (Muslim) Mamluk rule, a shared foe to Westerners and Mongols. The Christians welcomed Kitbuqa's appointment as governor of the region, and the history of Christianity in the Middle East may have turned out differently had the Mamluks not defeated Kitbuqa at the Battle of Ain Jalut in 1260, which was the first major defeat of the Mongol Empire. According to historian Christoph Baumer, the "victorious Mamluks . . . carried out a bloodbath among the Christians as revenge" after the battle went in their favor.[18]

After Hulagu's death in 1265, leadership passed khan to khan for the next seventy years. Many of the khans initially supported Christianity, though they did not practice it to the exclusion of other religions. And as was the case with Mongolian rulers in China, they sought alliances with Christians in Europe against the Mamluks. Over time, however, the khans converted to Islam and turned cold toward Christianity. When the Ilkhanate collapsed in 1335, various successor states, none favorable to the church, arose in its place. In what is now Iran and Iraq, the church never recovered and has remained marginal under the rule of more powerful non-Christian governments.

THE WANING OF ASIAN CHRISTIANITY

By the fifteenth century Christianity had become severely weakened across Asia. Other than in India, it's possible that the church diminished in size and spiritual vigor in every region of Asia. The Crusades were a microcosm of Christianity in the region: Though starting off strong and expanding rapidly, Christian presence was eventually halted and ultimately overwhelmed. In

---

[17]Foltz, *Religions of the Silk Road*, 116.
[18]Baumer, *Church of the East*, 219.

Central Asia a series of regional empires, all non-Christian and increasingly Muslim, were forming in the wake of the collapse of the Mongol Empire. The church was simply unable to cope with the dreadful effects of the Black Death, theological division and hostile political rule. The state of the Church of the East had become so dire by the fourteenth century that the "seat of the catholicos moved from one location to another, depending upon where he believed he was most secure."[19]

Around the same time period in Eastern Asia the Ming Dynasty was overtaking the Yuan Dynasty and disrupting the Christian community there. In Southern Asia we have copper plates in India giving partial testimony of the church, but no church structures exist from that time period. More partial is the state of Christianity in Southeastern Asia, a region that did not produce any long-term Christian communities until the arrival of Europeans. In Western Asia, where Christianity was practiced widely among various people groups, a whole series of Islamic empires took the place of Christian ones. Although Christianity did survive intact in Armenia, Cyprus and Georgia, it did so at a great cost, bearing wounds inflicted during this challenging time, from the expansion of the Islamic empires in the seventh century to the collapse of the Byzantine Empire in 1453 at the hands of Ottoman Turks. Although most Arab Christians gradually converted to Islam, and all virtually adopted Arabic as their official language, certain communities clung tightfisted to their Christian faith despite ongoing pressure to convert, enduring to this day in a hotly contested and often violent part of the world. These Christians scattered across the Middle East, in what is now Israel, Palestine, Lebanon, Syria, Iraq and parts of the Arabian Peninsula, are proud of their heritage and quick to point out that they are Christian Arabs of a noble past.

---

[19]Wilhelm Baum and Dietmar Winkler, *The Church of the East: A Concise History* (New York: RoutledgeCurzon, 2003), 104.

five

AFRICA

There is no reason to suppose that all the conquered territories converted to Islam at the same rate ... since the lands involved were inhabited by peoples with varying religious, linguistic, and social identities.

RICHARD BULLIET,
CONVERSION TO ISLAM IN THE MEDIEVAL PERIOD

A FAITH STARVED OUT

The Arab Muslim conquests profoundly shaped Africa. Although some still imagine angry, sword-wielding armies rushing across the African desert and foisting Islam on innocent victims, historical records present a different picture. "The Arabs," wrote Egyptian historian Aziz Atiya, "were essentially interested in ... state revenues," not converts.[1] Rather than denounce, kill or convert dhimmis, Arabs simply taxed them at higher rates as a substitute for military service. Most Christians in the first generations under Arab rule were found "to care little about [Arab] religious beliefs."[2] Because the former ruling Byzantine Empire legally enforced doctrinal decisions arising from the ecumenical councils and harassed those Christians disagreeing with them, Arab rule provided relief from religious oppression. Many African Christians, in fact, welcomed their new Muslim overlords, reasoning that political rule from non-Christian rulers would be better than that offered by Christians. As one historian notes,

---

[1] Aziz Atiya, *History of Eastern Christianity* (Notre Dame, IN: University of Notre Dame Press, 1968), 83.
[2] John Tolan, *Medieval Christian Perceptions of Islam: A Book of Essays* (New York: Garland, 1996), xii.

While the 6th century marked the isolation of the Coptic Church from the larger Orthodox world, it also deepened a greater sense of Coptic "national" unity and cohesive identity. The strained relations between Egypt and Constantinople made the Copts ready to accept the divorce that occurred after the Arab invasion of the peninsula. In some instances the Copts received improved treatment under the Arabs; they were granted religious freedom, their taxes were greatly reduced (even if they had to pay the *dhimmi* which separated them as "protected" religious people under Shariah [Law]), and they were given many important posts within the government.[3]

The fact that many individuals and communities eventually abandoned Christianity in favor of Islam need not surprise us. When put in historical perspective it took about as long for Islam to become the dominant religion in Eastern and Northern Africa as it did for Christianity centuries before. In Egypt, for instance, collective memory maintains that Christianity entered in the first century. If correct, it still took hundreds of years before most Egyptians abandoned centuries-old religious practices in favor of the foreign religion of Christianity. In fact, in Egypt, it arguably took longer for Islam to unite the people than it did for Christianity. Although conversion of Christian Copts to Islam occurred intermittently, not until after the Crusades did widespread conversion to Islam occur.[4]

The situation in Egypt shares some commonalities with other Eastern and Northern African regions. The strong ethnic-national indigenization of Christianity in modern Egypt, Ethiopia and Sudan kept the Christian tinder ablaze, so to speak, longer than in the Maghreb, where a combination of foreign Greek-Byzantine, Vandal-Arian and Roman Catholic rule cooled the fire of Berber-Donatist Christianity.[5] Whether or not this line of interpretation completely satisfies the historical realities, the continued existence of indigenous Christian communities across Africa almost fourteen hundred years after the Arab conquest underscores the fact that Islam did not completely extinguish Christianity

---

[3]Justin Lasser, "Coptic Orthodoxy," in *The Encyclopedia of Eastern Orthodox Christianity*, ed. John McGuckin (Oxford: Blackwell, 2011), 1:157.

[4]See the progression of anti-Coptic practices in Egypt under the Mamluk Dynasty in Jacques Tagher, *Christians in Muslim Egypt: An Historical Study of the Relations Between Copts and Muslims from 640 to 1922* (Postfach, Germany: Oros Verlag, 1998), 142-64.

[5]At least, this is a commonly held view most capably articulated by W. C. H. Frend in *The Donatist Church: A Movement of Protest in Roman North Africa* (Oxford: Oxford University Press, 2003).

in Africa.[6] To its credit, Christianity, though greatly diminished, survived amidst an escalation of Islamic empires from the eighth to the fourteenth centuries.

CHAPTER OVERVIEW

In this chapter we will continue our discussion of the diminishment of Christianity. The causes of the church's decline in Africa were similar to those in Asia, but in a more concentrated form. In Asia Christianity eventually became a minority religion over the course of centuries of rule under various non-Christian governments, not just Islamic ones. In Africa, by contrast, other than in Ethiopia and in parts of the Sudan, Christianity found itself under Islamic rule from around the seventh century onward. It has not changed since then. As you read about the medieval history of the African church, try to imagine how long it would have taken you, had you been an African Christian, to contemplate converting to Islam given the great political, economic, physical and social benefits such a conversion would offer not only you but also your extended family. Such were the considerations of Christians living in Africa during this time.

NORTHERN AFRICA

Although Christianity has likely existed in a continuous state in Northern Africa since the first century, the Arab conquests in the seventh century naturally affected the development, well-being and expansion of the church. Historian Richard Bulliet offers a helpful caveat when attempting to understand the religious change that took place after this transition from Byzantine to Arab rule (see this chapter's epigraph). We should not expect that Christian communities in Africa converted to Islam at the same time or for the same reasons. All of this underscores that there was no direct path from Christianity to Islam. The wide-ranging regional dynamics meant that Christians converted to Islam on various occasions at various stages for various reasons.

A case in point emerges in the Maghreb. Although it is commonly held that Christianity west of Egypt completely disappeared after the Arab conquests, historical evidence reveals another scenario. In the town of Tahart in southern Algeria, well after the seventh-century Arab conquests, "Christians formed

[6]Mark Handley, "Disputing the End of African Christianity," in *Vandals, Romans and Berbers: New Perspectives on Late Antique North Africa*, ed. A. H. Merrills (Aldershot, UK: Ashgate, 2004), 292.

part of the Imam's court, ... had their own church, were wealthy and involved in trade, [and] had a market."[7] The rulers of the region at this time were the Ibadis, a Muslim movement distinct from the dominant Sunnis and Shias. Today, they comprise the majority of inhabitants of Oman. When the Ibadis left Tahart in the tenth century, "the Christian population went with them."[8] Other reports of Christians living in what are now Libya, Morocco, Tunisia and elsewhere in the Maghreb centuries after the Arab conquest force us to acknowledge that Christian conversion did not follow a set path.

Sudan. The Nubian Christians lived in what is now Ethiopia and Sudan. Having been Christianized mostly by Egyptian and Ethiopian monks, they were naturally part of the Oriental Orthodox Church and were under the ecclesial jurisdiction of the pope of Alexandria. By the sixth century each of the three kingdoms of Nubia had made Christianity the state religion (see table 5.1). The expansion of Islam in the seventh century from the Arabian Peninsula, very close geographically to Sudan, naturally affected the Nubians' welfare. Nubia's first military encounter with the Arabs occurred in 642. This was less than a century since Nubia had officially adopted Christianity. An Arab military commander approached (Old) Dongola with an army of twenty thousand men, but due to the archery skills of the Nubians, the Arabs relented. It was the first halt of Arab expansion. Not deterred, a second Arab attack proceeded against the Nubians in 646. But after the Nubians defended themselves again against the Arabs, an agreement was brokered in 652 called the Treaty of the Baqt.[9] This treaty allowed the Nubians freedom from Arab rule in exchange for an annual tribute of slaves, protection of Muslims in Nubia and the safeguarding of the mosque in the capital city. Despite occasional breaches, this treaty remained intact for centuries.

With the Arab invasion of Nubia at bay, the Nubian Church embarked on a period of church growth and construction. Archaeologists have unearthed beautiful churches and monasteries in Sudan that give another dimension to medieval Nubian Christianity. In and around the Makurian capital of Old Dongola, colorful and ornately decorated churches attracted many pilgrims. At one church in

---

[7]Ibid., 303.

[8]Ibid.

[9]Hassan Abdelwahab, *Influence (Supremacy) of Religion on Sudan's Foreign Policy Decision-Making* (Bloomington, IN: AuthorHouse, 2012), 50.

Banganarti, just a few miles from Old Dongola at a pilgrimage site probably dedicated to the archangel Raphael, archaeologists discovered that some Europeans traveled thousands of miles to this church for the purpose of healing.

Table 5.1. Three kingdoms of Nubia (all Christian by the sixth century)

Nubian Kingdom	Location	Capital	Establishment of Christianity	Christian Tradition	Source of Evangelism
Alodia (Alwa)	South	Soba	580	Oriental Orthodox	Aksumite (Ethiopian) monks and Bishop Longinus
Makuria	Central	(Old) Dongola	569–570	Eastern Orthodox	Envoy from Byzantium
Nobatia	North	Faras	543	Oriental Orthodox	Father Julian

While the church was growing in Nubia, the political climate beyond Nubian borders was not favorable. Perhaps as a defensive posture against the Arabs, a series of independent Nubian kings expanded their power over the church. Although the Nubians did not display innovation in church leadership or structure, the Nubian kings served as ruler-priests who participated in church affairs and sought expansion beyond Nubian borders. King Merkurios, for instance, led the Nubian kingdom into great prosperity in the early eighth century. In order to secure added reinforcement against the Arab-Muslim threat up north, Nobatia and Makuria united to form the Kingdom of Dongola, with Old Nubian as its official language.[10]

King Merkurios, dubbed the "new Constantine" by some, rebuilt Faras Cathedral, the site of the head Nubian bishop.[11] In around 745 the Christian king Cyriacus of Dongola led an army against the Umayyad emir of Egypt. "The reason given for the war," one author notes, "was that the emir of Egypt imposed a tax on the population of Egypt and assigned the Coptic patriarch of Alexandria to supervise the collection of it."[12] Such a policy, referred to as the millet system, was common under Muslim regimes. In this system church leaders collected taxes from the Christians, who lived freely in their own neighborhoods. This policy sometimes put the heads of the

---

[10]Richard Lobban Jr., "Christianity in Nubia: The Missionary Period," in *Historical Dictionary of Ancient and Medieval Nubia* (Lanham, MD: Scarecrow Press, 2004), 115.

[11]Bengt Sundkler and Christopher Steed, *A History of the Church in Africa* (Cambridge: Cambridge University Press, 2000), 32.

[12]Abdelwahab, *Influence (Supremacy) of Religion*, 55.

Christian community in a precarious position, especially as taxes for Christians doubled or tripled to account for the decline of Christians who had converted to Islam for economic reasons.

King Cyriacus's intrigue with the Umayyads revealed his attempt to restore Christianity to Egypt. Later, King Georgios I expanded Dongola's border further than his successors had and likewise entered into conflict with Muslim Egypt. His reign also coincided with the colorful artistry of church buildings in a time period sometimes called Classic Nubia due to its high level of Nubian culture and grandeur.[13] In Nubia frescoes played a key role in communicating the biblical story and teaching key theological doctrines since most inhabitants could not read. The Nubians constructed their churches with purpose: Altars were located on the eastern side of churches to symbolize that Christ would return from the east, and pictures of Christ on the throne reinforced the centrality of Jesus in the church liturgy.[14]

Eventually, however, just as in many other parts of Africa, the Nubian monarchy converted to Islam and intermarried with Muslims. The last Christian king of Dongola was Kudanbes, whose reign ended in 1324. The monarchy's conversion to Islam, coupled with the covering up of churches in many towns and villages from sandstorms as well as the lack of ample communication between the pope of Alexandria and the Nubian churches, led to the decline of Christianity in Sudan in the fourteenth century. The apparent lack of sufficient indigenization of Christianity outside of the court elite may have contributed to this decline. What's more, the diminishment of the Coptic Church meant that it could not provide adequate leadership to the Nubians by means of deacons, priests and monks. The Mamluks from the north installed a Muslim king in the kingdom of Makuria in 1315 and converted the palace building in Dongola to a mosque in 1317. The Islamic Sultanate from the south then conquered the Christian kingdom of Alodia in 1504 along with its capital Soba. These two events initiated widespread Muslim immigration, which soon caused Muslims to outnumber Christians. However, a Christian presence in Sudan did survive at least until the eighteenth century.[15]

---

[13]P. L. Shinnie, "Christian Nubia," in *The Cambridge History of Africa*, vol. 2, c. 500 B.C.-A.D. 1050, ed. J. D. Fage (Cambridge: Cambridge University Press, 1978), 579.

[14]William Anderson and Ogbu Kalu, "Christianity in Sudan and Ethiopia," in *African Christianity: An African Story*, ed. Ogbu Kalu (Trenton, NJ: Africa World Press, 2007), 79-80.

[15]Lobban, "Christianity in Nubia: The Missionary Period," 112.

> **TRAIL MARKER**
> **Facing the Inevitable**
>
> What happened in Sudan happened everywhere in Northern Africa. Sooner or later, Islamic rule created a culture in which it was much easier for Christians to convert to Islam rather than remain Christians. Although it took longer to occur in Sudan than it did in the Maghreb, it seemed inevitable given the impressive expansion of Islam.

EASTERN AFRICA

The Nile River had long been a point of connection between Egypt and Ethiopia, but Arab Muslim occupation of Egypt from the seventh century onward disrupted communication between the Coptic Church and the Eastern African churches. Similar to the situation that developed between the Copts and the Nubians, this had the consequence of jeopardizing the health of the churches in the Christian Aksumite Kingdom (in Ethiopia) since the pope of Alexandria held jurisdiction over churches in this kingdom and appointed its top ecclesial leaders. Fortunately, the monastic base of these local churches provided support in times of limited communication, but it was only a matter of time before Islam extended its presence over large pockets of the land south and east of Egypt and eventually came to govern most of Eastern Africa.

Ethiopia. The Christian kingdom of Aksum in Ethiopia was flourishing when Islam emerged. Due to the refuge it provided for the earliest Muslim refugees, the Arabs did not attack the Aksumite Empire in the seventh century. Nevertheless, the Arabs did take complete control of the Red Sea, expanding all across the Horn of Africa (in what is now Djibouti and Somalia). This had the result of severing Ethiopia from trade and commerce, and forcing it to retreat inward into the Ethiopian highlands. Due to the custom of the pope of Alexandria appointing an Egyptian to Ethiopia's highest church official, the *abuna*, Ethiopia's isolation led to long stretches of time of inadequate, if any, leadership.

After years of political decline the foreign Zagwe Dynasty assumed control of Ethiopia around the year 900. This dynasty renewed international trading opportunities and increased pilgrimages to the Holy Land, something that had played an important part of Ethiopian Christianity since at least the seventh century—and there are still many Ethiopian Christian communities throughout Jerusalem. The most prominent Zagwe *negus* or king was a man nicknamed Lalibela, who began ruling around the year 1200 and who commissioned the construction of eleven magnificent rock-hewn churches in the town of Lalibela to "extol Christ, the New Testament and the Apocrypha."[16] King Lalibela fortified the sacred city of Lalibela under the conviction that he was building the new Jerusalem, thereby making the town a center of pilgrimage for Ethiopian Christians and a bastion of Christian learning.

Although the Zagwe Dynasty claimed descent "from King Solomon but through the line of [the] Queen of Sheba's royal handmaid," the Solomonic Dynasty claimed both Aksumite and Solomonic descent.[17] During this dynasty, the legendary story of the Queen Sheba's union with King Solomon arose anew in the popular consciousness, which had fueled the Jewish practices of Ethiopian churches for centuries. *The Glory of the Kings*, a fourteenth-century Christian document written in Ge'ez but based on centuries of oral tradition, became the framing narrative of Ethiopian culture. A work rich in detail and wonder, it aimed to prove three things:

1. That the lawful kings of Ethiopia were descended from Solomon, King of Israel.

2. That the Tabernacle of the Law of God, the Ark of the Covenant, was brought from Jerusalem to Aksum by [Menelik], Solomon's firstborn son.

3. That the God of Israel transferred His place of abode on earth from Jerusalem to Aksum, the ecclesiastical capital of Ethiopia.[18]

As the country became more isolated from its neighbors, Christian Ethiopia regarded itself as the successor to Israel. As one chapter in *The Glory of the Kings* describes:

---

[16]Sundkler and Steed, *History of the Church in Africa*, 38.

[17]Ephraim Smith, *The Ethiopian Orthodox Tāwahïdo Church* (Trenton, NJ: The Red Sea Press, 2013), 23.

[18]*A Modern Translation of the Kebra Nagast: The Glory of Kings*, ed. and trans. Miguel Brooks (Lawrenceville, NJ: Red Sea Press, 1995), xiii.

And after he slept there [with the queen of Sheba] there appeared unto King Solomon [in a dream] a brilliant sun, and it came down from heaven and shed exceedingly great splendor over Israel. And when it had tarried there for a time it suddenly withdrew itself, and it flew away to the country of Ethiopia, and it shone there with exceedingly great brightness for ever, for it willed to dwell there. And [the King said], 'I waited [to see] if it would come back to Israel, but it did not return.'[19]

Under the belief that they were the new Israel, Ethiopian churches adopted Old Testament regulations regarding dietary laws, circumcision and sabbath observance in addition to embracing New Testament customs. The Ethiopians, perhaps unlike any other Christian community before or after them, united the best of the Semitic and Christian cultures into one exuberant tradition.

TRAIL MARKER
Ethiopia and Israel

There has been a very long cultural and religious connection between Ethiopia and Israel. Judaism has long existed in Ethiopia, and it is rumored that the Ark of the Covenant is preserved in an Ethiopian church in the ancient Aksumite capital of Aksum, Ethiopia.

Because Ethiopia faced long spells without an *abuna*, monastic communities became the bedrock of Ethiopian piety. Ascetic practices characterized much of the Ethiopian Church, and monasteries served as educators of the clergy and the laity as well as curators of important literary documents and ancient relics. The confluence of Jewish ancestry and practices, pilgrimage, and monasticism made for a distinct Ethiopian identity. Together with the Coptic Orthodox Church, the Ethiopian Orthodox Church became a bulwark of Christianity in all of Africa until the arrival of European Catholics in the fifteenth century, during which time the Ethiopian Church experienced deep theological division as well as continued pressure of Muslim expansion into

---

[19]*The Kebra Nagast*, trans. E. A. Wallis Budge (New York, NY: Cosimo Classics, 2004), 35.

its borders. In other words, despite the many successes of the church in Ethiopia and its initial shelter from aggression due to the protection it offered Muhammad's earliest followers, Islamic expansion in the later Middle Ages hampered the growth of the Ethiopian Church.

REINFORCEMENTS ON THE WAY

The cumulative effect of Islamic rule over Africa from the eighth to the fourteenth centuries led to the gradual decline of Christianity in Africa. But despite diminishing and dying out in parts, it did endure in others. The fact that faithful Coptic and Ethiopian Christian communities exist to this day, whether in Africa or in the West, attests to the fact that Christianity has survived. At the same time, Islam inevitably became the predominant religion in Northern and Eastern Africa—an honor once reserved for Christianity. Islamic empires achieved this feat by Muslims giving birth to more children than their Christian counterparts, marrying into Christian families and mandating that the children be Muslim—and generally creating a culture that encouraged Christian emigration and enticed Christians to convert in order to receive economic breaks, political benefits and social prominence. The emergence of Arabic as the lingua franca in much of Africa, and certainly in Northern Africa, also eased entry into the Muslim community. As Nelson Mandela would later quip, if you talk to a person in his own language, whatever you say goes right to his heart.

The "tipping point," or moment of critical mass, for Islam occurred at different times in Eastern and Northern Africa, but the second millennium fell decisively in its favor.[20] In the Maghreb the tipping point occurred in the eleventh and twelfth centuries; in Egypt, Ethiopia and Sudan, it occurred around the fourteenth century.[21] By this time the mighty Portuguese Empire was sailing across the Atlantic Ocean and making landfall in Northern and Western Africa. This landing of Catholic Europeans in the fifteenth century forever changed the history of Africa and perhaps halted the spread of Islam below the Sahara.

---

[20]Malcolm Gladwell, author of *The Tipping Point: How Little Things Can Make a Big Difference* (New York: Back Bay, 2002), defines the term as follows: "The Tipping Point is the moment of critical mass, the threshold, the boiling point" (p. 12).

[21]For the Maghreb see Handley, "Disputing the End of African Christianity," 308; for Egypt see Tagher, *Christians in Muslim Egypt*, 148-61; for Ethiopia and Sudan, see Sundkler and Steed, *A History of the Church in Africa*, 31, 38.

six

EUROPE

*The creation of European Christendom was an
immensely complex and multi-faceted process.*

DANA ROBERT, *CHRISTIAN MISSION*

A MOMENTOUS SHIFT

The balance of world Christianity shifted around the turn of the first
Christian millennium. Whereas Christianity had taken shape like a ring
around the Mediterranean Sea in the first centuries of the Christian era, it
began to fade in the eastern and southern parts of that circle after the
second millennium, just as it began to shimmer in the western and northern
parts. Catholic Christianity, particularly in the West, culminated in the late
fifteenth century with the expansion of Catholicism into the African,
American and Asian continents. In Africa and Asia, meanwhile, the fourteenth and fifteenth centuries witnessed its greatest setbacks, exacerbating
the decline of the church in those regions.

Momentous changes were taking place in Southern and Western Europe
during the Middle Ages. On Christmas Day in 800, Pope Leo III crowned
Charlemagne the first Holy Roman Emperor. Charlemagne, or Charles the
Great, was of Frankish Germanic stock and ruled over a sprawling kingdom
stretching out over what are now Austria, Belgium, the Czech Republic,
France, Hungary, the Netherlands, northern Italy, northeastern Spain,
Switzerland and western Germany. The fusion of Germanic and Roman
cultures, forged by a common faith and an evangelistic and imperialistic

mindset, transformed medieval Christian European culture. Contemporaries even revived the ancient word *Europe* to celebrate the growing union of church and state.[1]

In the eastern part of Europe, the Byzantine or East Roman Empire expanded to its north and west for a season. As early as the fourth century the Eastern Orthodox Church, the official religion of the Byzantine Empire, had regarded the relationship between the church and state as symphonic—going so far as to use the Greek term *symphonia* to describe the interplay.[2] From its base in Constantinople, the Byzantine Empire drew smaller kingdoms into its orbit that adopted Eastern Orthodoxy—kingdoms that include today's Belarus, Bulgaria, Greece, Malta, Macedonia, Moldavia, Serbia, Romania and Russia. Though transmitting its faith to new people groups, the Byzantine Empire was losing its political grip. With every new people group and region the empire evangelized, it seemed to lose more of its authority; eventually it was too late and Byzantium was too weak to ward off the ongoing Muslim threat. The ultimate source of its downfall, the Ottoman Empire, advanced into southeastern Europe in the fourteenth century. This empire, a Sunni Muslim dynasty owing its origins to the Turkic ruler Osman, had been expanding in Western Asia for decades before gaining a foothold in Europe, where it would soon disrupt the Christian *oikoumenē* (community).

CHAPTER OVERVIEW

In this chapter I will provide an overview of Christianity in Europe during the Middle Ages. Such was the time when Christianity became inextricably linked with Europe, so much so that we may now begin thinking of Christianity as a native European religion and a foreign one in much of Asia and Africa. We all know, of course, that the reverse was true, but now things were beginning to shift. As you read about the development of medieval European Christianity in this chapter, try to imagine a world in which everyone you knew was a Christian and in which there was no one left to evangelize. The end of the world was probably coming soon, and life was very hard. Such was the world of many medieval Europeans.

---

[1]Norman Davies, *Europe: A History* (New York: HarperCollins, 1998), 302.
[2]Andrew Sharp, *Orthodox Christians and Islam in the Postmodern Age* (Leiden: Brill, 2012), 131.

EASTERN EUROPE

There were great religious changes taking place in Eastern Europe during the Middle Ages. For the most part the people who inhabited Eastern Europe accepted Catholicism or Orthodoxy, depending on their link with either the Holy Roman (Catholic) or Byzantine (Orthodox) Empires. Some regional rulers altered their allegiance to Catholicism or Orthodoxy based on their own political interests, just as the Byzantine and Holy Roman Empires lobbied for alliances with smaller kingdoms to expand their influence, create buffers between rival empires and stave off any preemptive strikes from their enemies. Over time a religious fault line—a confessional border, if you will—came to divide many modern countries of Eastern (and Southern) Europe. The Byzantine Empire introduced Orthodoxy to each of the modern countries on the eastern side of that fault line: Belarus, Bulgaria, Moldova, Romania, Russia and Ukraine. The Holy Roman Empire, by contrast, led to the transmission of Catholicism to the countries on the western side of the line: the Czech Republic, Hungary, Poland and Slovakia.

The Czech Republic. The migration of the Slavs into Eastern Europe between the sixth and eighth centuries reconfigured the church in Europe (see table 6.1). The Slavic people originated in the northeastern part of Europe and consisted of various tribes such as Bulgars, Moravians, Poles, Serbs, Slovenes and Rus. These tribal groups had migrated southward after the invasions of the Avars and Huns from centuries past. The Moravians settled along the Morava River separating the eastern part of the Czech Republic and the western part of Slovakia. There they established a kingdom in the ninth century called Great Moravia between Francia in the west and Bulgaria in the east.

Table 6.1. Slavic peoples

Classification of Slavs	Slavic People(s)	Modern Countries
East Slavs	Rus	Belarus, Russia and Ukraine
South Slavs	Bosniaks, Bulgars, Croats, Macedonians, Montenegrins, Serbs and Slovenes	Bosnia-Herzegovina, Bulgaria, Croatia, Macedonia, Montenegro, Serbia and Slovenia
West Slavs	Czechs, Poles and Slovaks	Czech Republic, Poland and Slovakia

The first ruler of Great Moravia, Mojmir, was baptized as a Catholic in the 820s under the influence of German Catholics. However, Mojmir's successor, Rastislav, feared Germanic expansion and sought an alliance with the Byzantine

Empire.[3] In response to a letter he received from Rastislav, the patriarch of Constantinople commissioned the Greek brothers Cyril and Methodius, two of the most prominent missionaries of the Orthodox Church, to introduce Eastern Orthodoxy to the Slavs in Great Moravia.[4] There they translated the Bible, liturgy and other Christian texts into (Old Church) Slavonic, establishing an indigenous Slavonic church. Like Ulfilas a few centuries before, Cyril and Methodius believed that translation of the Bible into the language of the people was essential to evangelization. They were right. In their prologue to the Slavonic Bible, Cyril wrote,

> As without light there can be no joy—
> For while the eye sees all of God's creation,
> Still what is seen without light lacks beauty—
> So it is with every soul lacking letters,
> Ignorant of God's law,
> The sacred law of the Scriptures,
> The law that reveals God's paradise.
> For what ear not hearing
> The sound of thunder, can fear God?
> Or how can nostrils which smell no flower
> Sense the Divine miracle?
> And the mouth which tastes no sweetness
> Makes man like stone;
> Even more, the soul lacking letters
> Grows dead in human beings.[5]

Despite Byzantine success, Germanic Catholic missionaries in Great Moravia regarded the Orthodox missionaries as intruders. In response to their harsh treatment, the Greek brothers appealed to Pope Hadrian II, and although the pope supported them, internal Christian missionary battles continued. The Germans imprisoned Methodius (Cyril had passed away in Rome), stymied his missionary efforts and eventually expelled the Orthodox

---

[3]Craig Cravens, *Culture and Customs of the Czech Republic and Slovakia* (Westport, CT: Greenwood Press, 2006), 24.

[4]For more, see Derek Cooper, *Twenty Questions That Shaped World Christian History* (Minneapolis: Fortress Press, 2015), 137-54.

[5]Cyril, "Prologue to the Gospel," in *Reading the Middle Ages: Sources from Europe, Byzantium and the Islamic World*, ed. Barbara Rosenwein (Toronto: University of Toronto Press, 2006), 146.

community after Methodius died. The third ruler of Moravia, Svatopluk, sought the protection of the Holy Roman Empire and deposed his uncle Rastislav. Unlike Rastislav, who favored Orthodoxy over Catholicism, Svatopluk had been colluding with the Germans and agreed to reinstitute Catholicism in Moravia once put on the throne. As a ruler, Slvatopluk mandated Catholicism and "enforced a papal ban on use of the Slavonic liturgy."[6] The subsequent union of the Moravians with the Bohemians (people who lived in the western Czech Republic) led to the adoption of Catholicism.

TRAIL MARKER
Medieval Tug-of-War Match

Keep these two things in mind when reading this section. First, there was a lot of religious back-and-forth among rulers and dynasties in the Middle Ages in what is now the Czech Republic. Great Moravia was a small kingdom caught between two larger ones, whose faith and politics clashed. Second, rulers in the ancient world—Christian or not—were violent and refused to see a separation between the church and state. One's religion was not a personal decision but was demanded under a sort of patronage system whereby the people under the ruler's authority were expected to be of the same religion, by force if necessary. The conversion of the ruler to a certain branch of Christianity all but required the conversion of the royal court and of the populace to that same branch.

The Bohemian duke Wenceslas reinforced the Catholic evangelization of what is now the Czech Republic. Although his brother, Duke Boleslav or Boleslaus, murdered Wenceslas, Boleslav expanded Catholic Christianity in Bohemia. He made Prague a bishopric in 967 and wed his Christian daughter to the leader of modern Poland and the first ruler there to endorse (Catholic) Christianity. The Piast Dynasty in Poland then sanctioned the Catholic

---

[6]Robert Bideleux and Ian Jefferies, *A History of Eastern Europe: Crisis and Change*, 2nd ed. (Oxford: Routledge, 2007), 54.

evangelization of the Polish state and formed a close relationship with the pope. Later, the king of Bohemia, Charles IV, became the Holy Roman Emperor. He established his headquarters in Prague, just a few decades before the Bohemian Catholic priest Jan Hus, whom Martin Luther appealed to as a great reformer, began preaching against some of the abuses of the Catholic Church. The Hussite Wars in the early 1400s estranged Czech Catholics from Rome, and the Czechs gained an independent church, giving a foreshadowing of things to come in Catholic Europe. Although Hus would lose his life at the Council of Constance in 1415 for his theological views, his legacy endured and his ideas gave fuel to the fire of Czech ecclesial independence. In the Articles of Prague (1420), the Czech Christians demanded that the Bible be freely proclaimed in Czech by its priests (rather than in Latin), for everyone to receive the Eucharist in both "species" (that is, in both the bread and wine) and for the Czechs to be in charge of their own church discipline.

NORTHERN EUROPE

Unlike in the east, Christianity developed in Northern Europe later than any other part of the continent. Of the three regions of Northern Europe, only inhabitants of the British Isles accepted Christianity during its first few centuries (see chap. 3). But once they did so, a strong church developed. In England, the archbishopric of Canterbury was the seat of religious authority. Occupants of this office such as Anselm and Thomas a Becket fiercely contended with a powerful English monarchy. Residents of the Baltics and Scandinavia, by contrast, were the last Europeans to embrace Christianity. Why did the Scandinavians eventually accept the Christian religion? The adoption of Christianity among the kingdoms of Denmark, Iceland, Norway and Sweden provided new commercial and political opportunities and ushered them into European Christian society. During the Middle Ages these Scandinavian kingdoms adopted Catholic Christianity and enforced it on their people, as other societies had done centuries before. Whereas the Scandinavian monarchs chose Christianity on their own volition (even though they did not give the same freedom to their subjects), the Baltic States of Estonia, Finland, Latvia and Lithuania adopted the Christian religion under duress. In the twelfth century, when crusades were fully operative in Europe (and not really gaining any success in the Holy Land), the papacy declared a crusade against the Baltics, a region steeped in paganism for millennia. A poem, written in Swedish from the second and third crusades against the Finns, gives a snapshot of the (Catholic) Christian mentality against the Baltic "heathens."

> And he who was fain to bow the knee
> And go to the font and a Christian be,
> They left him his life and goods to enjoy,
> To live at peace, without annoy,
> But the heathen who still denied Our Lord
> They gave him death for his reward.[7]

Despite, or more accurately, due to, the violent evangelism of the Baltic peoples, each nation in the region adopted Christianity as its state religion by the fourteenth century. We will see in chapter seven if such evangelism proved effective in the long run.

Scandinavia. The conversion of Scandinavian kingdoms to Christianity began at the turn of the first millennium. In the course of their seafaring invasions, Vikings had enslaved and imported Christians back to Scandinavia. In 821 Pope Paschal I permitted three bishops from modern France and Germany to evangelize the Danes. The pope's letter in from 822 revealed his intentions:

> Since we are aware that some peoples who dwell in the North do not yet have knowledge of God, nor have they been reborn in the water of baptism, and they live in the shadow of death, and they idly serve creature rather than the Creator, therefore, we have decided [to send the following] . . . to reveal the Truth.[8]

King Harald Klak of Denmark was the first Scandinavian king to be baptized. Klak had received asylum in Germany from Charlemagne's son, Louis the Pious, before returning to Denmark to regain control in 819. In 826 Klak traveled to Mainz to undergo baptism along with his court. The German monk Anskar later accompanied Klak to Denmark, where he planted a church and established a school for priests. Klak, however, was unable to defend his kingdom, and so Anskar traveled to Sweden in 829, where he established a church west of Stockholm. By the middle of the ninth century the Danes and Swedes generally allowed Christian missionaries to preach,

---

[7]Quoted in Eric Christiansen, *The Northern Crusades*, 2nd ed.(London: Penguin, 1997), 118.
[8]Paschal I, quoted in Anders Winroth, *The Conversion of Scandinavia: Vikings, Merchants and Missionaries in the Making of Northern Europe* (New Haven, CT: Yale University Press, 2012), 9.

baptize and establish churches unmolested.[9] Anskar's archbishopric of Hamburg-Bremen held spiritual jurisdiction over all of Scandinavia for the next centuries, and most of the bishops in Scandinavia hailed from either Germany or England.

Almost a century and a half passed before the next Danish king adopted Christianity. The German historian Widukind of Corvey described King Harald Bluetooth's conversion in 965 based on a miracle he observed a Christian named Poppo perform to contradict the Danes' belief that other gods existed who were mightier than Christ:

> As a result, the next day the king had a large piece of iron heated and ordered Poppo to carry the glowing iron for the sake of the catholic faith. Poppo took the iron and carried it as far as the king determined. He then showed his un-damaged hand and demonstrated to all the truth of the catholic faith. Conse-quently the king converted, resolved that Christ alone should be worshiped as God, ordered all people subject to him to reject idols, and thereafter gave due honor to priests and God's servants.[10]

King Harald's endorsement of Christianity enabled further Christian mis-sions into Norway and Sweden. Several decades later Knut the Great became king of England in 1016 and then of Denmark two years later. Knut attempted to eradicate the lingering pockets of paganism in Denmark and imported English missionaries to finish the task of Christianization. Knut founded Danish dioceses and also fought with the Christian king of Norway, Saint Olaf.

The official conversion of Norway generally proceeded along the same lines as in Denmark. The Norwegian king Olaf Tryggvason embraced and promul-gated Christianity more so than any other Norwegian before him. Saint Olaf, as many refer to him, converted to Christianity at the beginning of his brief reign and then imposed Christianity on Norway and nearby Scandinavian islands such as Iceland. Olaf was influential in the baptism of the first Eu-ropean discoverer of North America, Leif Ericson, as well as of the renowned Scandinavian poet of skaldic verse, Hallfred, who captured his change of fealty from pagan gods to the way of Jesus in the following poem:

---

[9]Birgit Sawyer and Peter Sawyer, *Medieval Scandinavia: From Conversion to Reformation, Circa 800–1500* (Minneapolis: University of Minnesota Press, 1993), 100.
[10]Widukind, quoted in ibid., 102.

It's the creed of the sovereign
Of [King Olaf] to ban sacrifices.
We must renounce many
A long-held decree of norns [women fates who ruled destiny].
All mankind casts [the god] Odin's words
To the winds; now I am forced
To forsake [the goddess] Freya's kin
And pray to Christ.[11]

By the late Middle Ages Christianity had firmly embedded itself in Denmark, Norway and Sweden. As we have seen, newly Christianized leaders were ill disposed toward religious diversity or anything that undermined the kingdom's unity. In those days religious nonconformity was not celebrated, it was squashed. One Scandinavian historian summarizes well the immediate history of Scandinavia after its adoption of the Christian faith:

> Once the conversion [of the three kingdoms] was completed, the institutions of monarchy grew up in a constant interplay with the power of the church; each state enjoyed a period or periods of expansion beyond its original frontiers; and all came to possess social and cultural characteristics which to some extent distinguished them as a group from the rest of medieval Christendom.[12]

TRAIL MARKER
Conversion at the Top

Each of the Scandinavian nations embraced Catholic Christianity around the turn of the second Christian millennium. As was the case in many parts, Scandinavian kings converted the populace in a top-down fashion, regardless if the people wanted to give up their pagan ways or not. During the Middle Ages, Scandinavian society became thoroughly Christian.

---

[11]Hallfred, quoted in Winroth, *Conversion of Scandinavia*, 4.
[12]T. K. Derry, *A History of Scandinavia* (Minneapolis: University of Minnesota Press, 2000), 16.

As in many other parts of Europe, monasticism played an important role in the formation and preservation of Christianity in Scandinavia. Convents and monasteries, in particular, proliferated among the urban and suburban landscapes. They also inspired lay piety and expanded the base of Christianity in Scandinavia. Birgitta of Sweden, who lived for seven decades in the 1300s— quite a long life at that time—emerged in this context as perhaps the most famous woman writer in medieval Scandinavia. She also bridged the gap between the laity and monastics. Married in 1316, Birgitta gave birth to eight children before her husband died in 1344. Like many other mystic Christian writers in the history of global Christianity, Birgitta received auditory "revelations" during her life, which she communicated to her Catholic confessors, such as when she witnessed Jesus' crucifixion.

> Round about her tenth year, on a certain occasion she heard a sermon preached in church about the passion of our Lord Jesus Christ. The following night she saw, in a dream, Christ as if he had been crucified in that same hour, and he said to her: "In such a way was I wounded." And she thought that this had happened at that hour and answered in her sleep: "O Lord, who has done this to you?" Jesus Christ answered: "Those who scorn me and neglect my love: they have done this to me." Then she came to herself; and from that day, she felt such affection for the passion of Christ that she could rarely recall the memory of it without tears.[13]

Birgitta moved to Rome in 1350, at a time when the Black Death was at its pinnacle, and when up to half of the population of any given city would die a horrific death. Beloved in the city for her good deeds and revered for her visions, Birgitta lived in Rome until her death 1373. The Birgittine order that she founded, which was eventually recognized by the pope, "changed the map of monasticism" by combining the best of the more well-known Cistercian, Dominican and Franciscan orders.[14] The Bridgettines are still active today.

SOUTHERN EUROPE

In contrast to Northern Europe, where the church emerged relatively late, Christians had been living in parts of Southern Europe since the first century.

---

[13]Birgitta of Sweden, *Life and Selected Writings*, trans. Albert Kezel (Mahwah, NJ: Paulist Press, 1990), 73.
[14]Philip Pulsiano, "Monasticism," in *Medieval Scandinavia: An Encyclopedia*, ed. Philip Pulsiano and Kirsten Wolf (London: Taylor & Francis, 1993), 417.

In the western part of Southern Europe, Catholicism, which had succeeded through the union of church and state, reigned supreme. The left hand of the church expanded into pagan lands through the sword while the right hand of the church triumphed through the evangelization of pagan tribes, the establishment of churches and the erection of monastic houses. The pope's coronation of Charlemagne in Rome in 800 officially wed the Franks and Romans together in an alliance known as the Holy Roman Empire. Their fruitful marriage generated a large number of Christian offspring on account of the pious—though violent—imperial-missionary efforts of Charlemagne and his successors.

In the eastern part of Southern Europe, by contrast, the Byzantine Empire experienced moments of domination, instability and finally collapse. Byzantium also found the union of politics and religion the most effective instrument in the conversion of Eastern and Southern Europeans on the one hand, and the expansion of the empire on the other. Between the eighth and fourteenth centuries the Eastern Orthodox Church became the state religion of many kingdoms in the Balkans, even as the Byzantine Empire was gradually losing its supremacy in the region. In the middle of the fifteenth century, that empire would be finally overcome.

Serbia. By the eighth century countless Slavic groups were living in the Balkans, which, depending on their locations, adopted Catholicism or Orthodoxy. Along the western end of the Balkan Peninsula, the Serbs established Slavic kingdoms independent of the Byzantine Empire and adopted Christianity in the late ninth century. Then, following "the rapid decline of the Byzantine Empire (after AD 1180) and its temporary collapse (AD 1204)," a new Serbian dynasty emerged that forever linked Serbian ethnicity with Orthodox faith.[15] The Nemanjić Dynasty was formed by Stefan Nemanja. Born in what is now Montenegro and baptized as a Catholic, he later converted to Eastern Orthodoxy and established it as the state religion of Serbia. Byzantium's diminishment allowed space for Stefan to create a national Serbian Church.

After forty years of rule, Stefan abdicated his throne, spending his remaining years in contemplation and prayer as a monk on Mount Athos in

---

[15]Sima Circovik, *The Serbs*, trans. Vuk Tosic (Oxford: Blackwell, 2004), xix.

Greece, where he and his monastic son—who was later named Saint Sava—founded a Serbian monastery. One of Stefan Nemanja's three sons, Stefan Nemanjić, reigned over this vast Serbian land while his younger brother Saint Sava built numerous churches, monasteries and schools. Saint Sava also established the Serbian Orthodox Church.

TRAIL MARKER
The Serbs

Southeastern Europe has a complex history. There were many different ethnic groups and kingdoms, but here's the thing to keep in mind about Serbia. The Serbs fully adopted the Eastern Orthodox faith in the Middle Ages, and Serbian identity became inextricably linked with the Serbian Orthodox Church. In many ways, to be Serbian was to be Orthodox, and many Serbians were willing to die for their faith and their independence as Orthodox Serbs. This explains, in part, the animus of certain groups in the Balkans today, which is a region roughly divided religiously into Orthodox, Catholics and Sunni Muslims.

Stefan Dušan became the most famous monarch to succeed Stefan Nemanja and his son Stefan Nemanjić. Born in 1307, Dušan had his father murdered and assumed rule. The Serbian Church and nation reached its apogee under Dušan's rule, which encompassed parts of what are now Albania, Bosnia and Herzegovina, Greece, Kosovo, Macedonia, Montenegro and Serbia. In 1346 Dušan assumed the title of tsar and elevated the Serbian Orthodox Church from an archbishopric to a patriarchate, with ecclesial headquarters in the modern city of Peć, Kosovo. Due to Dušan's expanding power, the Byzantine emperor invited the Muslim Turks to help fight the Christian Serbs—a great irony in hindsight.[16] All too eager to enter Europe, the Turks invaded the Balkans, leading not only to the end of the Nemanjić Dynasty at the Battle of Maritsa in 1371, but also the dismantling of the

---

[16]Tim Judah, *The Serbs: History, Myth and Destruction of the Yugoslavia* (New Haven, CT: Yale University Press, 1997), 24.

Byzantine Empire. The result of this invasion was the fragmentation of Bulgaria, Macedonia and Serbia—which became vassals to the Turkish sultans, who demanded heavy tributes and military assistance. Organized into the millet system, Orthodox Christians received protection from the Turks and fell under the jurisdiction of the patriarch of Constantinople.

Despite the continual onslaught of Muslim armies and the Serbian defeat in 1371, the Serbs did not retreat. At the Battle of Kosovo in 1389, Lazar of Serbia sought to resurrect the mighty Serbian kingdom against the Turks. With the full support of the Serbian Orthodox Church, he led the Christians to battle, dying as a martyr. Later, the notable Serbian poet Vuk Karadžić wrote a poem titled "The Downfall of the Serbian Empire," immortalizing Lazar's choice between the empires of heaven and of earth, the former of which he and Orthodox Serbs chose:

> Flying hawk, grey bird,
> Out of the holy place, out of Jerusalem,
> Holding a swallow, holding a bird.
> That is no hawk, grey bird,
> That is Elijah, holy one;
> Holding no swallow, no bird
> But writing from the Mother of God
> To the Emperor at Kosovo.
> He drops that writing on his knee,
> It is speaking to the Emperor:
> "Lazar, glorious Emperor,
> Which is the empire of your choice?
> Is it the empire of heaven?
> Is it the empire of the earth?
> If it is the empire of the earth,
> Saddle horses and tighten girth-straps,
> And, fighting-men, buckle on swords,
> Attack the Turks
> And all the Turkish army shall die.
> But if the empire of heaven
> Weave a church in Kosovo,
> Build its foundation not with marble stones,
> Build it with pure silk and with crimson cloth,

Take the Sacrament, marshal the men,
They shall all die,
And you shall die among them as they die."[17]

Due to the great epic tradition that linked "Serbdom" or Serbian nationality with Orthodox Christianity, Serbians did not convert to Islam as willingly as neighboring peoples did, such as the Bosnians, which perhaps due to a weak national church witnessed widespread conversions to Islam after the fifteenth-century conquests.

WESTERN EUROPE

The battle between Christianity and Islam raged not only in the Balkans but also in Spain, Portugal and France. In fact, the Crusades in the Holy Land were just one expression of the violent clash between Western Christians and Muslims; other crusades occurred in many places across Europe, including Western Europe. While the victory of the Franks over Arab and Berber forces at the Battle of Tours in 732 came to symbolize Western Europe's triumph over Islam, in truth it represented only one phase in the centuries-long process of the Christianization of Europe. In fact, even decades after the famed Battle of Tours, "Western Europe remained an impoverished backwater" that "lacked identity and cohesion."[18]

Identity and cohesion, however, were soon to come. This time the victory occurred not on the battlefield but in the bedroom. The hero at the Battle of Tours, Charles Martel, like all ancient rulers, recognized the act of procreation as the most important regal matter during his reign. He spawned a litter of rulers that lasted for centuries. This new Carolingian Dynasty, a term deriving from Charles's first name in Latin, Carolus, developed the Germanic notion of "royal blood" and divided its territorial units into counties overseen by counts. Martel's son Pepin the Short overthrew the Merovingian Dynasty, which had fragmented into three subpar subkingdoms that cast only a shadow of its former glory.

While procreation guaranteed the survival of the new Western European powerhouse of the Franks, the papacy legitimated it. The papacy blessed

---

[17]Vuk Karadžić, "The Downfall of the Serbian Empire," quoted in ibid., 34.
[18]Barbara Rosenwein, *A Short History of the Middle Ages*, 4th ed. (Toronto: University of Toronto Press, 2014), 1:58.

Pepin's new leadership in exchange for Pepin's defeat of the Lombards in the northern part of Italy, a Germanic people who had been a constant thorn in the pope's side. Whereas the Byzantine Empire had formerly aligned with the papacy, the papacy now linked with the Franks. This alliance became the basis of the Holy Roman Empire and indirectly led to the Crusades in both the Holy Land and in Europe. As the papacy gained power and prestige during the Middle Ages, it flexed its muscles by initiating and sponsoring the Crusades. Pope Urban II preached mightily for his cause. The union of religion and politics created a distinct Christian identity. It also introduced ongoing confusion as to the relation between secular and spiritual authority—sparking what has often been called the Investiture Controversy. Because church and state were so intimately connected in the Middle Ages, monarchs did not see any problem with appointing bishops without consulting the religious structures beforehand (if at all). This controversy was symptomatic of the larger struggle in the West between the papacy (and its bishops) and monarchs (and those under their patronage).

France. In addition to the cult of the saints, in which saints were venerated at Christian tombs (which many churches were eventually built over), the monastic movement played a central role in the education, evangelization and preservation of medieval Christianity in France. Monks "lived a life of daily martyrdom, giving up their wealth, family ties, and worldly offices."[19] Convents and monasteries sprang up by the hundreds—more than three hundred between the sixth and seventh centuries alone. While convents usually remained within city walls (to provide greater protection of the women), monasteries lined the countryside and led to the evangelization of country dwellers. Due to the spiritual malaise that had crept in after centuries of prosperity and the ongoing disputes between secular rulers (on whose land many monastic houses were standing) and abbots, different reform movements appeared throughout medieval France—before then spreading out into the rest of Europe. The two most significant medieval reform movements within monasticism were the Cluniac and Cistercian movements.

The Cluniac movement consisted of a confederation of Benedictine monasteries founded in the tenth century through an endowment of land. This

---

[19]Ibid., 1:27.

movement dedicated monasteries to the apostles Peter and Paul—and thus to the pope, who held jurisdiction over their relics—rather than a local lord. The Cistercian Order sought to address the growing worldliness among monasteries by stressing greater application of Benedict's Rule and by emphasizing manual labor and agriculture. Cistercians withdrew further into the French countryside, and within years had established hundreds of houses. The French abbot Bernard of Clairvaux founded a Cistercian monastery in 1115 and was one of the leading voices of Western Christianity.

During this time in France several fringe Christian groups emerged in protest to the Catholic Church. Among many others, this includes the Cathars, the Henricians and the Waldensians. While the Henricians criticized standard practices of Catholicism such as infant baptism, the Mass and church discipline, the Waldensians emphasized Bible reading, lay preaching (it was illegal to preach in the Middle Ages without a license from the Catholic Church) and voluntary poverty. Such groups were anything but novel in the Middle Ages. On the contrary, a constant flow of unauthorized Christian movements spread across Europe. Some of these, such as the Cathars and Henricians, did not outlive the Middle Ages; others, such as the Dominican and Franciscan orders, which originated around the same time, eventually gained the approval of Rome and became international Christian movements that invigorated the Catholic Church.

The emergence of many new Christian groups coincided with the rise of the urban movement, which sparked educational reform across Europe. The origins of the movement stemmed from Charlemagne's provision for the education of future monks and priests in the eighth century—just one of several reforms during the so-called Carolingian Renaissance. The cathedral schools that Charlemagne introduced offered education from the bishop, and they also led to the spread of Latin as the language of Christian learning as well as the spread of the Nicene Creed, Benedict's Rule and Christian Bibles. Over time, urbanization and the decline of (rural-based) feudalism led to the creation of secular Christian universities. Though originally attached to cathedrals or monasteries, the *universitas* ("guild" in Latin) referred to a group of students who paid individual masters to teach them. The *magistri* ("teachers" in Latin) soon eclipsed abbots, monks and priests by inaugurating a new era of theological inquiry. They lived in the cities, traveled freely, socialized with the aristocracy and gained reputations as important players in the new economic and social world of Western Europe.[20] The newly founded university also stimulated the bookmaking industry, creating the need for smaller, cheaper and portable Bibles for students to read and annotate for classes.

TRAIL MARKER
Changing Society

What we are witnessing in medieval France is the transition from a rural, feudalistic and faith-based culture to an urban, capitalistic and reason-based one. Europe was changing as a whole, and these larger changes greatly affected the development of theology.

By the twelfth century Paris, originally containing a hodgepodge of Christian churches and monastic houses, had become a center of this new learning largely on account of its size and location along the Seine River. One of the pioneers of this new urban movement, called scholasticism, was Peter Abelard. Originally from Brittany, Abelard traveled across the different cathedral and monastery schools and settled for a while in Paris as *magister*. There, thousands of eager students from all over Europe flocked to his lessons, enshrining him as the first celebrity professor. The university system that began in France spread across Europe, and some of the most influential theologians in the Middle Ages, such as Thomas Aquinas, studied in Paris. Although Paris soon became famous for its university and spell-binding professors, not all that glitters is gold. A fourteenth-century Dutchman named Geert Groote looked back with no twinkles in his eyes as he remembered his days at the University of Paris:

> Avoid and abhor every public disputation held simply to score a triumph or to make a good appearance, such as all those disputations of the theologians and arts in Paris. Do not be present even to learn. Clearly they disturb tranquility; they sink to quarrels and disputes; they are useless, ever inquisitive, and what

---

[20]See Marie-Dominique Chenu, *Nature, Man, and Society in the Twelfth Century* (Chicago: University of Chicago Press, 1968).

is worse, superstitious, bestial, diabolical, earthly, so that their teaching is rotten, harmful, and never useful, making them a waste of time.[21]

Although Groote was not alone in his assessment of the "rotten" teaching at Paris, students raced to the school. As elsewhere in Europe, students at Paris learned the key components of a liberal arts education: grammar, logic and rhetoric; and arithmetic, astronomy, geometry and music. The completion of these basic studies enabled students to then focus on law, medicine or theology, the latter of which cost the most and took the longest amount of time to master.

Meanwhile, in the larger religio-political context of the Middle Ages, France underwent its fair share of spiritual and secular challenges—once again, the twin conduits of authority in the ancient world. While the Crusades in the Holy Land were simmering down, a power struggle was brewing between Philip IV of France and Pope Boniface VIII. For centuries European monarchs had taxed clergy in order to finance their battles and crusades. The clergy grew to resent this practice, but it came to a head at the turn of the fourteenth century. When Philip IV sought to tax the clergy in order to pay for a war with England, the pope responded unequivocally: All clerics, and laymen who imposed payments on them, "shall, by [that] very act, incur the sentence of excommunication."[22] Although the French king attempted to arrest Boniface and drag him to France like a dog on a leash, Boniface escaped capture. His successors, however, were not as fortunate.

The fourteenth century was particularly devastating for medieval France. In Paris half of the population died from the Black Death. During this great social upheaval—which, of course, caused widespread religious anxiety and despair—the Catholic Church underwent its own woes. Just when the church was needed the most, it appeared, it was being strong-armed by the state. From 1309 to 1378, the so-called Avignon Papacy ruled over the Catholic Church from France rather than from Italy, but everybody knew that the popes were attached to the French monarch's leash. From 1378 to 1417, papal controversy continued. As the apostle Paul once stated, you reap what you sow. Rival popes, one based in Avignon and the other in Rome, vied for jurisdiction over

---

[21]Geert Groote, "Resolutions and Intentions, but Not Vows," in *Devotio Moderna: Basic Writings*, trans. John Van Engen (Mahwah, NJ: Paulist Press, 1988), 68.

[22]Rosenwein, *Short History of the Middle Ages*, 1:259.

the church. To make matters worse, a rival pope based in Bologna claimed succession to Saint Peter. This Great Schism caused widespread division, as nations acknowledged one pope or another "as their political affinities dictated."[23] While France, Naples, Scotland, Sicily and Spain favored the Avignon popes, Bohemia, England, Germany, Hungary, Poland and Scandinavia favored the Italian ones. This schism greatly impacted and further divided England and France—inveterate enemies—contributing to the Hundred Years' War. In the year this feud ended, Ottoman Turks scaled the walls of the capital of the Byzantine Empire, Constantinople. Europe, for its part, was slowly rising out of the ashes of death and war, and was about to enter the modern world.

THE FORMATION AND FRAGMENTATION OF A CHRISTIAN EUROPE

Despite ongoing internal and external challenges, Europe became the center of the worldwide Christian movement after the second millennium. This shift proved surprising given the strong reception Christianity received in Africa and Asia in the first several centuries. According to historian Barbara Rosenwein, "No reasonable person in the year 750 would have predicted that . . . Western Europe would, by 1500, be well on its way to dominating the world."[24] The emergence and ascendancy of the various rival Islamic empires in Africa and Asia, on the one hand, and the amalgamation of the Byzantine and Holy Roman Empires in Europe, on the other, created the space and time necessary for the shift. With most of Continental Europe safe from the perceived Muslim threat, Christianity expanded in the north, east and south over the course of several centuries. Again, however, this transition occurred step by step. It took seven hundred years after the Battle of Tours (732) before the last kingdoms in Europe adopted Christianity.

By the fifteenth century Europe had congealed more or less into its respective religious borders and enclaves: Catholicism in the southwest, northwest and west; and Orthodoxy in the southeast and northeast. Arianism had died out, and other religious sects such as Cathars and Waldensians were under the radar. For centuries Catholics and Orthodox competed with one another. Churches and convents arose, evangelism propelled converts into

[23]Williston Walker et al., *A History of the Christian Church*, 4th ed. (New York: Scribner, 1985), 376.
[24]Rosenwein, *Short History of the Middle Ages*, 1:58.

neighboring regions, and both prince and peasant alike adopted the Christian religion. The process took fifteen centuries to complete. And by this time Christianity was now a European religion, one replete with rituals, saints' days and feasts, churches and monasteries, and other customs melded over time with the pagan cultures of each region. But as we shall see in the next stage of European history, "European Christianity is a dangerous thing."[25] What could this possibly mean for the rest of the world?

---

[25]Mojola Agbebi, quoted in Lamin Sanneh, *Disciples of All Nations: Pillars of World Christianity* (Oxford: Oxford University Press, 2008), 143.

PART THREE

Christianity from the Fifteenth to the Twenty-First Centuries

How can we summarize the past six hundred years of world Christianity? It's not an easy task; this is the time period in which the church experienced unprecedented expansion. Although the church has always been global in outlook, Christianity truly became a worldwide phenomenon during this era. Between the fifteenth and twenty-first centuries there have come to be followers of Christ in every part of the inhabited world. And in these regions the doctrines and practices of the Christian churches that have developed vary considerably—some to the point of having little to do with the way other Christian groups practice their faith. If there were a handful of Christian traditions active during the early church, there are tens of thousands of smaller traditions now. Most pointedly, the traditions stemming from Protestantism have proliferated beyond imagination—so much so that it is nigh impossible to actually classify the various Protestant churches, denominations, cults and sects. As hinted at throughout this book, the different Christian groups across church history do not always see eye to eye on many issues, often allowing their differences to take precedence over their commonalities.

In this last section of the book we continue our whirlwind tour of worldwide Christianity. We will begin with the continent of Europe, since Europeans have been most active in the evangelization and colonization of the rest of the world since the 1400s—but certainly not before this time. Beginning in the fifteenth century trade and seafaring opened up like never before, and

Southern Europeans of a Catholic persuasion led the way. From Europe we will sail to the Americas, a region that was "discovered" by Catholic Europeans in the fifteenth century. In Oceania, a region representing only a small proportion of Christians worldwide, missionaries have been rolling in like waves since the eighteenth, nineteenth and twentieth centuries. Christianity on the many islands of Oceania is a microcosm of the global church. Despite its rather small population, there are colossal numbers of Christian traditions and denominations, with the result that Christians in Oceania are divided from one another based on European and American disputes that have little to do with life on the islands.

The last two chapters discuss Christianity in Africa and Asia. As we know, African and Asian Christians have been worshiping Jesus Christ since the first century. Despite many hardships, a remnant has survived from both Africa and Asia to this day. Some in these two regions were Christians well before people in Europe began converting from paganism. Nonetheless, during the Middle Ages, a confluence of factors converged that brought about the diminishment of Christianity throughout Africa and Asia, halting its otherwise impressive expansion and increase. Meanwhile, Europe witnessed explosive growth. By the time European and Northern American missionaries arrived in Africa and Asia a few hundred years ago, Christianity might as well have been a novel religion. For not only was European and American Christianity different in many ways from the way it was practiced in Africa and Asia in the earliest centuries after Christ, but it was largely forgotten.

seven

EUROPE

*The world has changed more in the last five hundred
years than in all of previous human history.*

DOUGLAS JACOBSEN, THE WORLD'S CHRISTIANS

FROM THE CENTER TO THE PERIPHERY

Europe's monopoly over world Christianity lessens day by day. The place that
served as the center of global Christianity a few hundred years ago now inches
closer to the periphery. Although the Christian religious skeleton—what
Philip Jenkins calls "residual Christianity"—remains intact, Christianity plays
a considerably less important role in the life of Europeans than it once did.
Today, atheism, secularism and an increasingly large number of non-Christian
communities have crowded out the monolithic Christian market of Europe,
making it one of the greatest missionary fields of any world region. Despite
their Christian past, an increasing number of native Europeans claim no religion at all, and many of those who do identify with Christianity attend
church nominally at best and never at worst. Jenkins writes, "Contemporary
[European] churches are surviving on accumulated capital, which is evaporating at an alarming rate."[1]

The collapse of European hegemony over Christianity took several centuries. Five hundred years ago Europe, though never completely unified, was
the center of the global Christian map. Its key was written in Latin, and the

---

[1]Philip Jenkins, *The Next Christendom: The Coming of Global Christianity*, 3rd ed. (Oxford: Oxford
University Press, 2011), 119.

terms were largely decipherable from the perspective of Europe. Despite the fracturing of the Catholic Church due to the European Reformations, the Catholic Church experienced its greatest successes as it expanded into a new world. Catholicism, in fact, held a strong presence over what are now France, Hungary, Ireland, Italy, Spain, Portugal and Poland. Yet over time costly geographic-political-religious wars fractured the European continent. The subsequent formation of nation-states transferred Christian religious allegiance from the church to the secular state. Civic religion became the new state religion. National anthems replaced Christian songs, flags replaced Bibles, politicians replaced ministers and dying for one's country replaced martyrdom for the faith. The Enlightenment, deism, political and scientific revolutions, and theological liberalism further, in fits and starts, redirected the religious fervor of the continent.

In the East the formation of the Soviet Union hamstrung the Eastern Orthodox Church. This antireligious, socialist empire killed countless millions of Eastern Europeans, and it also uprooted religious identity from the hearts of the people and in its place forcibly planted atheism. The USSR's decades-long siege against religion partially explains the high degree of secularism in its former states today and the irrelevance of the Orthodox Church in the lives of generations of Eastern Europeans. In the central and western part of Europe a different set of circumstances caused a similar religious effect. Today, formerly Catholic nations such as the Czech Republic, France and Slovakia contain exceptionally high rates of atheism, just as formerly Protestant nations in Scandinavia such as Denmark and Sweden do. Put negatively, it appears that Catholicism, Orthodoxy and Protestantism have overstayed their welcome in Europe and will now enter a steady era of neglect and cultural irrelevance.

To add to this decrease of Christian faith, Europe has both the lowest fertility rate and the oldest population in the world, meaning that it cannot sustain itself under current conditions. Put positively, however, continued immigration could provide the vehicle necessary to re-Christianize Europe and force older Europeans to reexamine their faith.[2] The rising numbers of immigrants have brought their own forms of Christianity—often Pentecostal or Catholic—to complement the majority of immigrants who practice other

---

[2]See Philip Jenkins, *God's Continent: Christianity, Islam, and Europe's Religious Crisis* (Oxford: Oxford University Press, 2007), 287-89.

religions, even though evidence suggests that these minority religious communities will not readily assimilate into the majority population.[3]

CHAPTER OVERVIEW

In this chapter I will provide an overview of the past five hundred years of Christianity in Europe. Naturally, a detailed study of Christianity at this time in Europe is well beyond the scope of this book, so we will focus on the most basic features of European Christianity. As we do so, try to imagine a continent completely divided in terms of ethnicity and language, but with a largely Christian culture intact. As the centuries pass and ideas, movements and brutal wars both enhance and devastate society, many Europeans begin to shy away from their Christian past and instead turn toward an uncertain religious future.

EASTERN EUROPE

Political instability and war marked Eastern Europe from the sixteenth to the twentieth centuries. Borders shifted regularly as different empires emerged, expanded, diminished, retreated and morphed. The Ottoman and Hapsburg Empires overpowered many smaller kingdoms in the region, but they did not get along. With the aid of the Polish-Lithuanian Commonwealth, the Hapsburgs drove the Turks across Romania and Hungary and back into the Balkans at the Battle of Vienna in 1683. This symbolized the defeat of Muslim advance in Eastern Europe and the rising alliance of the Austrians and Hungarians. The Austro-Hungarian alliance kept the province of Transylvania, part of Romania, Catholic, whereas Romania's other provinces of Moldavia and Wallachia remained Orthodox. Prussia, based largely in modern Germany, encompassed many parts of Eastern and Northern Europe, while the Polish-Lithuanian Commonwealth established a strong presence over northeastern Europe. The Russian Empire, meanwhile, extended its borders across a sprawling countryside before communists took control and expanded its base even further in the early twentieth century. Since the end of communism its borders have eroded.

Russia. After the collapse of the Byzantine Empire in 1453, the Russian Empire regarded itself as Byzantium's successor—the Third Rome. With

---

[3]David Martin, *Pentecostalism: The World Their Parish* (Oxford: Blackwell, 2002), 67.

great fanfare, the monk Philotheus of Pskov advocated the Russian theory of political-spiritual succession to Rome in his letter to Tsar Basil III in 1510:

> This present church of the third, new Rome, of [your] sovereign empire: the Holy Catholic Apostolic Church . . . shines in the whole universe more resplendent than the sun. And let it be known to [your] Lordship, o pious Tsar, that all the empires of the Orthodox Christian faith have converged into [your] one Empire. [You are] the sole Emperor of all the Christians in the whole universe.... For two Romes have fallen, the Third stands, and there shall be no fourth.[4]

Whether the Russian Empire should be regarded as the Third Rome or not, the art and worship of its churches certainly mirrored the grandeur of the Byzantine Church. As Russian envoys stated after they staggered starstruck out of Hagia Sophia in Constantinople back in 987, "we did not know whether we were in heaven or on earth. For on earth there is no such splendor or such beauty."[5] If that were the sole criteria for succession to the Byzantine Empire, the Russian Empire's religion may very well qualify. Well known for its ornate architecture, emotive music, beautiful iconography and rapturous liturgy, Russian services could continue for hours on end, with church attendees being caught up in worship as if in a dream.

Besides its beauty we do see connections between the Russian Empire and the Byzantine Empire in terms of wealth and sheer size. The Russian Church became quite wealthy as the Russian Empire expanded into neighboring lands. In fact, the church's landholding "increased at a phenomenal rate" during the fifteenth and sixteenth centuries,[6] precipitating a theological crisis since church monasteries now controlled more than a third of the land in Russia. What are those who have renounced all material wealth supposed to do with hundreds of acres of land? There were two general responses. The so-called possessors, monks who, of course, had no personal possessions since they had taken vows of poverty, favored monastic holdings of land under the belief that the money acquired through land ownership could be used to take care of the poor; while the nonpossessors opposed monastic

---

[4]Philotheus of Pskov, quoted in Geoffrey Hosking, *Russia: People and Empire, 1552-1917* (Cambridge, MA: Harvard University Press, 1998), 6.

[5]*The Russian Primary Chronicle: Laurentian Text*, trans. Samuel Cross and Olgerd Sherbowitz-Wetzor (Cambridge, MA: Medieval Academy of America, 1953), 112.

[6]Nancy Kollmann, "Muscovite Russia 1450–1598," in *Russia: A History*, ed. Gregory Freeze, 3rd ed. (Oxford: Oxford University Press, 2009), 37.

ownership of land under the conviction that it would distract monks from their vocations of prayer and worship.

The arrival of the seventeenth century led to continued controversy for the Russian Church. The mentally unstable Ivan the Terrible oppressed the church and ordered the deaths of leading officials, while multiple claimants to Ivan's throne upon his death threw the empire and church into confusion. The chaos ended only with the emergence of the Romanov dynasty in 1613. As co-regents, Tsar Michael I and his father Patriarch Philaret linked the church and state like a metal chain, though their successors would never attain to the same level of *symphonia*.

The Russian Church entered an era of confrontation during the reign of the long-term tsar Peter the Great. When the holder of the office of patriarch died in 1700, Peter did not appoint a replacement, and instead established a Holy Synod to manage the affairs of the church that lasted for two centuries. Peter founded St. Petersburg and moved the headquarters of the state out of Moscow to this new, Western-friendly and largely secular city, launching a new era of church-state relations whereby the state assumed authority over many areas the church had historically overseen. Peter also liquidated the spiritual treasure of Russian Orthodoxy—the monasteries and its monks. The church "lost its position as a supreme moral authority" and increasingly came to serve the interests of the state.[7] Peter's successors, such as Elizabeth and Catherine II, continued to levy heavy restrictions on monks and monasticism, though the church experienced bursts of evangelistic and spiritual reinvigoration through the likes of well-known Christian authors such Seraphim of Sarov, Alexis Khomiakov, Theophan the Recluse, Fyodor Dostoevsky, Leo Tolstoy and the anonymous author of *The Way of a Pilgrim*.

In the early twentieth century secularism and atheism made their first national victories. The Marxist Bolshevik Party seized power in 1917 just as the Holy Synod absolved itself in exchange for a patriarchate. Saint Tikhon became the first person to hold that office in more than two centuries. Nonetheless, by the time the Soviet Union coalesced in 1922—the same year it arrested Saint Tikhon—the Marxist government had already formed an aggressive antireligious campaign. Not only did it nationalize all the extensive

---

[7]Wallace Daniel, *The Orthodox Church and Civil Society in Russia* (College Station: Texas A&M University Press, 2006), 18.

lands the church possessed but it also banned state subsidies to clergy and church bodies, canceled the church's status as a judicial body, denied legal standings to baptisms, church marriages and divorces, outlawed organized religious education of the youth and made it virtually impossible for them to attend church, seized church bank accounts, and separated the church from the state.[8] What was the church then? It was now a hollow tree.

TRAIL MARKER
The Russian Orthodox Church

The Russian Orthodox Church has been the most dominant religious institution in Russia for more than a thousand years. At the same time the past century has witnessed the eclipse of Russian Christianity by atheism and secularism. Combined with the rise of Protestantism, it's not at all clear which path Russians will take in the future in terms of religious orientation: Orthodoxy, secularism, Protestantism or something else.

The number of martyred Russian bishops, priests, monks and nuns reached well into the tens of thousands. Between 1917 and 1943 alone, "forty-five thousand priests were martyred,"[9] while the number of martyred laypeople ran into the millions—leading to mass emigration among those with means. Although Christians experienced periodic streaks of tolerance, particularly during World War II, the state completely undercut the missionary and prophetic witness of the church. The decades-long siege against Christianity ended at the end of the twentieth century. In 1988 Mikhail Gorbachev assisted the Church in the celebration of Russia's one-thousand-year anniversary of Christianity, an event foreshadowing the collapse of the Soviet Union in 1991 and the cessation of governmental persecution against religion.

[8]Nathaniel Davis, *A Long Walk to Church: A Contemporary History of Russian Orthodoxy* (Cambridge, MA: Westview, 2003), 2.
[9]Paul Mojzes, "Orthodoxy Under Communism," in *Twentieth-Century Global Christianity: A People's History of Christianity*, ed. Mary Farrell Bednarowski (Minneapolis: Fortress, 2010), 7:141.

Yet the church's new freedoms have also introduced new challenges. To begin with there has been considerable confusion among churches, as countless Protestant denominations have arisen in the wake of the Soviet collapse, and even many Catholic and Orthodox churches have sought independence from the patriarchate of Moscow. Such fragmentation has forced the Russian Orthodox Church—historically *the* church of the Russian people—to "face competition from all sides" of Christian theological traditions.[10] What's more, the decades-long attack against religion under Soviet rule has left an enduring impression on the Russian populace. Although many have rejoined the Russian Orthodox Church in the past couple of decades, or one of the Protestant varieties filling its void, many have not returned—and likely never will. That's because the empire that once held to the Christian faith with such fervency now contains, somewhat embarrassingly on the heels of its one-thousand-year celebration of Christianity's presence, one of the highest secular populations in the world.

Northern Europe

In contrast to the Orthodoxy exemplified in Russia, Protestantism has been closely linked with Northern European countries for almost half a century. Lutheranism, which originated in Saxon Germany in the early sixteenth century, soon began to impact every country in Catholic Northern Europe. Lutheran theology spread by means of the newly created printing press, widespread use of the Latin language and via Northern European Lutheran converts and missionaries. Lutheranism particularly appealed to inhabitants of what are now Denmark, England, Estonia, Finland, Iceland, Latvia, Norway, Scotland and Sweden, yet for different reasons.

Despite the religious dynamism of the European Reformations, the twentieth and twenty-first centuries have seen a gradual decrease in public religion and increase in secularism across Northern Europe. Inhabitants of Scandinavia and the Baltics illustrate this trend well. In Sweden, less than 5 percent of the population attends church on a regular basis, and there has been a precipitous decline in religious organizations. In nearby Estonia, a nation under foreign occupation for centuries before the communists took over in the twentieth

---

[10]Timothy Ware, *The Orthodox Church* (London: Penguin, 1997), 163.

century, more than half of the populace claims no religious identity at all—making it one of the most irreligious nations in the Western hemisphere.

England. Great changes characterized the English Church as it transitioned from the medieval to the modern world. Though not often recognized, Catholicism commanded a high degree of devotion among the English well into the sixteenth century.[11] The Mass, though spoken in a foreign language (Latin) and not often offered in both species (bread and wine) to the laity, was regarded as the centerpiece of the Christian life. At the same time, as early as the fourteenth century, certain individuals and movements questioned the Mass and challenged the authority of the pope. A small English reform movement, known as Lollardy and often associated with the thought of the Oxford professor John Wycliffe, regarded the Catholic Church as corrupt and in need of liturgical, moral and theological reformation.[12] The Lollards used the so-called Wycliffe Bible and lingered for two centuries in underground networks of mostly laypeople. In response the Church banned all English Bibles in 1407, persecuted Lollards and even dug up Wycliffe's bones to burn them for heresy.

A century later King Henry VIII, growing quite accustomed to getting what he wanted, became the first modern European monarch to officially reject the pope's authority after Pope Clement VII refused to annul his marriage to Catherine of Aragon. Through the left (political) hand of Henry's chief adviser Thomas Cromwell and the right (theological) hand of archbishop of Canterbury Thomas Cranmer, the English Parliament nullified its relationship with Rome just as the new and independent Anglican Church annulled Henry's marriage. Passed in November 1534, the Act of Supremacy read as follows:

> Albeit the King's Majesty justly and rightfully is and oweth to be the Supreme Head of the Church of England, and so is recognized by the clergy of this realm in their Convocations, yet nevertheless for corroboration and confirmation thereof, and for increase of virtue in Christ's religion within this realm of England, and to repress and extirp all errors, heresies, and other enormities and abuses heretofore used in the same; be it enacted by authority of this present

---

[11]See Eamon Duffy, *The Stripping of the Altars: Traditional Religion in England 1400–1580*, 2nd ed. (New Haven, CT: Yale University Press, 2005).

[12]G. R. Evans writes that Wycliffe "was apparently merely a contributor"—rather than the originator—of Lollardy. See her *John Wycliffe: Myth and Reality* (Downers Grove, IL: InterVarsity Press, 2005), 248, 255.

Parliament, that the King our Sovereign Lord, his heirs and successors, kings of this realm, shall be taken, accepted, and reputed the only Supreme Head in earth of the Church of England, called *Anglicana Ecclesia*, and shall have and enjoy, annexed and united to the imperial crown of this realm, as well as the style and title thereof, as all honours, dignities, pre-eminences, jurisdictions, privileges, authorities, immunities, profits, and commodities, to the said dignity of the Supreme Head of the same Church belonging and appertaining; and that our said Sovereign Lord, his heirs and successors, kings of this realm, shall have full power and authority.[13]

The Protestantization of England took decades to complete, stretching well into the reign of the last Tudor monarch, Elizabeth I. During her reign a growing debate emerged between Episcopalians and Puritans regarding the extent of the reformation of the Anglican Church.[14] Although Elizabeth managed to tenuously hold these factions together, the next ruling dynasty, the House of Stuart, was unable. An independent Puritan faction in Parliament assumed control of the government during the English Civil War and beheaded King Charles I on charges of treason. In 1660 a new royalist-leaning Parliament restored the monarchy, unleashing a string of strict legislation against Puritans and other Nonconformists such as Baptists and Presbyterians. A cadre of dissenting and popular-level Protestant groups, ranging from Diggers to Muggletonians to Ranters, was the theological product of the civil war.

The ascendancy of the Whig Party in the eighteenth century led to the secularization of the church in English society. The English increasingly came to treat Christianity "as a private matter" rather than as a public one.[15] An innocuous yet telling shift in English religious culture can be seen in how the more generic term *religion* came to replace the term *faith* in English book titles.[16] Before long, leading thinkers in England were questioning not only the authority of the Bible but even the very existence of God. The so-called Age of Reason (or the Enlightenment), which boasted an innate confidence in human reason along with a deep suspicion toward tradition, spread like

---

[13]"Act of Supremacy," in *Documents of the English Reformation*, ed. Gerald Bray (Cambridge: James Clarke, 1994), 113-14.

[14]For a distinction between these two groups, see Derek Cooper, *Thomas Manton: A Guided Tour of the Life and Thought of a Puritan Pastor* (Philipsburg, NJ: P&R, 2011), 24.

[15]C. John Sommerville, *The Secularization of Early Modern England: From Religious Culture to Religious Faith* (Oxford: Oxford University Press, 1992), 15.

[16]Ibid., 16.

wildfire across the British Isles. Even though it emerged from within a Christian context, the Enlightenment had a tendency to substitute science for religion, reason for tradition and certainty for faith.

Deism, a form of free-thinking rationalist Christianity, appealed to a whole generation of weary Europeans. Religious squabbling and religious wars, most notably the devastatingly brutal Thirty Years' War, had led to a darkening of traditional religion. The Deists, by contrast, were enlightened by recent discoveries in mathematics, science and new currents of philosophical thought. The English deist Matthew Tindal wrote several influential writings that advocated deism, including *Christianity as Old as the Creation* (1730). This popular deist book, though at face value lauding Christianity as true, undercut historic Christianity and subordinated it to human reason:

> If God will judge mankind as they are accountable, that is, as they are rational, the judgment must hold an exact proportion to the use they make of their reason. And it would be in vain to use it if the due use of it would not justify them before God. And men would be in a miserable condition, indeed, if whether they use it or not they should alike be criminals. And if God designed that all mankind should at all times know what he wills them to know, believe, profess and practice; and has given them no other means for this but the use of reason; reason, human reason, must then be that means. For . . . God has made us rational creatures, and reason tells us that it is his will that we act up to the dignity of our natures. . . . What God requires us to know, believe, profess and practice must be in itself . . . reasonable.[17]

Over time thinkers who extolled the human mind reasoned away Jesus' virgin birth, miracles and resurrection from the dead—foundational tenets of historic Christianity.

While reason held sway over pockets of the English Church, spiritualism, pietism and the Evangelical Revival invigorated other ones. The seventeenth-century apprentice to a cobbler, George Fox, criticized the English Church and asserted that following one's "inner light" surpassed church tradition and reason. Opponents to Fox's teaching pejoratively called his followers Quakers since they quaked fanatically when the Spirit led them to speak. Later, the Evangelical Revival (the First Great Awakening in America) came through the

---

[17]Matthew Tindal, *Christianity as Old as the Creation* (London, 1730), 1:6. Note: I have modernized spelling and punctuation in this quote.

outdoor preaching of two Anglican clergy who were friends—John Wesley and George Whitefield. Although both men remained within the Church of England, they gave birth to an international movement: evangelicalism.

Meanwhile, dissenting Christian traditions ranging from Baptists to Unitarians competed with the Church of the England for converts. Dissenting evangelicals responded to social ills that industrialization and urbanization had caused by forming organizations like the YMCA and Sunday schools. In 1865 the Methodist preacher William Booth founded the Salvation Army along with his wife Catherine to reach "the lowest of the low."[18] As for Catholicism, tensions among the Protestant majority eased and the Catholic Church grew and gained in importance due in part to England's closer ties to Ireland in the Act of Union in 1801. Parliament rescinded antiquarian, anti-Catholic legislation in the Catholic Emancipation Bill of 1829, and immigration of Irish Catholics increased. Similarly, widespread immigration of Eastern Orthodox believers in the twentieth century gave a boost to the Orthodox Church in England, although its first parish in England dates to the seventeenth century.

In the past decades, historic English churches have decreased in size and number while immigrant churches are on the rise. Stated differently, Anglican, Baptist, Catholic and Methodist churches are declining precipitously, while Pentecostal churches are growing. And even though Christianity's religious skeleton remains intact, recent surveys indicate that almost half of all Britons claim "no religion."[19] Overall, less than 5 percent of the British population attends church on a regular basis, meaning that there are as many religiously active Muslims in England as there are Anglicans.[20] In fact, one of the growing problems that these immigrant communities face—whether consisting of Muslims or Christian Pentecostals—involves finding a sufficient location for their services while, ironically, many historic churches are being sold and set up as art shops, clinics, community centers, homes, libraries, museums, pubs, restaurants and theaters.[21]

---

[18]Norman Murdoch, *Origins of the Salvation Army* (Knoxville: University of Tennessee Press, 1994), x.
[19]Jenkins, *Next Christendom*, 118.
[20]Joel Fetzer and J. Christopher Soper, *Muslims and the State in Britain, France and Germany* (Cambridge: Cambridge University Press, 2005), 2.
[21]Doreen Rosman, *The Evolution of the English Churches, 1500–2000* (Cambridge: Cambridge University Press, 2003), 313.

SOUTHERN EUROPE

In the fifteenth and sixteenth centuries the Catholic kingdoms of Spain and Portugal were the richest in Europe. The crown of their achievement was not only their occupation of lands from the Americas to Africa and Asia, but the legislative and papal-approved right to appoint their own priests and bishops over their new empires—a practice called patronage. On the other side of Southern Europe, in Italy, the series of popes occupying the throne of Peter found themselves sitting on a gold mine of wealth thanks to kingdoms such as Spain and Portugal. At the same time, the papacy was reeling from a spiritual battle in its own back yard, as inhabitants of many European kingdoms were abandoning the Catholic Church in great numbers in order to form Protestant ones. The Catholic Church has faced a dizzying array of challenges in the centuries since then. Yet over the course of devastating wars, the rise of modern nations and growing numbers of non-Catholic religious movements, the Catholic Church has managed to thrive and even expand its influence across the world.

The Former Yugoslavia. The southeastern European region referred to as the Balkans is one of the most religiously and politically volatile sections in all of Europe. Religiously, the Balkan nations are a crossroads of three ancient faiths—Catholic Christianity, Orthodox Christianity and Sunni Islam. In a related way there are three major groups who share a common language and ethnicity in the Balkans who now are very different from one another due to religious and political divisions. These three major groups—each of them Slavs—are Bosniaks, Croats and Serbs, and they exemplify some of the heated divisions in the Balkans.

In order for us to understand some of the controversies surrounding these people groups today, we must first turn to the past. When the Turks conquered the Serbs in what is now Bulgaria in 1377 and again in Kosovo in 1389, many Serbs emigrated to nearby lands controlled by the Catholic Hapsburg Dynasty. After the Hapsburgs defeated and pushed back the encroaching Turks from Eastern Europe, the Austrians encouraged Serbians to live in Austrian territory. Regrettably, this led to Serbian persecution on two fronts: first, Catholic Austrian persecution of the Orthodox Serbs living under the authority of the Hapsburgs; and second, external persecution of Serbs who remained in their land and who lived under the authority of the Ottomans. This twofold persecution caused Serbian nationalists to declare an independent Serbian country in 1830, and although most Serbs chose to live outside of the state under the reign of the Habsburgs, the creation of Serbia offered an ethnic, historic and religious imagined community, which preserved (Orthodox Christian) Serbian identity in the midst of larger ethnic, political and religious realities.

While a large portion of the Orthodox Serbs emigrated out of Ottoman-occupied territory, the Bosniaks mostly remained and converted to Islam within 150 years. Many of these Slavic Christians adopted Islam under the devshirme system, a system whereby Ottoman Turks collected (Christian) boys from the Balkans to receive a Muslim education in Turkey for imperial service. Such a practice decimated the Christian population. From the fifteenth to the seventeenth centuries the Turks conscripted at least 200,000 boys, meaning that such boys not only never married Christian women and had Christian children, but converted to Islam.[22] As one Serbian historian notes, "Those [Serbian Christians] who left Orthodox community were forsaken by the Serb people; they no longer shared their tradition, they had a different attitude toward the Ottoman Empire and its authorities, and completely changed their way of life."[23]

TRAIL MARKER
Religion in the Balkans

The interpretation of the complicated history of the Balkans is hotly debated among scholars. Speaking in terms of religion, one historian writes, "Religion has made the Slavs of southeastern Europe what they are. Catholic Slavs in the region of the former Yugoslavia became Slovenes or Croats; Orthodox [Slavs] became Serbs and some of them, more recently, Macedonians and Montenegrins; [and Muslim Slavs] . . . are called Bosniaks."[a]

[a]Tim Judah, *Kosovo: What Everyone Needs to Know* (Oxford: Oxford University Press, 2008), 17.

---

[22]Noel Malcolm, *Bosnia: A Short History* (New York: New York University Press, 1996), 46.
[23]Sima Circovik, *The Serbs*, trans. Vuk Tosic (Oxford: Blackwell, 2004), xx.

Although it was not the policy of the state to convert people to Islam, economic and political incentives were compelling. Other than Slavic Bosniaks, Albanians (a non-Slavic people claiming descent from pre-Roman tribes) became the largest group of Europeans in the Balkans to convert to Islam. Of the three majority-Muslim nations in the Balkans—Albania, Bosnia and Herzegovina, and Kosovo—the Albanians comprise the majority of Albanian and Kosovar multiethnic groups. The shifts in religio-political boundaries that formed produced ongoing conflicts, as now, for instance, largely Catholic Croats, Orthodox Serbs and Muslim Bosnians clashed with one another despite their common ethnic, historic and linguistic identities.

More recently the Yugoslav Wars ripped apart what are now Bosnia and Herzegovina, Croatia, Kosovo, Macedonia, Montenegro, and Serbia (the former Yugoslavia; see table 7.1). President Slobodan Milošević sought to resurrect a former Serbian empire by attacking and killing non-Serbs, leading to his international condemnation. The nation of Serbia declared its independence in 2006, and Kosovo, a majority-Albanian Muslim population, seceded from Orthodox Christian Serbia in 2008. Serbia, however, refused to recognize this secession.

Table 7.1. Modern nations out of former Yugoslavia

Modern Country	Capital	Year of Independence	Major Ethnic Groups	Dominant Religious Tradition
Bosnia and Herzegovina	Sarajevo	1992	Bosniaks (dominant), Croats and Serbs	Sunni Islam
Croatia	Zagreb	1991	Croats (dominant) and Serbs	Roman Catholicism (with high Protestant minority)
Kosovo	Pristina	2008	Albanians (dominant), Bosniaks and Serbs	Sunni Islam
Macedonia	Skopje	1991	Albanians, Macedonians (dominant), Roma (Gypsies), Serbs and Turks	Eastern Orthodoxy (with high Sunni Islam minority)
Montenegro	Podgorica	2006	Albanians, Bosniaks, Montenegrins (dominant) and Serbs	Eastern Orthodoxy (with high Sunni Islam minority)
Serbia	Belgrade	2006	Bosniaks, Hungarians, Roma and Serbs (dominant)	Eastern Orthodoxy

Today, the Serbian Orthodox Church claims members throughout Serbia and the Balkan Peninsula, especially in Bosnia and Herzegovina, Croatia, Kosovo, Macedonia, and Montenegro. Montenegro, which shares a common heritage and faith with Serbia, contains a majority Eastern Orthodox population. However, a

Table 7.2. Sample of Catholic reform movements before Martin Luther's reform

Century of Origin	Reform / Movement	Description	Representative
11th	Nominalism	Universals do not exist and things are only mental constructs and given names.	William of Ockham (d. 1347)
12th	Conciliarism	Ecclesial authority resided with ecumenical councils and cardinals, not the pope.	Marsilius of Padua (d. 1342)
12th	Waldensians	Emphasized preaching, Bible study, laity and vernacular translations; reaction to Catholic views on transubstantiation, authority and excess, and purgatory.	Peter Waldo (d. 1218)
13th	Mendicant Orders	Designed to counter heresy, minister to the cities and preach to the public.	Stephen of Bourbon (d. 1261)
13th	Apostolic Poverty	Clergy should live in poverty and not have possessions.	Michael of Cesena (d. 1342)
14th	Modern Devotion	Renewal focusing on inward spirituality and piety, Scripture reading, and solitude.	Geert Groote (d. 1384)
14th	Lollardy	Rejection of papal authority, transubstantiation and Latin-only liturgy and Bible.	John Wycliffe (d. 1384)
15th	Hussitism	Bohemian (Czech) reaction to Catholic teaching, authority and sacraments.	Jan Hus (d. 1415)
14th	Humanism	Focus on texts, morality and language.	Erasmus (d. 1536)

Perhaps the persistent backing of Lutheranism by strong secular leaders distinguished the success of this reform movement in Germany from others. From its beginning Lutheranism gained support from or purposely aligned with political rulers who protected the fledgling movement. The fact that Luther departed unharmed after the Diet of Worms (1521) had condemned him and his writings—under the watchful eye and capable hand of Emperor Charles V, no less—testifies to the protection Luther received from Frederick the Wise, his secular lord. The Catholic Frederick simultaneously secured Luther's safe conduct to Worms and snuck him away to Wartburg Castle once Luther's death appeared all but certain. Later, after Frederick had preserved his celebrity monk, the Lutheran movement aligned with the Schmalkaldic League.

The Schmalkaldic League consisted of influential German Lutheran princes and leaders who banded together against the Catholic Holy Roman Empire and fought for theological and political freedom. This happened after Charles V had decided against the Protestants at Augsburg in 1530. Now liberated from political menacing and no longer captivated by the constraints of the Catholic Church, Lutheran theologians in Germany knocked on more than church doors by hammering out a new Protestant theology during and after Luther's peaceful demise in 1546. As happens at the death of many great founders of movements, controversy and division marked early Lutheranism as varied Luther(an)-influenced groups proffered rival articulations of what it meant to be Lutheran. As elsewhere in Europe, confessionalization of independent Protestant traditions after their reformations produced what scholars call Protestant orthodoxy or scholasticism. Accordingly, "intellectual assent to correct doctrine" came to dominate Lutheranism in the late sixteenth and early seventeenth centuries.[27]

Lutheran scholasticism provoked various spiritual reactions to rationalist thinking. Jacob Boehme, the son of a German Lutheran family, claimed to receive visions from God at an early age. He soon put pen to paper and re-corded his visions. Response from church authorities ranged from utter de-nunciation to complete bafflement as to what Boehme meant—an excerpt of his writing follows:

> Beloved soul, if you will be earnest without intermission, you shall certainly obtain the favor of a kiss from the noble Sophia (or Divine Wisdom) in the holy name of Jesus. For she stands ever before the door of the soul, knocking and warning the sinner of his wicked way. Now if it once thus desires her love, she is ready for it and kisses it with the beams of her sweet love, from where the heart receives joy. But she does not presently lay herself in the marriage-bed with the soul. That is, she does not presently awaken the extinguished heavenly image in herself, which disappeared in Adam in Paradise. No, there might be danger to man in that. For if Adam and Lucifer fell, having it mani-fested to them, the same may easily happen to man, who is still so strongly enthralled to vanity. . . . Christ was tempted in the wilderness. And if you will put on him, you must go through his whole progress or journey, even from his incarnation to his ascension.[28]

Meanwhile, a less controversial but more lasting reaction to Lutheran or-thodoxy manifested itself in the form of Pietism. Lutheran writers such as Jacob Arndt, Philipp Jakob Spener, August Francke and Nicolaus Zinzendorf gave direction to this new movement centered on individual holiness, faith over rationalism, Bible reading and spiritual reflection. Of these many Pietists,

[27]Carter Lindberg, *The European Reformations* (Oxford: Blackwell Publishing, 1996), 358.
[28]Jacob Boehme, *The Way to Christ* (1622; repr., New York: Cosimo, 2007), 27. Note: I have modern-ized the spelling and punctuation.

Count Zinzendorf became the protector and landowner of the Moravian Church, indigenous to the Czech Republic from the fifteenth century. Under Zinzendorf's leadership as bishop, the Moravians initiated the first large-scale international missionary ventures of Protestantism. The Pietist movement also inspired many Protestant denominations in Europe and abroad.

While various theologians offered different visions for Lutheranism in the seventeenth century, a bloody war was taking place in the Holy Roman Empire. Known as one of the most destructive wars in European history, the Thirty Years' War (1618–1648) devastated Germany as Protestant and Catholic states in the empire fought with one another. The Peace of Westphalia ended this European interreligious bloodbath in 1648 by allowing each state or territory to establish its own tradition of Christianity based on the ruler's preference, allowing the large yet Catholic minority of Germany to exist alongside the majority of Protestants, who by now consisted of more than just Lutherans. These religio-political divisions shaped the development of Christianity all across Europe for centuries.

While the northern part of Germany embraced Protestantism, the southern part remained staunchly Catholic. Germany, of course, like other "countries" in Europe at the time, consisted of numerous independent states and larger kingdoms. This only changed after the domineering prime minister of Prussia, Otto von Bismarck, unified Germany into a republic in 1871 amid widespread European nationalism. Although Bismarck's new Germany included a high percentage of Catholics, he relegated their influence in the so-called *Kulturkampf* (cultural struggle) between the Protestant majority and the Catholic minority. Bismarck's anti-Catholic campaign led to the arrest and imprisonment of priests and bishops, the expelling of Catholic religious orders and the seizure of Catholic property. Rather than destroying the Catholic Church in Germany, however, this campaign merely strengthened it.[29] The Catholic Church, in fact, experienced a renewal in the nineteenth century in broader Europe, just as it did in Germany. A growing number of shrines dotted the European countryside as a result of an unprecedented number of Marian apparitions—divine visitations from the Virgin Mary, usually to common people (and even children). Of note among

---

[29]See Michael Gross, *The War Against Catholicism: Liberalism and the Anti-Catholic Imagination in Nineteenth-Century Germany* (Ann Arbor: University of Michigan Press, 2004).

these apparitions, Our Lady appeared to three village girls in Marpingen, in 1876, at the height of the *Kulturkampf.*

World Wars I and II seriously disrupted the German Christian community—both Catholic and Protestant. The heavy conditions that Allied victors placed on Germany after World War I "planted the seeds that would later grow in the Nazi Party and World War II."[30] Fascism and totalitarianism sprang from European soil in places like Italy and Germany. Adolf Hitler founded the Nazi Party and rose to power in the 1920s until he became the chancellor of Germany in 1933 and dictator the following year. He implemented an aggressive agenda of German expansion and domination in Europe. Pope Pius XI, in the midst of an explosive Europe, issued the encyclical *Mit brennender Sorge* (*With Burning Anxiety*) in German rather than the standard Latin as if to expedite its release from the Vatican. There was no time to wait for this important message to undergo delay in the renowned bureaucracies of Rome.

After the papacy smuggled it into Germany, the pope ordered Catholic priests to read the letter in the pulpit on Palm Sunday 1937. The letter publicly denounced Nazism, infuriating Hitler and causing him to respond in attacks against the Catholic Church he was baptized into in his native Austria. The encyclical read as follows:

> The peak of the revelation as reached in the Gospel of Christ is final and permanent. It knows no retouches by human hand; it admits no substitutes or arbitrary alternatives such as certain leaders pretend to draw from the so-called myth of race and blood. Since Christ, the Lord's Anointed, finished the task of Redemption, and by breaking up the reign of sin deserved for us the grace of being the children God, since that day no other name under heaven has been given to men, whereby we must be saved (*Acts* iv. 12). No man, were every science, power and worldly strength incarnated in him, can lay any other foundation but that which is laid: which is Christ Jesus (1 *Cor.* iii. 11). Should any man dare, in sacrilegious disregard of the essential differences between God and His creature, between the God-man and the children of man, to place a mortal, were he the greatest of all times, by the side of, or over, or against, Christ, he would deserve to be called prophet of nothingness.[31]

---

[30]Carl Koch, *A Popular History of the Catholic Church* (Winona, MN: Saint Mary's Press, 1997), 250.
[31]Pius XI, *Mit brennender Sorge* 17, The Holy See, March 14, 1937, www.vatican.va/holy_father/pius_xi /encyclicals/documents/hf_p-xi_enc_14031937_mit-brennender-sorge_en.html.

In addition to the papacy, certain segments of the Protestant churches likewise raised anxious concerns about the violent direction of Germany, including the German pastor Dietrich Bonhoeffer and the so-called German Confessing Church, which authored the Barmen Declaration in 1934 principally under the guidance of the Swiss theologian Karl Barth.

TRAIL MARKER
Christianity in Modern Germany and England

The history of Christianity in Germany parallels, in many ways, the history in England. Catholicism was the dominant religion for centuries before Protestantism emerged in the 1500s. For the next several hundred years Protestantism was very influential, though the Catholic Church retained a strong minority identity. Nonetheless, the seeds of secularism were planted by both Catholics and Protestants, and today England and Germany are largely secular.

Today, secularization pervades Germany. Although residual Christianity lingers privately and publicly, studies indicate that only about a million Germans, out of about eighty million overall, attend church on a regular basis. While Germans defect from the historic church and increasingly avow to have no religious persuasion, a fairly large immigrant population practices Islam and takes its religious identity quite seriously. Projections indicate that their faith will continue to transform the religious landscape of Germany on account of the high birth rates of immigrants coupled with the low birth rates of ethnic Germans. By 2050 it is projected that "Europe as a whole will have a Muslim minority of at least 15 percent, possibly as high as 20 percent."[32] A high percentage of this Muslim population will come from Germany.

---

[32]Jenkins, *Next Christendom*, 122.

European Christianity Experiences Religious Competition in a Flooded Market

Europe has witnessed great changes in the past five hundred years. From its former place at the center of world Christianity, it now nears the edges of the global map. Atheism, secularism and immigrant religion stand poised to seize the formerly indigenous European Christian population. So-called traditional European Christianity—whether Catholicism, Orthodoxy or mainstream Protestantism—appears underequipped to address the changes in modern society. Pentecostalism, though energizing a certain base of the European population, has succeeded mostly among the immigrant population rather than among the majority of indigenous Europeans wielding the most influence on society.

According to this line of thinking, "Pentecostalism is unlikely to be a major power in the developed world [of Europe] because it represents the mobilization of a minority of people at the varied margins of that world, whereas in the developing world it represents the mobilization of large masses."[33] Nonetheless, religion, or at least spirituality, is not dead in Europe. Some scholars believe that religious competition—such as one encounters in developed regions boasting high secular percentages partially on account of their high life expectancies, adult literacy and per capita incomes—creates "better religious products" than the "one size fits all" products of yesteryear.[34] If this perception is correct, European Christianity will not die any time soon, though it will look very different than it has in the past.

---

[33]Martin, *Pentecostalism*, 67.
[34]Frank Pasquale, "A Portrait of Secular Group Affiliates," in *Atheism and Secularity*, ed. Phil Zuckerman (Santa Barbara, CA: Greenwood, 2010), 63; and Donald Miller and Tetsunao Yamamori, *Global Pentecostalism: The New Face of Christian Social Engagement* (Berkeley: University of California Press, 2007), 36.

eight

LATIN AMERICA

The North American colonies were largely settled by persons fleeing the feudal restraints, royal absolutism, and clerical oppression of the Old World. In Latin America, in contrast, the conquistadores sought to re-create in the New World the feudal society, political authoritarianism, and religious orthodoxy they had carried over from medieval Europe.

HOWARD WIARDA, THE SOUL OF LATIN AMERICA

CARTOGRAPHY AND WORLD DOMINATION

Cartography, the study and practice of making maps, features significantly in the story of Christianity. The pursuit of wealth, which went hand in hand with maps, does as well. While in the past it was customary to begin the story of Latin America with the arrival of the Genoese native but Spanish-supported Christopher Columbus on the Caribbean coast in 1492, we will commence the Latin American Christian narrative with cartography. We pick up the narrative a couple of months after Columbus returned to Spain in 1493. Now that the Spaniards had discovered a "new world"—of course, the "Indies," as the Spaniards incorrectly called the Caribbean islands, had been inhabited for millennia—it was important to set the rules, as it were, of global domination. Who had the rights to the land? What about any future discoveries of nearby lands? What about other pesky European powers that might want to interfere?

The papacy established the rules of Europe's global expansion. Fortunately for the Spanish the newly elected pope, Alexander VI, was a native of

Valencia in a newly united Spain and a close friend of the Spanish crown. Through a spate of papal bulls and decrees, most notably *Inter Caetera* and the Treaty of Tordesillas, the pope eventually divided all newly discovered lands located outside of Europe along a meridian of 370 leagues west of Cape Verde between Spain and Portugal.[1] In typical language at the time, the pope threatened "the wrath of Almighty God and of the blessed apostles Peter and Paul" on any who interfered with his holy "recommendation, exhortation, requisition, gift, grant, assignment, constitution, deputation, decree, mandate, prohibition, and will."[2] Such is the story of how Portugal and Spain came to dominate the world, particularly Latin America: By drawing a few lines on a map and imprinting the papal impress on an ornately designed document, the world changed forever. The West went to Spain, while the East went to Portugal.

CHAPTER OVERVIEW

In this chapter we will discuss the five-hundred-year history of the church in Latin America. The major influence of Latin American Christianity came from Portuguese and, especially, Spanish Catholicism. Monks and priests were very active in the evangelization of many native tribes of Latin America, and the people were ruled by authoritarian and violent rulers. There was also a cultural and religious fusion of indigenous and European beliefs and practices, as well as a mixing of races, which led to a veritable caste system among Christians in Latin American society for hundreds of years. As you read this chapter, try to imagine what it would have been like to be part of a church with such a complicated structure and systemic imbalances. For such was the reality for many Latin American Christians.

Caribbean. The Spaniards first arrived in the Caribbean in 1492. Columbus described his encounter with the Arawak Indians this way:

> I gave gratuitously [to the natives] a thousand useful things that I carried, in order that they may conceive affection, and furthermore may be made Christians;

---

[1]The original bull and treaty called for Spain to receive all lands 100 leagues west of Cape Verde, but Portugal mitigated Spain's geographic reach to 370 leagues west of Cape Verde. Naturally, countries like France, for instance, were not pleased with the pope's unilateral decision to give the spoils of new territories to Spain (in the west) and Portugal (in the east). See John Schwaller, *The History of the Catholic Church in Latin America* (New York: New York University Press, 2011), 39-40.

[2]For the actual wording of the bull *Inter Caetera*, see www.papalencyclicals.net/Alex06/alex06inter.htm.

for they are inclined to the love and service of their Highnesses and of all the Castilian nation, and they strive to combine in giving us things which they have in abundance, and of which we are in need. And they knew no sect, nor idolatry; save that they all believe that power and goodness are in the sky, and they believed very firmly that I, with these ships and crew, came from the sky; and in such opinion, they received me at every place where I landed.[3]

On Columbus's second trip to the Caribbean in 1493, he brought with him the first Christian missionaries. However, a division soon emerged between the settlers, who sought material things, and the missionaries, who sought souls. The *encomienda* system, which lawfully allowed Spanish settlers jurisdiction over natives (since "slavery" was illegal) for service in exchange for protection and Christianization, became the main conduit of evangelization for many early native peoples. Though viewed as a win-win situation from the eyes of Spain (since the natives would receive protection and Christ, while the Spaniards would obtain fortune and wealth), it was a dreadful practice foreshadowing hundreds of years of mistreatment. Such exploitation has led one Latin American historian to lament, "There is no evidence from anywhere in the region for a single pastoral endeavour starting from respect for the indigenous cultures as a pre-condition for evangelization."[4]

The exploitative character of such colonization led Spanish monks to criticize the practices of settlers. When three Dominicans arrived in Hispaniola (current Haiti and the Dominican Republic) in 1510, for instance, they immediately denounced the harsh treatment of the indigenous people. In a fiery sermon he gave during the third Sunday in Advent in 1511, the Dominican priest Antonio de Montesinos condemned settlers for their mistreatment and exploitation of the natives:

> I am the voice of one crying in the wilderness. . . . This voice . . . declares that you are in mortal sin, and live and die [in it] by reason of the cruelty and tyranny that you practice on these innocent people. Tell me, by what right or justice do you hold these Indians in such cruel and horrible slavery? . . . Are they not men? Do they not have rational souls? Are you not bound to love them as you love

---

[3]Christopher Columbus, "Letter to Luis de Sant' Angel," in *America Firsthand*, vol. 1, *From Settlement to Reconstruction*, ed. Robert Marcus and David Burner, 2nd ed. (New York: St. Martin's Press, 1992), 5-6.

[4]Armando Lampe, "Christianity in the Caribbean," in *The Church in Latin America 1492–1992*, ed. Enrique Dussel (Maryknoll, NY: Orbis, 1992), 203.

yourselves? How can you lie in such profound and lethargic slumber? Be sure
that in your present state you can no more be saved than the [Muslim] Moors
or Turks who do not have and do not want the faith of Jesus Christ.[5]

Other Spanish friars joined de Montesinos in their spiritual assault against
Spanish practices. Bartolomé de las Casas, who had arrived in the Caribbean
in 1502 as a conquistador but only became a Dominican priest in 1515, later
wrote a scathing narrative about the destruction of the Indians at the hands of
the Spaniards: "I have already said and I repeat . . . no measures were taken for
the conversion of Indians and no more was done about the matter nor any
more thought given to it than if the Indians were sticks, stones, cats or dogs."[6]

Despite the ongoing criticisms of these friars, priests benefited from the
system of slavery. The first African slaves arrived in Hispaniola in 1505. Spaniards had imported African slaves to work the sugar mills due to the high death
rates among the local populations, whom the Spanish (unsuccessfully) attempted to enslave and force to work the mills. Incredibly, by 1509 between 70
percent and 95 percent of the local population in Hispaniola had died out due
to the Spaniard's harsh treatment, susceptibility to European diseases and
physical duress.[7] The Catholic Church, for its part, was not just a silent
partner when it came to the business of slavery and sugar plantations:

> Many mills on the larger islands had their own chapels, with chaplains paid by the
> proprietor. Production needs, however, did not always coincide with those of the
> Church, which led to numerous conflicts over issues such as working on feast days.
> But the one could not manage without the other: the mill needed the religious
> justification for slavery, this being that the main reason for bringing black pagans
> from Africa was to teach them the way of Christian salvation; the Church had
> powerful interests in the sugar mills: the seminary of Havana, for example, still
> drew its revenue from the sugar industry in the nineteenth century. So the dom-
> inant factor was the alliance between the Church and the sugar producers, with
> the former preaching a message of submission to discourage black rebellion.[8]

---

[5]Antonio de Montesinos, quoted in Bartolomé de las Casas, "History of the Indies," trans. Andree
  Gollard, in *Religion in America: A Documentary History*, ed. Lee Penyak and Walter Petry (Maryknoll, NY: Orbis, 2006), 23-24.
[6]De las Casas, "History of the Indies," 21.
[7]Ondina González and Justo González, *Christianity in Latin America: A History* (Cambridge: Cambridge University Press, 2008), 30.
[8]Lampe, "Christianity in the Caribbean," 204.

Eventually the slave trade in the Caribbean came to a halt in the islands as the English and Dutch colonies entered the region. Whereas the Spanish-speaking countries in Latin America have always maintained a steady Catholic population, the arrival of the English, Dutch and North Americans beginning in the seventeenth centuries created a sizeable Protestant presence. Not surprisingly, given Christianity's history elsewhere, Caribbean islands fragmented along national and ecclesiastical lines: Anglican, Presbyterian and Methodist churches formed in British colonies like Barbados and the Bahamas, just as the Dutch established Reformed churches in colonies like Curaçao and Bonaire. Later in the nineteenth and twentieth centuries, Seventh-day Adventist, Baptist and Pentecostal missionaries from North America planted churches in Haiti, Jamaica and the Dominican Republic.

TRAIL MARKER
Slavery in Latin America

The history of Christianity in the Caribbean has been marked by the church's collusion in slavery, and it has also been divided island to island based on the ethnicity and religious persuasion of the Christian colonizers. For instance, because the English colonized Jamaica, it is a majority Protestant nation and the natives speak English; meanwhile, the Dominican Republic natives speak Spanish and the nation is a majority Catholic since the Spaniards colonized that nation.

Cuba. The island nation of Cuba is a reflection of the different European and African populations that traveled through the Caribbean after the sixteenth century. In terms of religion Cuba has one of the lowest percentages of Christians in the Caribbean. Three main factors account for this: the enduring presence of African religious beliefs and practices such as Santeria, the historic inability of the Catholic Church to connect with the locals as well as the church's close association with Spanish hegemony, and the rule of communism.[9] The first two factors intersect. In contrast to the history of many other Latin American countries, Cuba was a latecomer in colonization. Originally, the island served as a "sparsely populated . . . strategic stopover" that generated no wealth of its own for Spanish fleets.[10] Things changed after the Haitians, the greatest producers of sugar in the world, rebelled against European powers in the 1790s and abolished slavery. In place of Haiti, Cuba became ground zero for sugar production. Spaniards began importing hundreds of thousands of African slaves to provide the menial work needed in the sugar plantations, just as Creoles entered Cuba to purchase land and make money. Over time this created "two Cubas—one steeped in Spanish cultural traditions and ritual practices like Catholicism . . . and the other centered in African santería, a syncretic popular religion."[11]

Given such a negative opinion of Catholicism among those of African ancestry, it is no surprise that Afro-Cubans did not historically seek refuge in Mother Church. Nor does it come as a shock that they did not raise more clamors of concern more than a century later when Fidel Castro took over the country and demoted the Catholic Church's societal importance. As one religious scholar notes, "Cubans have historically viewed the institutional Catholic Church as urban, white, upper class, and anti-revolutionary."[12] Such a view hardly inspires favor with the many black and poor Cubans who have called the island home.

Without doubt, the Cuban Revolution that Castro completed in 1959 has stymied Christianity's health and growth. Indeed, Cuba has been the only communist country in the Western hemisphere. The consequences of the revolution—though most Cubans enjoyed freedom from the former dictator Fulgencio Batista—have resulted in impoverishment for not only the people in general but also the church. Many of the Catholic and Protestant clergy— as well as the elites of society—fled the island after Castro took control. Before Castro's revolution, in fact, Protestant missions had made great progress on the island after Cuba gained its independence from Spain in 1898.

---

[9]Virginia Garrard-Burnett, "Central America and the Caribbean," in *Introducing World Christianity*, ed. Charles Farhadian (Oxford: Wiley-Blackwell, 2012), 164.

[10]Benjamin Keen and Keith Haynes, *A History of Latin America*, vol. 2, *Independence to the Present*, 9th ed. (Boston: Wadsworth Cengage Learning), 239.

[11]Ibid., 235.

[12]Garrard-Burnett, "Central America and the Caribbean," 165.

It was actually so successful that, at the time of the revolution, Cuba contained "one of the largest Protestant populations and most indigenized Protestant Church establishments of any country in Latin America."[13] How would Christianity look differently had Cuba never encountered communism and the Protestants grew in popularity?

Today, the Cuban government demonizes religion less than it formerly did. In 1992 the government amended the Cuban Constitution from an atheistic state to being a secular one.[14] Recently, the number of *evangélicos* (or Protestant evangelicals) has increased dramatically. This contrasts with the decline of mainstream Protestant churches in Latin America like the Methodists, who influenced the nation before the revolution. The country has also witnessed a growing number of *casas cultos* or "house churches" that congregate under the radar of the Cuban government. House churches have been gaining momentum for the past many years, and perhaps more than fifteen thousand Cubans frequent these house churches, especially around Havana.[15]

As for the Catholic Church, the historic visit of Pope John Paul II to Cuba, which took years to negotiate, led to the building of a new seminary, the first Catholic structure the government has allowed since Castro took over in 1959. Although the government forbids Christians to proselytize in Cuba, many Cubans hope that presidential attendance at the inauguration of the seminary in 2010—as well as Pope Benedict XVI's visit to and celebration of mass in Havana in 2012—presages an era of increased openness to Christianity. With Fidel Castro gone from power and the opening up of trade with the United States continuing apace, religion in Cuba is likely to undergo change in the years ahead.

Central America

In contrast to the Caribbean, Mexico—the largest and most influential of the Central American countries—boasts the highest percentage of Catholics and the lowest percentage of Protestants in Latin America. The rest of the countries of Central America, however, contain the reverse: one of the highest percentages of Protestants and least amount of Roman Catholics. Much of this stems from the nationalist loyalty on the part of the Mexicans for the Virgin of Guadalupe

---

[13]Ibid., 167.
[14]Ibid., 166.
[15]Ibid., 168.

as well as its strong sense of nationalist (Catholic) identity. But still, some of it has to do with the rise of Protestantism, particularly Pentecostalism, in Central America in the twentieth century. In fact, in only thirty years, from 1960 to 1990, Protestantism (including, of course, Pentecostalism) rose from 2 percent to 30 percent of the Christian population in most Central American countries.[16] Though Protestantism is on the rise in Mexico, it has been slower to take root.

Like elsewhere in Latin America, Spanish colonization went hand in glove with evangelization to the native peoples of Central America. Bartolomé de las Casas, who had emigrated from Hispaniola to New Spain (Mexico) and who eventually became the bishop of Chiapas in 1544, received permission for an experiment in the conversion of the natives by peaceful means rather than by force. There, both secular and regular clergy competed with one another over authority of the indigenous population. Regrettably, the Spaniards frequently exploited the native inhabitants of Central America.

Over time the Catholic Church came to dominate the region. The church built banks, convents, churches, monasteries, schools and towns. The church also collected tithes and taxes, making it the "largest single landowner" in Central America by the end of the eighteenth century.[17] This all changed, however, after the different nations achieved independence from Spain in the early 1800s. Like so many Latin American countries, Central America as a whole followed liberal agendas of separation of church and state and enacted similar policies of restricting the church's influence and appropriating its wealth.

In the twentieth century Pentecostalism soared to new heights while Catholicism began its descent from cultural and religious supremacy. The origin of Pentecostalism in Central America can be traced to El Salvador. Spreading from this small country, Pentecostalism has become the fastest-growing segment of Christianity in several Central American countries. It appeals to not only the poor but also to the affluent middle class. In fact, over the past few decades Pentecostalism has been inching forward the percentage of Protestants in several Central American countries close to 40 percent of the population—the highest by far of any Spanish-speaking region of the world.

---

[16]Adrian Hastings, "Latin America," in *A World History of Christianity*, ed. Adrian Hastings (Grand Rapids: Eerdmans, 1999), 265.

[17]Garrard-Burnett, "Central America and the Caribbean," 156.

Mexico. On Good Friday 1519, Spanish conquistador Hernán Cortés landed in Veracruz, Mexico, from Cuba with five hundred to six hundred men and sixteen horses. He proceeded to burn the eleven ships carrying his men to Mexico to signify that he would not leave before accomplishing the mission of acquiring great riches. As the Spanish saying goes, *A lo hecho, pecho*— loosely translated as, "in the face of things done, just stick out your chest." Cortés stuck out his chest. By burning his ships he did the unthinkable; he was not going to shrink back from the task at hand. After Friar Bartolomé de Olmedo celebrated High Mass on Easter Sunday, the Spaniards readied themselves for conquest and conversion. Although the Aztec army outnumbered Cortés and his men by more than fifty thousand to one, the Spaniards would eventually succeed in not only reaching the capital of the Aztec Empire, Tenochtitlán—the regal city built on a lake with a quarter of a million inhabitants—but also in destroying it and setting up a Spanish government and forming a Christian society. From the ashes of pagan Tenochtitlán would rise the phoenix of Catholic Mexico City.

Despite setbacks, the Spaniards overtook the Aztec Empire within two years. The settlement and expansion of Christianity in Mexico began in earnest. Although the Spaniards built their first church in Tlaxcala in 1522, they did not begin mass evangelization of Mexico until 1524—the year twelve Franciscan friars arrived in the Valley of Mexico at the request of Cortés himself. The Franciscans carried out their work seriously and urgently under the conviction that they were ushering in the arrival of the kingdom. The end times were fully expected to occur. But as time wore on, Franciscans (including friars from other religious orders as well as secular priests) arrived in droves. These monks oversaw conversions and baptisms by the thousands, stirring the beginnings of Mexican Christianity.

The Spanish established the diocese of Mexico City in 1530. The diocese's first bishop, Juan de Zumárraga, was in the midst of his own political and religious battles when the most unexpected yet crucial event in the history of Mexican Christianity occurred. The elderly Juan Diego, a local who had converted to Christianity with his (now deceased) wife just a few years prior, had a vision of the Virgin Mary. Unlike many representations of the Holy Mother in Europe, the Virgin of Guadalupe was dark-skinned with black hair. Zumárraga originally discounted Diego's story about meeting the Virgin but accepted it after he saw an image of the Virgin in Diego's *tilma* (an outer garment worn by Aztec men at the time). For almost five hundred years Mexicans have preserved the tilma of Juan Diego in the Basilica of Our Lady of Guadalupe, a shrine which represents the religious heartbeat of millions of Mexican Christians.

The appearance of the Virgin of Guadalupe to Juan Diego in 1531 was the turning point of Christianity in Mexico. The gentleness and warmth of the dark-skinned Virgin of Guadalupe appealed to and contrasted with the severity and strangeness of the God and cultic saints the Spanish conquistadors heralded. The appearance of the Virgin Mary not only became the means by which millions of Mexicans became Christians but it also served as the rallying cry for independence against Spain in the early nineteenth century. The year was now 1810. After the Creole priest Miguel Hidalgo rang the church bells and preached a fiery sermon against Spanish conquest to his flock of mestizos and Indians, he voiced the *grito de Dolores* (the cry in Dolores): "Long live our Lady the Virgin of Guadalupe! Death to bad government! Death to the *gachupines* [a derogatory term for Spanish peninsulars]!"[18]

TRAIL MARKER
Latin American Caste System

The Latin American caste system was used to measure one's social status. From the top of the tier to the bottom some of the more common castes were: peninsular (European born in Old Word), Creole (European born in New World), mestizo (half European and half Indian) and mulatto (half European and half African). For most of the history of Catholicism in Mexico (and Latin America in general), only the peninsulars and creoles—in other words, the Europeans—were allowed to be ordained and to lead in the churches and monasteries.

[18]Mary Jo Weaver and David Brakke, *Introduction to Christianity*, 4th ed. (Belmont, CA: Wadsworth, 2008), 176; Schwaller, *History of the Catholic Church in Latin America*, 117.

When the Mexicans finally achieved independence from Spain a decade later, the church was at a crossroads. In a circumstance repeated across Latin America, two major ecclesiastical obstacles appeared. First, because on the one hand the Catholic Church had gained considerable wealth during the colonial period and on the other the new independent governments were financially strapped, the government stripped the church of its land, money and resources. Second, because the Spanish crowns alone had legal rights to make clerical appointments, new governmental dictators—either audacious enough to appropriate that privilege for themselves or foolish enough to leave sees vacant for years on end—appointed their own puppet bishops or appointed none at all. Either way, this led to the languishing of the church.

Throughout the nineteenth century, especially after liberals deposed the conservative General Antonio López de Santa Anna in the 1850s, the church became the target of further scorn. New laws abolished ecclesiastical courts, confiscated church property and restricted the common practice of charging money for priestly services such as baptisms and funerals. In protest the priests withheld the sacraments from the masses. Nevertheless, the rising tide of liberal, church-state separation proved unstoppable.[19] Liberal and indigenous president Benito Juárez, no friend of the Catholic Church, nationalized it and relegated its importance (though it regained some of its standing later during his reign).

TRAIL MARKER
The Bygone Wealth of the Church

The Catholic Church, so dominant for centuries, was removed from the pedestal of power in the nineteenth century in Mexico. A revolving door of dictators appropriated much of the wealth, property and resources of the church for themselves or doled it out to the highest bidder, causing all kinds of turmoil in the process that would not go away even after the dictator had died.

---

[19]Schwaller, *History of the Catholic Church in Latin America*, 147.

During Juárez's tenure as president Protestant missionaries made their way into the country. Between the 1860s and 1870s denominations ranging from Congregationalists to Presbyterians to Baptists and Disciples of Christ arrived. Although they did not gain many converts, Protestants played an important role in the Mexican Revolution. They also fought alongside Juárez's men to oust the French from the country in the 1860s. The conservatives, by contrast, who were generally supportive of the Catholic Church, opposed Juárez and experienced hardship during the succession of power from the Porfiriato, referring to the modernizing tenure of Mexican president Porfirio Díaz, to the Mexican Revolution and beyond—the culmination of which was perhaps the Cristero Rebellion, where fighting between the government and the Catholic Church led to almost one hundred thousand deaths.

While the Catholics favored conservatism, the Protestants generally favored liberalism and its core tenets of freedom of speech and of religion. Therefore, as long as the liberalism-conservatism battle was brewing (and liberals were in control), the Protestants fared well. However, when this ideological battle died down in the twentieth century as liberal values became widespread and the Mexican authorities made peace with the Catholic Church, they minimized the Protestant influence. Today, the *evangélicos* represent less than 10 percent of the Christian population in Mexico. And, unlike most of Central America, most Protestants are not Pentecostals. Of the five largest non-Catholic churches in Mexico, the Jehovah's Witness, the Seventh-day Adventists and the Church of Latter-day Saints (Mormons) are leading the way.[20]

SOUTHERN AMERICA

The Catholic origins of South America share commonalities with its origins in Central America. The Spanish conquistador Francisco Pizarro began colonizing South America in the early 1530s. Together with the Aztec Empire in Central America, the Inca Empire—which encompassed current-day Peru, Bolivia, Chile, Argentina and Ecuador—was the apple of Spain's eye. The Portuguese, by contrast, who discovered Brazil in 1500, did not settle it until decades later. Throughout the 1530s different religious orders flooded South America in the attempt to establish Christianity. Over time the Catholic

[20]Douglas Jacobsen, *The World's Christians: Who They Are, Where They Are, and How They Got There* (Oxford: Wiley-Blackwell, 2011), 220.

Church came to dominate the religious landscape of the region just as it had done in Central America. During the eighteenth and nineteenth centuries, despite its tenuous relationship with the perpetually changing cadre of political leaders, the Catholic Church amassed a fortune for itself and maintained a strong presence in the land. Depending on the country and context, totalitarian regimes played Catholic bishops and priests like pawns. Prophetic voices of critique against injustice, exploitation and corruption arose with marginal success.

Protestantism, the results of European immigration and Western missionary ventures, came late to South America. It did not arrive until the nineteenth century, and it only became part of the larger culture in the twentieth century. In contrast to Pentecostals, who tended to be poorer, Protestants made up much of the middle class. James Thomson, better known as "Diego," pioneered Protestant missions in South America. A Scottish teacher with the British and Foreign School Society, Thomson gallivanted across South America, traveling from one country to another during the height of Latin American independence, selling Bibles and introducing Western and liberal models of education (but not establishing churches). He was a welcomed and honored guest almost wherever he went.

Since the twentieth century, liberation theology and Pentecostalism have influenced Latin American Christianity more than anything else. Beginning with the former, scholars often link the official date of liberation theology to the Conference of Latin American Bishops in Medellín in Colombia in 1968 and the 1971 publication of Peruvian priest Gustavo Gutiérrez's book *A Theology of Liberation*. In truth, however, the struggle for liberation has been a part of Latin American society since the Spanish arrived in the late fifteenth century. In fact, many assert that the church was complicit in the continuation of poverty under the conviction that the church has been closely associated with European-descended elite from the beginning of colonization. Pentecostalism, though, was hugely successful in the twentieth century in South America. Pentecostal Christianity can be traced back to at least 1910 in this region, particularly in Chile and in Brazil, where Pentecostalism is transforming the society.

Brazil. Although South American Pentecostalism did not originate in Brazil, the nation boasts one of the highest numbers of Pentecostals of any country in the world. A recent survey discovered that 61 percent of all churches in Rio de Janeiro were Pentecostal.[21] Brazilian Pentecostalism is traced to the Italian American Luigi Francescon, a man who established Pentecostal churches in São Paulo beginning in 1910 while still living in the United States. The Assemblies of God, the largest of the Pentecostal denominations, began work in Belém in the same year. Since this time the Pentecostal varieties of Christianity in Brazil have only increased.

Brazilian Pentecostalism boomed in the 1950s and 1960s. Unlike the history of the Catholic Church in Latin America, which took hundreds of years before it opened up leadership to indigenous peoples, it took almost no time for native, independent Pentecostal churches to arise. This is certainly part, but not all, of Pentecostalism's success. Perhaps the most influential of these Pentecostal churches today is the Universal Church of the Kingdom of God (UCKG), which Edir Macedo founded in 1977 in Rio de Janeiro. This "prosperity-oriented healing and deliverance" ministry is the fastest-growing group of churches in the country.[22] It holds the hearts of millions of poor Brazilians, many of whom have left Catholicism (and even indigenous religions) due to the Catholic Church's perceived inability or unwillingness to address religious and economic concerns. UCKG churches exist in more than fifty countries worldwide, and they maintain five thousand churches in Brazil alone. In the megacity of São Paulo the UCKG constructed a church—*Templo de Salomão*—based on Solomon's temple in Jerusalem. It competes with any church in all of world Christianity. In competition with Protestant Pentecostal churches like the UCKG, many charismatic Catholic churches have sprouted in Brazil. Father Marcelo Rossi, for instance, celebrates Mass to a daily crowd of thirty thousand people in his church in São Paulo.

It is, of course, impossible to predict how Christianity will fare in Brazil in the future, but it is certain that Protestant Pentecostalism and charismatic Catholicism are "catering to a vast public hunger," with no apparent indications that the people are yet satiated.[23] At the same time, although intense religious fervor characterizes this segment of the Brazilian people, it is also the

[21]Allan Anderson, *An Introduction to Pentecostalism*, 2nd ed. (Cambridge: Cambridge University Press, 2013), 78.
[22]Ibid., 73.
[23]Philip Jenkins, *The Next Christendom: The Coming of Global Christianity* (Oxford: Oxford University Press, 2002), 82.

case that secularism and spiritism are not dead. On the contrary, both are on the rise. Spiritism is growing each decade among the Afro-Brazilian population just as secularism is among the Euro-Brazilian one.[24] And if the enormous percentage of European-descended Uruguayans is any indication on where Brazil is headed in the future—"Uruguay is in fact the least Catholic and least Christian of any Latin American Spanish—or Portuguese-speaking country"—then the church will face an upward battle in the years to come.[25]

THE ONGOING RELIGIOUS DIVERSITY OF LATIN AMERICA

As we will see in chapter nine on Northern American Christianity, *diversity* is a term that aptly describes the religious landscape of Latin American Christianity. Whether large groups of descendants of German Mennonites in Paraguay, Waldensian Italians in Argentina, Shinto-Buddhist Japanese in Peru, American Protestants in Panama, Hindu Indians in Suriname, Chinese Catholics in Cuba, Pentecostals of all ethnic origins throughout Central and South America, European-descended secularists in Uruguay or practitioners of voodoo in Haiti, Latin America teems with religious diversity.

In other words, although Roman Catholicism remains the largest of the Christian traditions—as well as the largest overall "religion"—Latin American Christianity is incredibly diverse. The concomitant effects of democracy, globalization, immigration and missionary work in Latin America have produced a veritable religious buffet table, where one can just as easily choose to become Buddhist, practice Candomblé, recapture Maya rituals or simply profess atheism as choose to become a religiously exclusive disciple of Jesus Christ. As these religious options become even more attractive in Latin America and compete with Christianity, it is unlikely that either the Catholics on the one hand or the *evangélicos* or Pentecostals on the other will ever recapture the Christian hegemony it commanded over the Latin American peoples for many centuries.

---

[24]"Brazil," in *World Christian Encyclopedia: A Comparative Survey of Churches and Religions in the Modern World*, vol. 1, *The World by Countries: Religionists, Churches, Ministries*, ed. David Barrett et al., 2nd ed. (Oxford: Oxford University Press, 2001), 132, 134.

[25]"Uruguay," in *World Christian Encyclopedia*, 1:790.

nine

NORTHERN AMERICA

America is a nation of immigrants.

JAMES FISHER, *COMMUNION OF IMMIGRANTS*

A MELTING POT OF RELIGIOUS CULTURES

The church in Northern America is a melting pot of Christian cultures and traditions. In all probability Northern America remains the most diverse Christian region in the world. The four main countries or territories in Northern America—Bermuda, the United States, Canada and Greenland—have obtained the vast majority of their populations through immigration. This has produced not only a vibrant multiethnic populace but also an eclectic Christian mix that changes with each passing century. Beginning with Bermuda, a British Overseas Territory, it contains great ethnic and religious diversity in proportion to its small size. Because the British colonized Bermuda two centuries before the slave trade ended in the early nineteenth century, they imported large numbers of Africans and Native Americans to the islands. Bermudans practice endless varieties of Protestantism, but a growing segment practices spiritualism or no religion at all.

In Canada, English Protestants and French Catholics divided the country and attempted to convert the "heathen souls" of the native peoples.[1] The French Jesuits, in particular, proved unique in their ability to minister to the Native Americans in the New World. The English and French imported their

---

[1]Jon Butler, Grant Wacker and Randall Balmer, *Religion in American Life: A Short History* (Oxford: Oxford University Press, 2006), 12.

centuries-long feuds from the Old World. Although the Seven Years' War (1756–1763) gave victory to the English in Northern American soil, the French remained. This established two distinct European ethnic-religious groups: English Protestants and French Catholics. When the British divided the nation into Lower Canada (mostly French-speaking and Catholic) and Upper Canada (mostly English-speaking and Protestant) in 1791, this produced two ethnic, linguistic and religious communities. Immigration among non-Europeans in subsequent centuries, however, has yielded a more religiously diverse crop beyond the French-English and Catholic-Protestant divide.

Finally, although Greenland is among the most sparsely populated countries in the world, it actually boasts the longest Christian history in Northern America. The Norseman Eric the Red lived in Greenland in the late tenth century, a time period coinciding with Scandinavia's adoption of Catholicism. The fervent Catholic king Olaf Tryggvason of Norway, the native homeland of Eric the Red, sent missionaries to Greenland in the tenth century. Leif Ericson, a man many remember from secondary school history textbooks, adopted Catholicism under the auspices of King Olaf. However, his father, Eric the Red, remained a pagan. According to tradition, Leif Ericson explored nearby Nova Scotia (now Canada) but later returned to Greenland, where he reportedly spread his Christian faith. In the twelfth century the first (Catholic) bishopric in Greenland arose, and the arrival of the Scandinavians in the eighteenth century led to the dominance of Lutheranism.

CHAPTER OVERVIEW

In this chapter I will limit our discussion of Northern America to the largest and most influential country in this region, the United States. For many the history of the United States is a familiar one. However, I will highlight portions of the church's past that have been historically overlooked, while also attempting to include major common themes and motifs. As you read about the history of Christianity in the United States, try to recognize just how incredibly diverse Christianity is in this country, as well as how Christianized it is in relation to others. For not only is the United States perhaps the most theologically diverse and religiously free country in the world, but it is also the one with the largest number of Christians. Its influence on world Christianity has been nothing short of remarkable.

THE UNITED STATES

Despite the prominent role Protestant European Americans have played in the drama of American history, Spanish and French Catholics, Native Americans and African Americans have reprised more than supporting roles. I will begin by pointing out a little-recognized fact: Spanish Catholicism in North America boasts a history twice as old as the United States proper. That is to say, Spanish Catholics held settlements in the southern parts of Northern America from the early sixteenth to the mid-nineteenth centuries (more than 300 years), while the United States of America has only existed since the late eighteenth century (less than 250 years). This means, among other things, that Spanish Catholicism is just as much a part of American history as any form of Protestantism is. And thus, rather than being an anomaly in the American story, the growing number of Catholic Hispanics in the United States reflects a return to a grander yet often ignored American narrative.

The Catholic Church. Aside from Norse settlers in Greenland and Nova Scotia at the turn of the first millennium, Spanish Catholics were the first European Christians to enter Northern America. The Spaniards arrived in the southern United States and established missions to Native Americans in states such as Arizona, California, Georgia, Kansas, New Mexico, Florida and Texas decades before Pilgrims and Puritans landed in New England in the early 1600s. The Spaniards were mostly in search of wealth when they arrived in the early 1500s.

Hernando de Soto, born and raised in the so-called Cradle of the Conquistadors, in southwestern Spain, came to enslave more than save. Arriving in the Americas as an adolescent, De Soto sought adventure in Panama and Peru before entering Florida in 1539 with hundreds of armed Spaniards, a dozen Spanish priests and countless slaves. In reply to de Soto's request to speak with the Indian Timucua chief, the latter responded,

> Others of your accursed race have, in years past, poisoned our peaceful shores. They have taught me what you are. What is your employment? To wander about like vagabonds from land to land, to rob the poor, to betray the confiding, to murder in cold blood the defenseless. No! with such a people I want no peace— no friendship. . . . As for me and my people, we choose death—and yes! a hundred deaths—before the loss of our liberty and subjugation of our country.[2]

---

[2]Acuera, quoted in *Great Speeches by Native Americans*, ed. Bob Blaisdell (Mineola, NY: Dover, 2000), 3.

To be sure, Chief Acuera's response to Hernando de Soto neither represented the resolve of all Native Americans nor the violent hatred of all Spaniards. Dynamics between the Spanish Catholics and Native Americans varied. Both sides displayed generosity and hostility. Although Spaniards recorded some missionary success, their achievements came at the expense of many missionaries' lives. The outbursts of violence the Franciscan and Jesuits missionaries experienced required garrisons and armed authorities. Long accustomed to conversion by conquest, however, the Spaniards responded violently in turn. Yet between 1580 and 1690, Catholic missionaries established more than thirty missions in Florida, where they taught thousands of Indians. But by the early eighteenth century the British had all but obliterated the Spanish Catholic settlements.

TRAIL MARKER
Catholic History in the United States

The Catholic history of the United States is often overlooked, but there is no doubt that Catholicism has played an important role in American Christianity. Consider the following cities that emerged out of Catholic missions: St. Augustine, Florida (1565); Santa Fe, New Mexico (1610); St. Ignace, Michigan (1671); Mobile, Alabama (1702); New Orleans, Louisiana (1718); San Antonio, Texas (1718); San Diego, California (1769); San Francisco, California (1776).

A similar history of Spanish Catholicism played itself out in other parts of the south and southwestern part of the United States. The Spanish missionaries struggled to contextualize their religion, and many missionaries found it easier to house and educate Indian children in missions away from their families. In California the Franciscan Junípero Serra established nine of twenty-one missions to Native Americans. Almost five thousand Indians lived in the missions he founded when he died. Serra, for his efforts, was canonized as a saint by Pope Francis is 2015, despite protestations among some that Serra destroyed native Indian culture and brutally imposed Catholicism. Whatever the case, missions Sera founded attempted to reach the Native Americans with Christianity as well as inculcate a growing number of European American Catholics. As in other parts of the Americas the Spaniards employed the system of *encomienda* ("entrusting" in Spanish), whereby the Spaniards offered protection and Christian instruction in exchange for Indian labor. Over time this policy led to the conversion of tens of thousands of Indians, but it also bred resentment.

In addition to the Spanish there was a growing French Catholic population in the United States. The Jesuit Jacques Marquette converted many Indians and established missions in present-day Michigan, Wisconsin and Illinois before disease ended his life. Meanwhile, other French Catholics had settled around the Mississippi Delta in places like New Orleans and Mobile, Alabama, by the early eighteenth century. There the French evangelized Native Americans as well as converted and cared for enslaved Africans. The Louisiana Purchase in 1803 incorporated large numbers of "black and white French- and Spanish-speaking Catholics"[3] into the church, further stitching Catholic identity into the fabric of American Christianity.

The nineteenth century was a turning point for the Catholic Church in America. Millions of Catholic immigrants entered the United States in the late nineteenth century, particularly Germans, Italians and Irish. By around 1890 Catholics surpassed the Methodists as the largest single Christian denomination in the country. A veritable Catholic revival was taking place across the United States, led by the religious orders of the "Redemptorists, Paulists, Jesuits, and Passionists."[4] Although this Catholic revival differed from the Protestant ones of the same century and before, it was highly evangelistic, deeply spiritual and garnered widespread appeal.

Even after becoming the single largest Christian denomination, Catholics remained on the fringe of the American religious story. Catholics often felt like they lived on an island in a sea of Protestants. Such a mindset led many American Catholics to spend "much time, energy, and money constructing a 'Catholic mini-state'—a vast network of schools, colleges, hospitals, [and]

---

[3]Patrick Carey, *Catholics in America: A History* (Westport, CT: Praeger, 2004), 24.
[4]Roger Finke and Rodney Stark, *The Churching of America, 1776–1990: Winners and Losers in Our Religious Economy* (New Brunswick, NJ: Rutgers University Press, 1992), 125.

orphanages."[5] One of the most significant acts Catholicism achieved, however, was not the construction of a ministate but rather the deconstruction of the megastate of Protestantism. Around the middle of the nineteenth century, John Hughes, archbishop of New York, forced the release of Protestantism's tight grip on the New York state educational system, which had become a thoroughly Protestant and anti-Catholic structure. Hughes, an Irish immigrant, adroitly learned how to advance religion through politics. As he said to a mob of angry Catholic parents in 1841 in New York City:

> Our adversaries [Protestants in favor of Protestant religious instruction in public schools] accuse us of acting with interested motives in this matter. They say that we want a portion of the school fund for sectarian purposes, to apply it to the support and advancement of our religion. This we deny, as we have done heretofore. . . . There is no such thing as a predominant religion, and the small minority is entitled to the same protection as the greatest majority. No denomination, whether numerous or not, can impose its religious views on a minority at the common expense of that minority and itself. That was the principle from the unjust operation of which we desired to be released.[6]

Although Hughes's fight to gain equality before the law prevailed, anti-Catholic sentiments lingered in the popular Protestant consciousness. Why did Protestants, who held much of the American political power, discriminate against Catholics? For the most part Protestants, biased against Catholicism since the European Reformations, feared that Catholic leaders were nothing more than puppets of the pope. They also thought it an oxymoron to be a faithful Catholic and a good American. In the 1928 presidential election, for instance, Protestant ministers maligned Democratic candidate Alfred Smith in the pulpit just as Ku Klux Klan members lampooned him in papers and pamphlets.[7] As one Protestant minister said to a Protestant audience, "Shall we have a man in the White House who acknowledges allegiance to the Autocrat on the Tiber [the pope], who hates democracy, public schools, Protestant parsonages, individual rights, and everything that is essential to independence?"[8]

---

[5]Mark Massa and Catherine Osborne, eds., *American Catholic History: A Documentary Reader* (New York: New York University Press, 2008), 45.

[6]John Hughes, quoted in ibid., 47.

[7]Wyn Craig Wade, *The Fiery Cross: The Ku Klux Klan in America* (Oxford: Oxford University Press, 1998), 253.

[8]Quoted in Jay Dolan, *The Irish Americans: A History* (New York: Bloomsbury, 2008), 214.

Such a comment not only spoke to the prejudice of many Protestants against Catholics but also to the fact that Catholicism was now becoming a more main-stream religious option among the American populace, as illustrated by the election of Catholic candidate John F. Kennedy to the White House in 1960.

African American Churches. Like Catholics, Africans entered the United States before either the Pilgrims or the Puritans, and their religious traditions have arguably played just as important a role in the history of American Chris-tianity. The first Africans arrived in 1619 as indentured servants, but within a century slavery had become widespread. European Americans largely accepted the institution of slavery as part and parcel of American society, and it was sanc-tioned by the government. As David Walker, an African American Christian abolitionist, lamented in his book *Appeal* in 1829, "Mr. [Thomas] Jefferson . . . has in truth injured us [African Americans] more, and has been as great a barrier to our emancipation, as anything that has ever been advanced against us."[9]

Though the term "the Black Church" suggests a monolithic institution, Af-rican American Christianity is quite diverse historically—as well as today.[10] Some Africans who arrived in America as slaves were Christians, while the others were deeply religious. In terms of religion Africans typically affirmed a supreme being; venerated ancestors; made use of music, song and dance in rituals; and did not radically distinguish the sacred from the profane. African Americans who embraced Christianity were nurtured by Negro Spirituals, hymns that drew their inspiration from biblical themes and the experiences of slavery. Black theologian James Cone writes that the "spirituals enabled blacks to retain a measure of African identity while living in the midst of American slavery, providing both the substance and the rhythm to cope with human servitude."[11] As a few verses from the celebrated spiritual "Go Down Moses" illustrate:

When Israel was in Egypt's land,
Let my people go;
Oppressed so hard they could not stand,
Let my people go.

---

[9]David Walker, *Appeal: To the Colored Citizens of the World, but in Particular, and Very Expressly, to Those of the United States of America* (New York: Hill & Wang, 1965), 27.

[10]Anne Pinn and Anthony Pinn, *Fortress Introduction to Black Church History* (Minneapolis: For-tress Press, 2002), vii. See Albert Raboteau, *Canaan Land: A Religious History of African Americans* (Oxford: Oxford University Press, 2001), 50, for mention of black Catholics in America.

[11]James Cone, *The Spirituals and the Blues: An Interpretation* (Maryknoll, NY: Orbis, 1992), 30.

Go down, Moses, 'way down in Egypt's land;
Tell ole Pharaoh
Let my people go.[12]

Although slave religion did not have ample access to the Bible or other liturgical books such as the Book of Common Prayer, biblical stories, songs and verses were passed down orally from generation to generation. Stories about the book of Exodus, particularly the section narrating God's liberation of enslaved Israel from Egypt, were favorites among African Americans who longed for freedom.

The black church grew considerably in the nineteenth century. In the First Awakening (1730s–1740s), white revivalists such as George Whitefield "emphasized the immediate experience of conversion as the primary requirement for baptism and so made becoming Christian a less time-consuming and difficult process."[13] Meanwhile, the lawyer-turned-revivalist Charles Finney exemplified the Second Awakening (1790–1840) by means of his anti-Calvinist, charismatic, individualist, pragmatic, populist and racially inclusive style. The aftereffects of the awakenings led to the rapid growth of black churches. Many African Americans saw parallels between African culture and revivalist Christianity, though the individualistic nature of white Christianity clashed with the communal nature of African society. There was also reluctance among slaves to embrace the religion of their slaveholders—to be sure, the religion of oppression. James Cone put the issue starkly, "How could whites confess and live the Christian faith and also impose three-and-a-half centuries of slavery and segregation upon black people?"[14] This is certainly a question that contemporary African Americans asked, yet black affiliation among traditionally white denominations experienced a spike during the nineteenth century. The Baptist and Methodist traditions in the North particularly appealed to African Americans because of their abolitionist stances, warmer reception of free and enslaved blacks, shorter membership requirements, licensure of black evangelists and their ability to better incorporate blacks into existing white congregations.[15]

---

[12]"Go Down Moses," cited in Howard Thurman, *Deep River and the Negro Spiritual Speaks of Life and Death* (Richmond, IN: Friends United Press, 1975), 19.

[13]Raboteau, *Canaan Land*, 17.

[14]James Cone, *The Cross and the Lynching Tree* (Maryknoll, NY: Orbis, 2011), xvii.

[15]Nathan Hatch, *The Democratization of American Christianity* (New Haven: Yale University Press, 1989), 102-5.

Black preachers who received licenses from white churches evangelized fellow blacks—both freemen and those enslaved—and established Christian communities in plantations across the country. Many of these converts originally attended white churches while others met in black-only fellowships, where music, song and rhythm "was a constant feature."[16] For blacks who attended predominantly white churches—even ones where black populations were in the majority[17]—ongoing discrimination, racism and segregation caused African American leaders to eventually withdraw from European American churches and establish their own black-led congregations. The formation of the Free African Society in Philadelphia in 1787 by Absalom Jones, Richard Allen and others who had been victims of racism and discrimination at their church in Philadelphia sowed the seed for a great African American Christian harvest. Black churches sprouted across America, just as many other new Christian communities arose among largely European American inhabitants.

TRAIL MARKER
Historic Black Churches

African American Christianity has been an important part of American Christianity. The most historic black denominations are the African Methodist Episcopal Church, African Methodist Episcopal Zion Church, Christian Methodist Church, Church of God in Christ, National Baptist Convention, USA, and National Convention Baptist Convention of America. Like other churches in America, many of these historic churches are the result of church splits.

Although other factors contributed, the rise of the black church led to a growing rift between pro- and antislavery Christian communities. All Protestant denominations—whether Baptist, Methodist or Presbyterian—experienced

---

[16]Estrelda Alexander, *Black Fire: One Hundred Years of African American Pentecostalism* (Downers Grove, IL: InterVarsity Press, 2012), 42.
[17]C. Eric Lincoln and Lawrence Mamiya, *The Black Church in the African American Experience* (Durham, NC: Duke University Press, 1990), 24.

church splits due to their views regarding slavery. Though not always the case the Mason-Dixon line served as the geographic fault line dividing the largely antislavery North and proslavery South. Some historians believe that the secession of denominations in antebellum America "presaged and to some extent provoked" the secession of the South from the North.[18] Whatever the case, despite unprecedented bloodshed on American soil, the Civil War did not at all end issues of discrimination and racism in America or in Christian theology. In fact, the migration of many African Americans to the North after the Civil War (before this time, the overwhelmingly majority of African Americans lived in the South) led to racial conflicts.

In addition to the growth of the black church in the nineteenth century, a great revival took place at the turn of the twentieth century that brought race to the forefront. Between 1906 and 1909 a man named William Seymour led one of the most influential Christian revivals of all times. Seymour, the son of freed slaves from Louisiana, moved to Los Angeles in 1906 in order to serve as a pastor of a black Holiness Church. Despite some initial challenges, including being locked out of the church, Seymour found a location to begin his all-inclusive and world-famous revival. The location of his church, situated on 312 Azusa Street, was a two-story rectangular building, which had been used for a variety of purposes over the years, and no doubt was regarded as an eyesore in the nonresidential black part of town. There, on the street that would become synonymous with the movement, Seymour—leading services three times a day, seven days a week—fanned the flames of God's Spirit for three years without interruption. Thousands of people across the country and across the world—of all colors and ethnicities—rushed to the destination like spiritual prospectors eager to mine for themselves the spiritual gold in that church. Others came simply as curious onlookers. One white observer of the movement famously noted, "The 'color line' was washed away in the blood [of Christ]."[19] Uncharacteristic of the times, "People of different races . . . worshiped side-by-side without the constraint of segregated seating."[20]

[18]C. C. Goen, *Broken Churches, Broken Nation: Denominational Schisms and the Coming of the Civil War* (Macon, GA: Mercer University Press, 1985), 13, 8-9.

[19]Frank Bartleman, *How Pentecost Came to Los Angeles* (Los Angeles: Frank Bartleman, 1925), 54; quoted in Charles Fox and Vinson Synan, *William J. Seymour: Pioneer of the Azusa Street Revival* (Alachua, FL: Bridge-Logos, 2012), 36.

[20]Alexander, *Black Fire*, 122.

Although there was no racial (or class or gender) stratification at the Azusa Street Revival, there was no escaping the racial politics of the early twentieth century. After all, it took place during the atrocious "lynching era (1880-1940)" of American history, when Jim Crow laws segregated blacks from whites in public with the support of both church and state.[21] Even the dozens of Pentecostal denominations that emerged out of the black-led Azusa Street Revival soon gave way to separating along racial lines. For the most part Pentecostal churches were either mostly black or mostly white. The two largest Pentecostal denominations in America—both of which derived from the Azusa Street Revival (the Church of God in Christ and the Assemblies of God)—still comprise mostly African Americans and Caucasians respectively.

The centuries of legal segregation in America came to an end in the second half of the twentieth century. In 1954, *Brown v. Board of Education* ruled the segregation of public schools unconstitutional. A year later Rosa Parks refused a public bus driver's command to vacate her seat in the "Colored Section" for a white person whose section was full. This incident struck a chord with a young black Baptist preacher living in Alabama, Martin Luther King Jr. Although many other Christian leaders were active in this struggle against racism, King led protests for civil rights that enshrined him in the popular consciousness as a nonviolent defender of justice and equality before the law. Writing from the Birmingham jail after his arrest on Good Friday in 1963, King wrote with clear disappointment about the lack of support among white churches:

> There was a time when the church was very powerful—in the time when the early Christians rejoiced at being deemed worthy to suffer for what they believed. In those days the church was not merely a thermometer that recorded the ideas and principles of popular opinion; it was a thermostat that transformed the mores of society. Whenever the early Christians entered a town, the people in power became disturbed and immediately sought to convict the Christians for being "disturbers of the peace" and "outside agitators." But the Christians pressed on, in the conviction that they were "a colony of heaven," called to obey God rather than man. . . . Things are different now. So often the contemporary church is a weak, ineffectual voice with an uncertain sound. So often it is an arch-defender of the status quo.[22]

---

[21]Cone, *Cross and the Lynching Tree*, 3.
[22]Martin Luther King Jr., "Letter from Birmingham Jail—April 16, 1963," in *African American Religious History: Documentary Witness*, ed. Milton Sernett (Durham, NC: Duke University Press, 1999), 531-32.

The assassination of Martin Luther King Jr. in 1968 (and of Malcolm X three years earlier) illustrated just how pervasive racism still was in American society. In the past fifty years legal segregation has ended, but discrimination and racism have not. During this time, the black church has undergone extensive changes. In addition to the emergence of a black theology of liberation, many historic black denominations have seen defections of younger men and women to Islam, indigenous African religious traditions, secularism and even the Catholic Church, while many black Pentecostal churches have seen increases in attendance.

European American Protestant Churches. Since the Civil Rights movement, and certainly before, larger cultural and political issues have severely divided Christians in European American churches just as in African American ones. As with the black church, revivalism provided white churches with their largest increases. Before Catholicism became the single largest denomination, Methodism was the single largest Christian tradition in America for much of the nineteenth century. It was at this same time that a hodgepodge of distinct yet parallel religious communities emerged, ranging from Christian Scientists to Mormons to Jehovah's Witnesses to Seventh-day Adventists and renewalists. Each of these communities formed their own churches and institutions. Many were offshoots of other movements, and all of them made universal claims about religious truth to the exclusion of rival groups. Such were the dynamics of Christianity in America, where denominationalism was invented, and where separation of church and state allowed thousands of sects and denominations to flourish in peace with protection from the law.

TRAIL MARKER
The Home of Denominationalism

American Christianity is truly the home of denominationalism. There are more denominations in America than any other country. In the 1800s there was a spike in new denominations among European Americans, including Christian Science, the Church of Jesus Christ of Latter-day Saints, the Jehovah's Witness, the Seventh-day Adventists and the Unitarian Universalist Church.

Among the white Protestant population a noticeable rift was forming between so-called conservative and liberal factions of the church. This division had been forming for some time and stemmed from issues related to the nature and inter- pretation of the Bible, culture, gender roles, science and theology. The debate between these rival Protestant groups culminated in a public spectacle in Dayton, Tennessee, in 1925, during the so-called Scopes (Monkey) Trial, when a school teacher was brought up on charges of teaching evolution in defiance of state law. This modernist-fundamentalist controversy greatly shaped white Protestant imagination. According to some historians the conservatives or fundamentalists lost this battle and retreated from the public, while the liberal or mainline Chris- tians won and saw many of their views fuse with the wider public.

These two so-called liberal and conservative factions pursued different courses during the twentieth century. According to historians of American re- ligion Randall Balmer and Lauren Winner mainline churches "invested heavily in the ecumenical movement and in such political causes as civil rights, oppo- sition to the war in Vietnam, and the pursuit of equal rights for women."[23] Meanwhile, the evangelical church followed a different path, which led to "a flourishing subculture of [conservative] colleges and seminaries, missions and publications."[24] In fact, increasingly since the late twentieth century, evangelical Christianity has become more mainstream than mainline Christianity.

Despite its past history and controversies, American religion is changing. There is a growing non-Christian strand. In particular, a noticeable group of religiously unaffiliated individuals or "nones," ranging from those who claim to be spiritual but nonreligious to those who profess agnosticism and atheism, stands at 20 percent of the population.[25] This percentage is expected to in- crease, particularly as the younger generation boasts the highest percentages of "nones." In fact, secularism and non-Christian religions are also expected to grow in the future, though not at the pace as in Europe since many American immigrants already practice Christianity or eventually convert.

In addition to the growth of non-Christian religion and spirituality, there has also been an increase in the number of nonwhite churches. For instance,

[23]Randall Balmer and Lauren Winner, *Protestantism in America* (New York: Columbia University Press, 2002), 29.
[24]Ibid., 35.
[25]"'Nones' on the Rise," *Pew Research Center*, October 9, 2012, www.pewforum.org/2012/10/09 /nones-on-the-rise/#_ftn3.

the large Hispanic immigrant population has a strong (Catholic) Christian identity, whose offspring have—and will continue to—boost both the Catholic and Protestant numbers in America. It is projected that American churches will increasingly reflect the larger culture by "steadily moving from a black-and-white affair to a multicolored reality."[26] In the past fifty years the number of immigrants has more than doubled. Based on these trends it is anticipated that whites will cease to be the majority by the middle of the twenty-first century, meaning that unless many denominations "see growth among the ethnic minority population, . . . they will experience steady decline."[27] In many ways, the increase of Hispanics in the United States—most of whom are Catholic and who will soon constitute a quarter of the population—represents a return to the multicultural narrative of American Christianity, where Spanish Catholics played the first parts.

THE DIVERSITY CONTINUES IN ALL OF NORTHERN AMERICAN CHRISTIANITY

Diversity remains the thread that weaves throughout the history of Christianity in Northern America. As one historian notes, speaking mostly of the United States, "North America provided special opportunities for religious innovation."[28] Despite its relatively short history, the United States has produced an astounding number of Christian entrepreneurs. The First Amendment to the Constitution—which reads in part, "Congress shall make no law respecting an establishment of religion, or prohibiting the free exercise thereof"—has sanctioned and protected religious freedom. Homegrown peddlers of Christian innovation in America proved especially active in the nineteenth century. Canada also enacted legislation to protect religious freedom, though it has not experienced the same religious innovation as in America. Either way, Northern America's cultural tolerance and legal protection of religion have made it one of the most diverse religious regions in the world.

---

[26]Philip Jenkins, *The Next Christendom: The Coming of Global Christianity* (Oxford: Oxford University Press, 2002), 117.

[27]Soong-Chan Rah, *The Next Evangelicalism: Freeing the Church from Western Cultural Captivity* (Downers Grove, IL: InterVarsity Press, 2009), 74.

[28]Paul Conkin, *American Originals: Homemade Varieties of Christianity* (Chapel Hill: University of North Carolina Press, 1997), vii.

ten

OCEANIA

*The life that was emerging [in Oceania] blended
what was brought with what was found.*

STUART MACINTYRE,
A CONCISE HISTORY OF AUSTRALIA

A TALE OF TWO STORIES

Christianity in Oceania is the tale of two stories. The first one begins with
British colonists from the Old World who rapidly constructed a modern world
in Australia and New Zealand. Though foundational in the early years, Christianity plays a less prominent role in the lives of its citizens there today. The
contemporary concerns of Australians and New Zealanders reflect issues
facing many modern and Western nations such as ecology, economics, gender
roles, sexuality, technology and laws promoting tolerance. The other story of
Christianity in Oceania deals more intimately with the native inhabitants of
the islands in Melanesia, Micronesia and Polynesia. There Christianity has
taken center stage in the religious theater. Though one of the last evangelized
regions on earth, it boasts some of the highest percentages (per capita) of
Christians anywhere in the world. The challenges these islanders encounter
have to do with discovering a new identity between the premodern world of
their ancestors and the modern world of their descendants.

The term *Oceania* refers to thousands of islands in the Pacific Ocean, the
largest body of water in the world. The endless islands of Oceania have served
as historic dividers between the thousands of people groups who call this

region of the world home. Four general clusters of islands constitute Oceania, though this term does not adequately encompass the diversity of people groups and cultures living in this oceanic expanse: Australia and New Zealand, Melanesia, Micronesia and Polynesia. Westerners are probably more familiar with Australia and New Zealand than with any other of the two dozen countries and territories in this region. Despite their vast ethnic, linguistic, religious and historical differences, what unites these disparate islands is European colonization, which always gives birth to twins who suffer from sibling rivalry: the more spiritually minded brother who wants to convert the natives and inculcate the settlers, and the more financially oriented brother who wants to explore a new world and exploit those in their path.[1] In that respect, the story of Australia and New Zealand resembles the histories of European colonization in other parts of the world, particularly Northern America. The other grouping of islands—Melanesia, Micronesia and Polynesia—share much in common with Southeastern Asia. Christianity, though on the decline in Australia and New Zealand, is virtually an unrivaled religion in the other cluster of islands.

Christianity came to Oceania in two waves. The first wave introduced Catholic Christianity beginning in the seventeenth century, though Spanish explorers had arrived before then. The center of Spanish Catholicism became Manila in the Philippines, the most Christianized country in all of Asia (and very close to Oceania). Due to a variety of factors, Catholic missions to Oceania did not develop strength until the nineteenth century. Two of the most active Catholic missionary societies in Oceania, the Congregation of the Sacred Hearts of Jesus and Mary, and the Society of Mary, had just emerged out of the politically volatile modern France. The second wave of Christianity introduced Protestantism to the islands beginning in the eighteenth century, though it too made its largest splashes in the nineteenth century. The Protestant evangelization of Oceania should be understood in the context of the emergence of the modern Protestant missionary movement in the late eighteenth century, when evangelical Protestants understood the evangelization of such remote regions as Oceania as necessary in order for the return of Christ on earth to take place.

---

[1]See John Williams, *A Narrative of Missionary Enterprise in the South Sea Islands* (London: J. Snow & J. R. Leifchild, 1837), 8.

CHAPTER OVERVIEW

In this chapter I will offer an overview of Christianity in Oceania, the youngest Christian region on earth. As you read about the history of Christianity in Oceania, try to imagine a world surrounded by water and isolated from other people groups on neighboring islands. Much of the interaction among different tribes, since time immemorial, was violent in character, as tribal warfare in the Pacific islands was incessant. But now, rather than being tribal enemies, most people in Oceania are united by a common religious tradition: Christianity. But how do the long-standing rivalries among European and Northern American Protestant groups contribute to divisions of Christians in Oceania?

AUSTRALIA AND NEW ZEALAND

Australia and New Zealand boast some of the highest standards of living in the world. They are also two of the world's youngest countries. Australia shares the distinction of possessing the largest island in Oceania and the largest number of inhabitants. Although no Europeans inhabited the continent and country until the late eighteenth century, the majority of its population today sailed from Europe in the nineteenth and twentieth centuries. Due perhaps to its history as a penal colony for British convicts, a strand of irreligion has endured from 1788 to the present. The majority of Australians self-identify as Christians, but that number decreases each year, as does the number of Australians who attend church on a regular basis. Immigration after World War II has led to an increase in the number of Catholic and Orthodox Christians as well as the number of non-Christians, while secularism has weakened historic Australian denominations such as Anglicanism, Methodism and Presbyterianism.

The earliest missionary to New Zealand was the Anglican priest Samuel Marsden. Through the Anglican Church Missionary Society, he successfully evangelized the Maori people of New Zealand beginning in 1814. As elsewhere, Christianization and colonization went hand in hand in Australia and New Zealand. Missionaries often interpreted the local inhabitants' perceived disinterest in Western culture—whether in clothing, customs, farming techniques or tools—as indicative of their lack of religiosity. Clashes between the Europeans and the Maori led to a series of battles during the nineteenth century, even though the British managed to convert the Maori to Christianity. The British also created a Maori alphabet and introduced literacy into the oral culture, a phenomenon that occurred throughout the Pacific islands and which proved an effective tool in the evangelization and instruction of local inhabitants. The first Catholic missionary to New Zealand arrived in 1838 and demonstrated sensitivity to the Maori people by allowing native dress, respecting Maori chiefs, not imposing Christianity too quickly and too rigidly, and not usurping Maori land. Catholicism, however, suffered from ethnic Irish-French conflict and never made up a large percentage of the population (as distinct from in Australia).

Australia. Hundreds of Aboriginal groups were living in Australia when the first Europeans arrived in 1770. Captain James Cook of the Royal Navy, the famous British explorer who mapped out the Pacific, wrote in his journal upon arrival in Australia that year:

> From what I have said of the natives of New Holland [western part of Australia], they may appear to some to be the most wretched people on earth, but in reality they are far more happier than we Europeans, being wholly unacquainted not only with the superfluous but the necessary conveniences so much sought after in Europe. . . . They live in a tranquility which is not disturbed by the inequality of [their] condition. . . . In short, they seemed to set no value on anything we gave them, nor would they ever part with anything of their own for any one article we could offer them. This, in my opinion, argues that they think themselves provided with all the necessities of life and they have nothing superfluous.[2]

The British began to populate Australia with convicts (and other settlers such as merchants, military men and missionaries) from 1788 until 1868. Perhaps because of its recent loss of the American colonies, the British uncharacteristically claimed seizure of the whole land of Australia rather than bargaining with the native inhabitants.[3] They claimed it as *terra nullius*, a void land belonging to no one.[4] The British came "with their sense of superiority of the inheritors of Western civility and bearers of Christian revelation enhanced by the further advantages of scientific knowledge, industrial progress and liberty."[5]

---

[2]James Cook, *James Cook: The Journals* (London: Penguin, 2009), 174. I have modernized spelling and punctuation.

[3]See Stuart Banner, *Possessing the Pacific: Land, Settlers, and Indigenous People from Australia to Alaska* (Cambridge, MA: Harvard University Press, 2007), 13-46. Banner gives additional reasons for the British seizure of the land.

[4]Ibid., 13.

[5]Stuart Macintyre, *A Concise History of Australia*, 3rd ed. (Cambridge: Cambridge University Press, 2009), 19-20. See also Banner, *Possessing the Pacific*, 20-25, for the prejudice and racism of the British for the Aborigines.

As in other parts of the New World, interaction between Europeans and native inhabitants was stricken with conflict. As church historians Stuart Piggin and Peter Lineham write, "the cultural clash between Western civilization and that of the indigenous peoples of Australia has been one of the nation's most intractable problems."[6] The British devastated Aboriginal populations, and Captain Cook delayed missions to Aborigines for decades based on the faulty premise that they "trouble[d] themselves very little about [religion]."[7] The European colonizers experienced difficulty learning local languages, keeping the native people in one location, eliminating their former religious practices and inculcating them into the Christian faith. Despite the perceived challenges, however, the Aborigines eventually abandoned their animistic religious practices and adopted Christianity, so much so that the majority of Aborigines today are Christians.[8]

The Anglican Church represented the largest Australian Christian body for almost two centuries. It held an ecclesial monopoly for decades and paid its clergy from governmental taxes. Although the British government regarded the imposition of church services on the general populace as morally beneficial, convicts and settlers "endured" church services "as part of their punishment [as convicts]."[9] "Male convicts," writes one historian, "were known to use Bibles and prayer books to make playing cards; women convicts turned tracts into hair curlers."[10] Before long, the Anglican Church in Australia would face more than apathy. The passing of the Church Act of 1836 led to the construction of non-Anglican churches and the funding of their ministers through state funds, which signaled the end of the Anglican Church's religious domination.

Methodist missionaries from the London Missionary Society arrived in 1798. Methodism, which emerged out of the Church of England in the early eighteenth century, emphasized personal conversion and active evangelism. It was part of a larger global evangelical movement, which aimed at the conversion

---

[6]Stuart Piggin and Peter Lineham, "Australasia and the Pacific Islands," in *Global Evangelicalism: Theology, History and Culture in Regional Perspective*, ed. Donald M. Lewis and Richard V. Pierard (Downers Grove, IL: InterVarsity Press, 2014), 253.

[7]Cook, *James Cook*, 118.

[8]According to a 1996 census, 70 percent of Aborigines practiced Christianity. See "Australia," in *Religious Freedom in the World*, ed. Paul A. Marshall (Lanham, MD: Roman & Littlefield, 2008), 72.

[9]David Hilliard, "Australasia and the Pacific," in *A World History of Christianity*, ed. Adrian Hastings (Grand Rapids: Eerdmans, 1999), 509.

[10]Macintyre, *Concise History of Australia*, 48.

of the whole world, particularly in newly discovered lands like Australia. The growth of Methodism went hand in hand with the Australian gold rush in the 1850s, which attracted tens of thousands of American, European and Asian adventurers eager to get rich fast. The wealth accumulated during the middle of the nineteenth century symbolized Australia's increasing status as a global power. In the 1850s, Victoria, the area with the largest deposits of the metal, "contributed more than one-third of all the world's gold output."[11]

While miners dug for gold, Christian missionaries preached for converts. Because of its rugged and pioneering foundational spirit, Methodist missionaries succeeded in the difficult outside conditions by camping alongside miners, ministering to the settlers and establishing schools and churches for those who had families. Communities began popping up all around Australia, with church buildings always being located in the center of new towns. Revival occurred across many leading cities. Christianity gained considerable influence in the late nineteenth and early twentieth centuries, at which time Protestant denominations such as the Anglicans, Baptists, Methodists and Presbyterians prospered alongside the growing Australian communities and towns.

TRAIL MARKER
The Anglican Church in Australia

The Anglican Church was the largest and most influential Christian body in Australia from 1788 until the next century. It slowly began losing its influence through state legislation (specifically the Church Act of 1836), the growth of other Christian bodies and the continued immigration of non-British Europeans and Asians.

Although Protestantism has predominated in religious matters, Roman Catholicism has existed in Australia since the First Fleet's arrival in 1788. Its earliest adherents were Irish convicts, who represented about a third of the convicts transported to Australia as punishment. These majority-Irish

---

[11]Ibid., 87.

Catholic practitioners faced discrimination among the largely Protestant English, and they did not have a consistently designated cleric available to them since neither Catholic nor Protestant authorities in Britain "were . . . interested in convict well-being,"[12] even though Catholicism lived or died based on priests who could administer necessary sacraments such as baptism, confession and last rites.

The governor of New South Wales finally allowed Catholic priests to enter in 1820. This, coupled with continued immigration, led to the growth of the Catholic Church. William Ullathorne, a Benedictine, served as one of Australia's first Catholic bishops upon his arrival in Sydney from England in 1833. Ullathorne authored many writings and became a public champion of Roman Catholics during their trials as a religious minority through his role as Vicar-General.

Roman Catholics were actively engaged in Australian politics, especially after the two World Wars. Longstanding Irish-Catholic animus toward England and Protestantism caused Catholicism to generate considerable support for an independent Australia. "As the faith of a minority group with little fondness for British rule, [Roman Catholicism] was also a strong force for Australian nationalism."[13] In the late nineteenth century, at a time when schools were forming all across Australia, Roman Catholics established their own Catholic schools as a protest to the Protestant-dominated public school culture (just as in the United States). Numerous individuals from religious orders such as the Bridgettines, Sisters of Mercy, Dominican Sisters and Marists immigrated to Australia in order to staff Catholic schools.[14] By 1990 Roman Catholicism had become the largest single denomination in Australia—due in part to the immigration of Catholic Asians, Europeans and high Catholic birth rates relative to the rest of the population. Even today, Catholics are considered the largest single Christian body, making up about 40 percent of the Australian population.[15]

Two noticeable yet religiously distinct Christian branches that have risen to prominence in the twentieth century in Australia are the Orthodox and

---

[12]Ian Breward, *A History of the Churches in Australasia* (Oxford: Oxford University Press, 2001), 19.
[13]Macintyre, *Concise History of Australia*, 116.
[14]Tracy Rowland, "Oceania," in *The Blackwell Companion to Catholicism*, ed. James Buckley et al. (Oxford: Wiley-Blackwell, 2011), 224.
[15]Douglas Jacobsen, *The World's Christians: Who They Are, Where They Are, and How They Got There* (Oxford: Wiley-Blackwell, 2011), 262.

Pentecostal traditions. Most of the Orthodox community immigrated to Australia after World War II. They have come from places like Armenia, Egypt, Russia and Serbia. The Greeks, however, have historically boasted the highest number of Orthodox immigrants, and Greek Orthodox Churches in Australia are numerous. In fact, the city of Melbourne has become "the world's third-largest Greek city after Athens and Thessaloniki."[16] The other side of the Christian continuum includes the growing numbers of Pentecostal churches across Australia (as elsewhere in the world). Although the Pentecostal tradition commands a long history in Australia, dating back to the late nineteenth century and thus preceding the American Pentecostal movement, it has become more established in the past few decades due to its resonance with a certain segment of the Australian culture.[17] Its churches, filled with lively music, charismatic leaders and tech-savvy individuals, have especially appealed to the younger generation. Hillsong Church, founded in 1983 and located outside of Sydney, has defied national religious trends by attracting thousands of churchgoers each week to its multiple campuses. Among this number includes many Aboriginal Christians who, though constituting a small percentage of the Australian population as a whole, have largely converted to Christianity.

As elsewhere in largely European populations, Christianity no longer commands the importance it did a century ago in Australia. It likely peaked in the 1950s and 1960s, at a time when churches, youth programs and Sunday schools appealed to those moving to the suburbs and when revivalists such as the Catholic priest Patrick Payton and the evangelical Protestant evangelist Billy Graham attracted large rallies and crowds.[18] Although Pentecostalism has achieved some success, it represents an Australian subculture in the midst of a larger religiously secular and tolerant dominant culture. Mainline Protestantism, the religious engine of Australia since its inception in the late eighteenth century, has been spurting for decades with no expectation of an overhaul. As one historian writes about nineteenth-century Australian Protestantism, "the ending of

---

[16]Barbara West, *A Brief History of Australia* (New York: Facts on File Books, 2010), 9.
[17]Stuart Piggin, *Spirit, Word and World: Evangelical Christianity in Australia* (Victoria, Australia: Acorn Press, 2012), 64.
[18]Macintyre, *Concise History of Australia*, 221.

state aid, and the separation of Christianity's leaders from the responsibility of government, helped to secularize politics, privatize religion, and turn the churches inward."[19]

Today, this legacy endures. Less than ten percent of the Australian population attends church on a weekly basis.[20] Traditional forms of Christianity "are increasingly treated with disdain for being 'antimodern and rigid.'"[21] Australians celebrate openmindedness and tend to think independently. Poet Charles Harpur noticed this "individualizing process" as early as the mid-nineteenth century.[22] Altogether secularism and immigration from practitioners of other religions have contributed to historic Christianity's decline in Australia, adherence to no faith at all remains at an all-time high—at around 30 percent.[23] In hindsight this strand of religious indifference goes back to the inception of the country (though nearby New Zealand never existed as a penal colony yet shares religious commonalities with Australia).

TRAIL MARKER
Reversals in Religiosity

There are two interesting dynamics at work in Australia. On the one hand multigenerational Australians are becoming increasingly secular and are leaving traditional churches. On the other hand recent immigrants are more religious. They are responsible for the growth of Catholic, Orthodox and Pentecostal churches as well as non-Christian religions.

As the English-born Methodist missionary Ralph Mansfield wrote in the early days of Australia, in the late nineteenth century, "Men in general seem to consider that all religions are the same—that it matters not what sort of

---

[19]Breward, *History of the Churches in Australasia*, 271.

[20]Marion Maddox, "Christianity in Australia and New Zealand: Faith and Politics in a Secular Soil," in *Introducing World Christianity*, ed. Charles Farhadian (Oxford: Wiley-Blackwell, 2012), 203.

[21]Marshall, "Australia," 73-74.

[22]Macintyre, *Concise History of Australia*, 116.

[23]West, *Brief History of Australia*, 10.

opinions they entertain upon subjects of the most vital importance; a degree of apathy which approximates to entertaining no religion at all."[24]

Whether or not it is profitable to draw comparisons between the early history of Australia and its religious condition today, the trend away from organized Christianity and toward unaffiliated Christianity, other religions and no religion will markedly change the religious landscape of Australia for years to come. This means, quite possibly, that "Australia in the future may well be a country of four or five major religious (and nonreligious) traditions."[25]

MELANESIA, MICRONESIA AND POLYNESIA

Although organized into the same region, the cluster of islands that make up Melanesia, Micronesia and Polynesia represent incredible diversity in terms of ethnicity, language and culture. If these clusters of islands were an arrowhead, Polynesia would be the head facing southeast toward Southern America, with Micronesia as the northern tail and Melanesia as the southern tail. The joint tail of Melanesia and Micronesia stand due north of Australia and east of Southeastern Asia. Many of the inhabitants of these islands migrated from other islands and regions of Southeastern Asia before settling down in places where Europeans began exploring in the nineteenth century. Catholicism and Protestantism both made their most formative ventures into these regions in the nineteenth century.

Melanesia (the "Black Islands" in Greek, due to the color of the inhabitants) consists of four archipelagos. In 1835 missionaries arrived first in Fiji buoyed by the great successes they had recently achieved in nearby Tonga, in Polynesia, by converting the king of Tonga. In addition to British missionaries the Tonga native Joeli Bulu, a convert in 1833, ministered in Fiji for four decades, serving as an indispensable bridge between British Christianity and Pacific islander culture. The conversion of one of the chiefs, Cakobau, enshrined Christianity as a powerful force in Fiji and enabled many other people to convert. Cakobau, a former cannibal, renounced cannibalism at his conversion in 1854. Today, Fiji is distinguished from every other country or territory in Oceania by its large Indian population, which practices Hinduism and Islam. Methodism, due to its early roots in the nineteenth century, claims the largest single Christian denomination.

---

[24]Ralph Mansfield, quoted in Piggin, *Evangelical Christianity in Australia*, 14.
[25]"Australia," in *World Christian Encyclopedia*, 1:84.

Micronesia (the "Small Islands" in Greek) contains the highest percentages of Catholic countries and territories in Oceania, as well as the most historic missions. Spanish Catholics entered Oceania in the early sixteenth century—well before Protestants—but Catholic missions did not begin until the seventeenth century. A group of six Jesuits landed in Guam in 1668, making Micronesia the earliest region of European missions in the Pacific. The Spanish Catholic legacy in Guam has continued, marking it as the territory with the highest percentage of Catholics in Oceania. The First Protestant missionaries evangelized the islands in the nineteenth century. Missionaries established schools for children and also created healthcare services in addition to teaching the Bible, the creeds and introducing the people to Western etiquette. Local Protestant churches with indigenous leadership always developed more rapidly than the Catholic Church because Catholicism required a lengthy and more rigid process toward ordination of priests than toward ordination of (Protestant) pastors. In both Christian traditions, however, the tribal nature of the islanders enabled close bonds to form very quickly among formerly rival tribes and clans once they adopted Christianity.

Polynesia (the "Many Islands" in Greek) includes the cluster of islands in the eastern part of the Pacific Ocean such as the Cook Islands, Hawaii, French Polynesia, the Samoan Islands and Tonga. Missionaries most actively evangelized Polynesia in the eighteenth and nineteenth centuries. Europeans encountered immediate challenges as different Polynesian tribes sought to involve them in intratribal wars and make use of their advanced weaponry. In French Polynesia missionaries from the London Missionary Society baptized King Pomare II in 1819, which led to the rapid adoption of the Christian faith in Tahiti, the largest of the French Polynesian islands. While European missionaries introduced positive changes to Polynesian culture such as ending warfare and slavery, Europeans whalers and merchants gained a reputation for bringing alcohol, a vigorous sexual appetite and disease—all of which devastated Polynesian populations. In Tonga, Methodism became the largest single Christian tradition, while Samoans found the distinct ceremonies of the Catholic Church attractive. Clashes occurred regularly between Catholics and Protestants since ethnic identity was so much a part of European missions.

Papua New Guinea. We will explore Christianity in the regions of Melanesia, Micronesia and Polynesia by focusing on the country of Papua New

Guinea. The island of New Guinea formed eons ago as the second-largest island in Oceania. European claimants of the island changed hands many times between the sixteenth and twentieth centuries. In the twentieth century Indonesia annexed the western portion of the island, West Papua, while Australia eventually took oversight of the eastern portion, Papua New Guinea, until the latter sought independence in 1975. Papua New Guinea bubbles over with cultural, ethnic and linguistic diversity, and its dense forests and ruggedness enabled hundreds of distinct tribes (with their own languages and customs) to remain separate from each other until European colonization.

As in all parts of Oceania, Catholic and Protestant missions to Papua New Guinea proceeded in different phases. Catholic missionaries arrived in 1847, but it was not until the 1880s that Catholicism was established. Catholic missionaries experienced dangers when evangelizing the different tribes, who constantly battled one another and ritually ate each other. We get a sense of how some native Papuans interpreted the arrival of missionaries in the following conversation held in 1880. On Kiwai Island, local chiefs deliberated whether to eat the missionaries who arrived since their appearance was interpreted as the cause of crop failure and sickness among the native people. One chief said,

> Why seek pigs in the bush or across the river whilst we have some here with us [referring to the missionaries]? Do you not see that we have had more sickness amongst us since the missionaries came with their God? They are the proper pigs to kill [and eat] for the feast.[26]

Although the missionaries in question escaped, many other missionaries lost their lives. Some Catholic missionaries even worked themselves to death for the sake of the gospel by emulating the life-giving sacrifice of Christ. One early missionary, Father Henri Verjus, wrote in his journal of 1885 "that the first missionary to New Guinea must be crushed and destroyed to assure the success of the Mission."[27] He achieved this goal by dying on the mission field at the age of thirty-three. It's a matter of one's theology to decide if such a sacrifice was necessary in order to produce a Christian harvest.

---

[26]Quoted in Breward, *History of the Churches in Australasia*, 225.

[27]Henri Verjus, quoted in G. W. Trompf, *Melanesian Religion* (Cambridge: Cambridge University Press, 1991), 165.

Many Western missionaries suffered death or violence by unwittingly committing cultural fouls such as violating territorial boundaries between different tribes, which were interpreted as invitations of war.[28] Other missionaries unknowingly disrupted trade networks or found themselves caught between intratribal wars. The outbreak of World War II further endangered the lives of missionaries when the Japanese occupied the islands from 1942 to 1945. Many missionaries fled the islands or risked death by staying. Despite the many setbacks, Catholic missionaries catechized many Papuans and baptized them into the Christian faith. The missionaries attempted to encourage ancient Papuan beliefs conducive to Christianity, such as beliefs in spirits and the immortality of the soul, while rejecting other practices in opposition to Christianity, such as killing young children and the wives of chiefs when the husband died.

The first Protestant missionaries came under the auspices of the London Missionary Society in 1871, but widespread Protestant missions did not develop until the turn of the century. John Williams of the London Missionary Society, formerly a missionary to Polynesia, had earlier written of Papua New Guinea, "It is reported to be a most beautiful island, rich in all the productions of a tropical climate, inhabited by several millions of immortal beings suffering all the terrific miseries of a barbarous state, and dying without a knowledge of God, or the Gospel of his Son."[29]

Like Catholic missionaries, Western Protestants encountered frequent setbacks due to a vast cultural divide separating them from Papuan tribes. There was also a lack of communication and native hostility toward outsiders. At the same time, the London Missionary Society did establish itself in the capital of Port Moresby by 1874 and was educating hundreds of children at its mission there within ten years.

German Lutherans erected their first mission at Finschhafen on the northeast coast of the Papua New Guinea in 1886. Although it did not last long there, German Lutheranism spread and left an enduring mark. The German Lutheran missionary Christian Keyser revolutionized missions in Papua New Guinea by encouraging the evangelization of whole tribes rather than individuals. Although

---

[28]John Dademo Waiko, *A Short History of Papua New Guinea* (Melbourne: Oxford University Press Australia, 1993), 18-19.
[29]Williams, *Narrative of Missionary Enterprise in the South Sea Islands*, 7.

this method was initially met with reluctance by the Lutheran pioneer missionary Johannes Flierl, Keyser recognized that Papuan culture lived communally and did not privilege individual thinking. After mastering the local Kate language, Keyser oversaw mass conversions in 1905 and 1906.

TRAIL MARKER
Evangelization of Papua New Guinea

The evangelization of Papua New Guinea was similar to that of many other islands in Oceania. Not only was there a great diversity of local religious cultures, peoples and languages, but European missionaries came from various countries and practiced different forms of Christianity. Although cannibalism among local tribes was widespread, the cannibalization of missionaries was rare.

Throughout the Pacific as a whole, Protestant missionaries often taught inhabitants the Bible and literacy, recruited and trained indigenous leaders, discouraged use of alcohol (which ironically was brought in by Westerners), encouraged sabbath observance, provided basic health services, and introduced agricultural and technological advances. They also attempted to end cannibalism, warfare, infanticide, sorcery and other practices that arrested Western mores. Missionaries struggled to explain why the God of the Bible was the only true deity, and they engaged in spiritual combat with indigenous sorcerers and magicians when necessary. In the end the missionaries advanced the living conditions of the Papuans, built roads, established currency, provided educational, medical and vocational structures, and persuaded the majority of the population to embrace the Christian faith. At the same time, the missionaries also introduced new customs that undercut traditional values and led to cultural fragmentation.

Christianity in Papua New Guinea underwent a turning point after World War II. The Japanese military, which occupied Papua New Guinea for three years, threatened the lives of missionaries and destroyed many Christian missions and schools. Before the war fewer Christian denominations ministered on the islands, and the ones that did generally honored an arrangement going back to the 1890s whereby denominations worked in designated "spheres of influence" in order to reduce friction among rival Christian groups.[30] This practice proved unsustainable after the war given the onslaught of so many Christian denominations, including, among others, Anglicans, Baptists, Catholics, Lutherans, Methodists, Nazarenes, independent fundamentalists and Seventh-day Adventists.

Indigenous churches also arose—some more firmly anchored in traditional Christianity than others—and Pentecostalism influenced new and existing churches, just as it does today. Many so-called cargo cults, religious movements headed by local visionaries that blend traditional customs with Christianity and materialism, popped up across Melanesia. In these cults local leaders performed rituals in order to supernaturally generate wealth, blessings and other material goods that Westerners brought with them—that is, "cargo."[31] The postwar efforts at Christianization—though never completely eliminating cargo cults and other indigenous rituals and religious rites— largely transformed a highly animistic and dispersed society into a thoroughly Christianized one by around 1960. The process of Christianization was aided when native Papuans assumed leadership. By the time Papua New Guinea achieved independence from Australia in 1975, most Papuans professed belief in Christianity. As in nearby Australia, Roman Catholicism is the largest single Christian denomination in Papua New Guinea. At the same time, Protestantism maintains the largest overall percentage of Christians. In less than two centuries Christianity has become a powerful institution in Papua New Guinea and the religion of the overwhelming majority of its people.

DISTINCT IDENTITIES IN OCEANIA

The Christianity that has emerged in Oceania over the course of the past few centuries has blended what was brought with what was found. The degree to which European Christianity blended with Pacific religious culture accounts for

---

[30]Chilla Bulbeck, *Australian Women in Papua New Guinea: Colonial Passages 1920–1960* (Cambridge: Cambridge University Press, 1992), 55.

[31]Holder Jebens, *After the Cult: Perceptions of Other and Self in West New Britain (Papua New Guinea)* (New York: Bergahn Book, 2013), 89-90. See also G. W. Trompf, ed., *Cargo Cults and Millenarian Movements* (Berlin: Walter de Gruyter, 1990). Trompf adopts the following definition of a cargo cult: "those 'activities arising from the expectation of abundant, supernaturally generated, Western-style cargo'" (p. 11).

the religious differences between the major regions of Oceania. In Australia and New Zealand this blend of European and indigenous cultures occurred to a much lesser extent than the blending of European and indigenous cultures in Micronesia, Melanesia and Polynesia. The prevalence of ethnic Europeans in Australia and New Zealand translates into an increasingly secular and post-Christian society. By contrast, a preponderance of ethnic Pacific islanders in Micronesia, Melanesia and Polynesia corresponds to a higher degree of Christian practice. The communal-mythical aspect of Christianity in Melanesia, Micronesia and Polynesia—where community precedes individuality and faith trumps reason—stands out as just one noticeable contrast between the individualistic-secular aspect of Christianity in Australia and New Zealand.

Pacific islanders incorporated Christianity into their existing religious social systems, which emphasized tribal identity, ritual, nature as a spiritual resource and a mythic view of history. Part of the success of Christianity in the Pacific formed from its tribal nature. This provided a lasting bond between formerly rival tribes and clans once they embraced Christianity. The emergence of a modern world filled with endless choices, constantly evolving freedoms and a move away from a tribal to an individualist outlook will likely lead to continued transformations of Christianity in the coming years. As historian of Oceanic Christianity Ian Breward concludes,

> Constructions of Christianity [in Oceania] have not yet finished. They never do. At the beginning of the third millennium, it looks unlikely that any one version of Christianity is likely to provide the shaping and unifying force in Oceanic cultures over the new century, comparable to what the various forms of Christianity did in the nineteenth century. Living with religious and cultural pluralism may be the foreseeable future, but individualism should not be taken as a final solution. Even the short history of Christianity in the region indicates how the hopes of the powerful are subverted by the unexpected, for the God of the Bible is full of surprises.[32]

Only time will tell what surprises the God of the Bible will bring to the highly and very recently Christianized culture of Oceania.

---

[32]Breward, *History of the Churches in Australasia*, 436.

eleven

AFRICA

The fact that African religions have emerged in Europe not as primal forms but in terms of Christianity is itself evidence of the growing strength of the Christian faith in modern Africa.

J. KWABENA ASAMOAH-GYADU,
"'BORN OF WATER AND THE SPIRIT':
PENTECOSTAL/CHARISMATIC CHRISTIANITY IN AFRICA"

FROM COLONIZATION TO AFRICANIZATION

Less than a century ago Europe governed most of Africa. Belgium, Great Britain, France, Germany, Italy, the Netherlands, Portugal and Spain all possessed colonies across the continent. In the words of one historian, "Deprived of the free use of black labor outside of Africa" after the international slave trade ended in the first half of the nineteenth century, "Europeans decided to put Africans to work for Europe's benefit within the borders of Africa itself."[1] How did this happen? Much of it goes back to a European-only conference held in Berlin, Germany, in 1884–1885, which was responsible for the otherwise arbitrary divisions of the African continent to this day. After dividing the continent of Africa, European nations rushed to Africa like gold miners (see table 11.1). The fact that Africans had lived in the land and ruled from it for millennia apparently factored little into Europe's decision to take oversight of the continent. Within a century, however, what began as a "scramble for Africa" turned into a scramble from Africa.

---

[1]Douglas Jacobsen, *The World's Christians: Who They Are, Where They Are, and How They Got There* (Oxford: Wiley-Blackwell, 2011), 158.

Table 11.1. European colonization of Africa

Colonizer	Current African Countries (and Names Under Colonizers)
Belgium	Burundi and Rwanda (Ruanda-Urundi) and Democratic Republic of the Congo (Belgian Congo or Zaire)
Great Britain	Botswana, Egypt, Gambia, Ghana (Gold Coast), Kenya, Malawi, Namibia, Nigeria, Lesotho, South Africa, Sudan and Uganda; Somalia (British Somaliland); Zambia and Zimbabwe (Southern and Northern Rhodesia)
France	Benin, Burkina Faso, Gambia, Guinea, Ivory Coast, Mali, Mauritania, Niger and Togo (French West Africa); Central African Republic, Chad, Gabon and Republic of Congo (French Equatorial Guinea); Algeria, Morocco and Tunisia (French North Africa); Comoros, Djibouti and Madagascar (French East Africa)
Germany	Cameroon and Nigeria (German Cameroon); Burundi, Rwanda and Tanzania (German East Africa); Namibia (German Southwest Africa); Ghana and Togo (German Togoland)
Italy	Eritrea, Ethiopia and Somalia (Italian East Africa) and Libya (Italian North Africa)
Portugal	Angola (Portuguese West Africa); Mozambique (Portuguese East Africa); Guinea-Bissau (Portuguese Guinea); Cape Verde, São Tomé and Príncipe
Spain	Equatorial Guinea (Spanish Guinea); Morocco (Spanish North Africa); West Sahara (Spanish Sahara)

It has been said that every story has at least two sides. Put bleakly, one side of the African story states that Europe divided Africa according to its own interests, colonized it and left when the situation became too challenging to maintain.[2] The other side asserts that European colonization paved the way for Africa to eventually become the most Christianized continent on the planet. As usual, the truth is probably somewhere in between—or a combination of both. World historian Lamin Sanneh argues that the church in Africa "unexpectedly grew and spread" once the Europeans left, and that the Bibles the Westerners translated into African languages "supplied the vocabulary for the politics of decolonization."[3] Whatever the case, there's no doubt that Christianity is on the rise in Africa, having increased greatly during the last half of the twentieth century. No longer colonial in leadership, African churches are thoroughly indigenized.

Taking into consideration the travesties the African continent endured over the course of colonization and missionization under foreign powers, the change of religious practices before and after colonization has been incredible.

---

[2]At the same time, Robert Woodbury has argued that Protestant missionaries were influential in the development of economically, socially and politically stable democracies around the world, particularly in non-Western countries. See Robert Woodbury, "The Missionary Roots of Liberal Democracy," in the *American Political Science Review* 106, no. 2 (May 2012): 244-74.

[3]Lamin Sanneh, "The Changing Face of Christianity: The Cultural Impetus of a World Religion," in *The Changing Face of Christianity: Africa, the West and the World*, ed. Joel Carpenter and Lamin Sanneh (Oxford: Oxford University Press, 2005), 3; and Lamin Sanneh, *Disciples of All Nations: Pillars of World Christianity* (Oxford: Oxford University Press, 2008), 154.

In 1900 only seven to nine million Christians lived in Africa. This amounted to about 2 percent of the worldwide Christian population. Most Africans practiced African traditional religions. A century later, however, after African nationals had taken the reins of the church, so the argument sometimes goes, more than 400 million Christians live in Africa. This accounts for 20 percent of the worldwide Christian population and more than 50 percent of the African population. With an annual Christian growth of 2.36 percent, scholars anticipate that Africa will soon boast the highest numbers of Christians in the entire world, leading Sanneh to write that "Africa is fast becoming a heartland for world Christianity."[4]

CHAPTER OVERVIEW

In this chapter I will offer an overview of African Christianity. Although Christianity has existed on the African continent since the first century, the arrival of Europeans beginning in the fifteenth century led to the reintroduction of Christianity into Africa. In the past century, after the ending of European colonization, there has been incredible growth in the African church, and it has been argued that the greatest contribution of Western Christianity was simply the translation of the Bible into local languages, which allowed Africans to gain immediate access to God in their own way of thinking. As you read about the history of Christianity in Africa, try to envision a world that is deeply religious and attempting to understand what it means to be both African and Christian.

CENTRAL AFRICA

By the time Christianity reentered Africa beginning in the fifteenth century, thousands of different ethnic and linguistic tribal kingdoms lived and moved across the African landscape. Religiously, Islam made inroads into the different African kingdoms beginning in the seventh century. The Islamic worldview offered a unifying religious narrative as well as political and economic benefit. In general, tribal peoples immediately south of the Sahara Desert embraced Islam while the rest practiced traditional African religions. The arrival of Western missionaries beginning in the fifteenth century posed

---

[4]Sanneh, *Changing Face of Christianity*, viii.

a serious challenge to both Islam and indigenous religious practices. As an exclusivist religion Christianity demanded an immediate and firm break with former religious customs and practices.

Europeans invaded Africa in search of natural resources, human slaves and territorial expansion. The missionaries among them also sought to enlarge their Christian empires by converting the indigenous Africans. Beginning in the seventeenth century and extending throughout the twentieth centuries, European (and later Northern American) Protestants entered Africa, proceeding along the same lines as their Catholic forebears did. From an African perspective, however, Dutch Reformed theology did not differ substantially from Portuguese Catholicism or British Anglicanism. In brief, the Portuguese transplanted Western or "white" Christianity in the sixteenth century, the Dutch in the seventeenth and the British and French in the nineteenth centuries. In the twentieth century Africans effectively dispossessed the Europeans and established independent countries. This century also witnessed the birth of African Initiated (or Independent) Churches, known as AICs. These Afro-Pentecostal churches have completely transformed the African continent and are partly responsible for the incredible growth of the African church in recent decades. They continue to convert not only non-Christian Africans but also influence and transform traditional European churches, whether Catholic or mainline Protestant.

Due to European occupation and colonization, most Central Africans practice some form of Christianity. Many residents, however, practice Islam and African traditional religions. Because European Catholic countries colonized Central Africa, their African colonies follow Catholicism more so than Protestantism. At the same time, both the indigenous African church movement and Pentecostalism have influenced the Catholic Church. Despite the high number of Christians per country, many Central African nations continue to struggle from warfare and political strife. In particular, the Central African Republic and the Democratic Republic of the Congo face sustained political and religious challenges in the years ahead.

Democratic Republic of the Congo. Christianity has existed in the region in and around the Congo River for more than half a millennium. The Congolese Catholic Church serves as the oldest of the sub-Saharan churches in Africa, just as the kingdom of Kongo is one of the most historic Christian empires in Central Africa. At its pinnacle this kingdom included parts of present-day Angola, both Congos and Gabon. The Portuguese arrived in the kingdom of Kongo in 1482. The *manikongo* or ruler of Congo, Nzinga Nkuwu, received the Portuguese warmly, and Portuguese Catholics baptized King Nkuwu in 1491, giving him the Christian name of João I. The Portuguese also baptized others in the royal court, including the manikongo's wife and sons. King João then sent two of his sons, Afonso and Henrique (their new baptized names, of course), to Portugal to receive a European Christian education. Afonso became manikongo of Congo in 1506 and made Christianity the religion of the empire; he renamed the capital São Salvador ("Holy Savior" in Portuguese), and made it a leading Christian city. The Portuguese ordained Henrique as a bishop before returning him to his homeland.

In accordance with tribal culture, the people in Kongo largely adopted Christianity as their religion under Afonso's reign, though many also maintained traditional African religious customs. The Portuguese presence in Congo came with as many curses as blessings. In addition to the introduction of Christian spirituality, the Portuguese became embroiled in the slave trade. By the middle of the sixteenth century they were exporting three to four thousand African slaves annually. This number increased each decade. The Portuguese also denied the manikongo's request for African clergy to educate and guide his people.

The Portuguese expanded their presence on the coast of Africa in the sixteenth and seventeenth centuries. They established a colony in Luanda in 1575, which is the capital and largest city of Angola today. This area belonged to the Bantu-speaking kingdom of Ndongo whose *ngola*, or king, gave his title to this present-day country.[5] From Luanda, Portuguese traders exported African slaves, mostly to the Americas, while Catholic missionaries, such as the Dominicans, Franciscans and Jesuits, worked with Africans. The missionaries baptized countless thousands of Africans, but they also clashed with African indigenous culture. They created schools to catechize the locals. In their attempts to communicate Christianity, the crucifix, images of the Virgin Mary and the saints often replaced traditional religious gods and images.

---

[5]Mark Shaw, *The Kingdom of God in Africa: A Short History of African Christianity* (Grand Rapids: Baker, 1996), 115.

The Portuguese monopoly over African trade and religion ended in the seventeenth century. Rome attempted to seize religious jurisdiction from the Iberian (Spanish and Portuguese) monarchy and provide better catechetical instruction for the people. Between 1645 and 1835 the papacy sent hundreds of mostly Italian friars of the Capuchin order to Western Africa. The Capuchins baptized hundreds of thousands of Africans and started many schools. The Capuchins sometimes baptized thousands of Africans simultaneously. Father Luca da Caltanisetta wrote of one of his experiences around the turn of the eighteenth century:

> As the people did not know the Sacred Baptism, they fled into the bush and it was in vain that we pleaded with them to receive Baptism, by which the sons of the Devil would become Sons of God and inheritors of Holy Paradise. Thus I could not manage to baptize more than 248.[6]

The Capuchins took a conservative approach to culture under the conviction that the kingdom of God and the kingdom of this world had nothing in common. They launched ongoing campaigns to destroy African fetishes (material objects in Africa believed to possess supernatural powers), undercut traditional religious beliefs and demonized local customs. Also at this time many African crucifixes, based on European prototypes, were manufactured. These copper alloy crucifixes depicted Christ with African features, and they were incorporated into burial and church rituals.

The Dutch arrived in the same century and threatened the Portuguese monopoly of the African slave trade and Christian missionization. Like the Portuguese, the Dutch established trading posts along the African coast. They were reluctant to colonize the African interior. As Reformed Protestants, the Dutch opposed Catholicism and sought to limit the sway it carried over the African continent. In their pursuit of riches the Dutch entered the lucrative enterprise of human trafficking and were soon exporting several thousand slaves a year. The Dutch captured Luanda for six years and destroyed much of the missionary work there before the Portuguese recaptured it in 1648. The Dutch Protestants expanded their power base, but mostly for economic and military reasons. This led to a civil war in Congo that endured

---

[6]Luca da Caltanisetta, quoted in Bengt Sundkler and Christopher Steed, *A History of the Church in Africa* (Cambridge: Cambridge University Press, 2000), 54.

for decades. The Congolese Church declined and divided among factions. Most Africans continued to practice traditional religions due to the lack of sufficient and unified missionary endeavors.

> ## TRAIL MARKER
> ### Along Ethnic and Religious Lines
>
> As in other regions the Christianization of Africa took place along ethnic and religious lines. While the Portuguese were Catholic, the Dutch were Protestant and so forth. Rather than viewing themselves as cousins in Christ, the different Christianized nations of Europe were enemies whose political and religious wars spilled over into their overseas colonies, in this case into places like the Democratic Republic of the Congo.

Protestant missionaries arrived in earnest toward the end of the nineteenth century. At the height of the "Scramble for Africa," King Leopold II of Belgium took possession of the Democratic Republic of the Congo (later called the Belgian Congo and also Zaire) in 1885.[7] Leopold's possession of the region was a human rights disaster. He exploited Africans for his own benefits, violently disciplined them, yet managed to amass a fortune for himself and Belgium in the process. Alongside Belgian rule came increased Catholic missionization, which explains why this country has eventually become one of the largest Catholic countries in the world. At the same time, Protestantism, in all its varieties, claims the allegiance of many Congolese Christians.

In the past fifty years in particular the Democratic Republic of the Congo has experienced failed governments, wars and constant social and political challenges. Religiously, Pentecostalism has positively affected church growth. African Initiated Churches, which the marriage of Pentecostalism and African nationalism has produced, continue to nurture the faith of millions of

---

[7]The term *Scramble for Africa* was possibly coined in 1884, the year the Berlin Conference began. See Thomas Pakenham, *Scramble for Africa: White Man's Conquest of the Dark Continent from 1876 to 1912* (New York: HarperCollins, 1991), xxv.

Congolese Christians. Simon Kimbangu, a Baptist who later started an independent ministry in the 1920s, is perhaps the most famous Congolese Christian of recent memory. Today the Kimbanguist Church claims more than 15 million members, and it serves as the largest African Initiated Church in all of Africa.[8] It "insists on monogamy, on abstinence from alcohol and narcotics, and on a radical renunciation of traditional religion."[9]

EASTERN AFRICA

Moving east from Christian-dominated Central Africa, Eastern Africa serves as an ongoing battleground between Christianity and Islam. Without fault, the religion that holds the majority of the people commands an overwhelming percentage of the overall religious population. Historically, Ethiopia, Eritrea and Sudan (which is now divided into two countries) share a common Christian heritage dating back to around the fourth century. Sunni Muslims, meanwhile, hold unrivaled possession of neighboring Djibouti and Somalia. Not surprisingly, tensions among these bordering countries persist and occasionally flare up. Whereas Islam emerged in Eastern Africa via nearby Saudi Arabia, recent Christian missions entered from Portugal.

The Portuguese sailed around the Cape of Good Hope and arrived in current-day Zimbabwe and Kenya at the end of the fifteenth century. They reached Mozambique and Kenya in 1498 and soon took control of the gold and slave trade. In Mozambique, the Dominicans were largely responsible for Christianization, but with marginal success. In 1560 the Portuguese Jesuit Gonçalo da Silveira traveled along the Zambezi River and made contact with the kingdom of Mutapa in current-day Mozambique and Zimbabwe. The tribal ruler, Chisamhura Nogomo, known as "the golden king" due to the gold he discovered there, welcomed the expedition. After a series of visions the king was baptized along with hundreds of his people. Within two months, however, Muslim traders convinced Nogomo that the Christian priest was a spy. Rather than flee and feed the hysteria, the priest remained and continued to evangelize and catechize. The newly baptized king then had da Silveira strangled in his sleep and his corpse thrown into the river.

[8]Jacobsen, *World's Christians*, 173.
[9]Elizabeth Isichei, *A History of Christianity in Africa: From Antiquity to the Present* (Grand Rapids: Eerdmans, 1995), 201.

Francisco da Gama, one of the grandsons of the famous explorer Vasco da Gama, sent Catholic missionaries, mostly from the Augustinian Hermits, to the kingdom of Mombasa (in current-day Kenya). They converted and baptized many Africans. They also worked on the nearby island of Zanzibar. From the beginning, however, the Christian Portuguese clashed with the Muslim populations. Blood was regularly spilt. In 1698, after years of fighting, the imam of the Sultanate of Oman, Saif bin Sultan, a recent convert to Christianity who converted back to Islam, captured and destroyed the Portuguese base of Fort Jesus. The sultan ordered the deaths of those who refused to convert to Islam, including missionaries. This ended Portuguese rule in that region, paving the way for the large Muslim population in Mombasa to this day. The further suppression of the Jesuits, coupled with the lack of a large indigenous Christian movement as in the Congo, led to the decline of Christianity in this region until the Protestants arrived in the next century.

The Scottish physician David Livingstone was the most famous Protestant missionary to Eastern Africa. Livingstone was the first European to view the Zambezi River in current-day Zambia. He reached Lake Malawi in 1859 and led the way for the establishment of Protestant missions in the 1860s and 1870s in the African interior. He died near Lake Bangweulu in 1873 in Zambia, where the locals buried his heart. Livingstone's disciple Henry Stanley traveled to the interior and reportedly converted Muteesa I, the king of Buganda (in current-day Uganda), to Protestantism despite attempts by both Roman Catholics and Muslims. Conflicts in this area continued for decades among the different Catholic, Muslim and Protestant factions until the British finally made Uganda a colony in 1894.

Ethiopia. The sixteenth century served as one of the most pivotal centuries in the history of Christianity in Ethiopia. By this time, after centuries of occupation of neighboring regions, Islam surrounded Christian Ethiopia. Many Muslims had already penetrated the Ethiopian highlands and established a large merchant community. Between 1529 and 1543, when a theological revolution was tearing apart Catholicism in Western Europe, a Muslim general and imam named Ahmad ibn Ibrahim al-Ghazi, nicknamed Gran (left-handed), invaded and waged a holy war, *jihad*, against Ethiopia. This man came from the neighboring Muslim kingdom of Adal (in present-day Somalia). Gran destroyed Christian churches, monasteries and villages. He forced the conversion of tens of thousands of Christians to Islam and massacred those who refused. He even razed the famed

Church of Our Lady Mary in Aksum, where Ethiopians had crowned their kings for centuries and where the Ark of the Covenant reputedly resides.

Who could help the Ethiopians against this Muslim onslaught? The Ethiopians appealed to the Catholic Portuguese. Exchange had existed between Westerners and Ethiopians for decades, but for different reasons: the Portuguese sought an alliance with "Prester John," a legendary figure who allegedly governed a Christian kingdom in the midst of Islamic kingdoms, while Ethiopians sought military protection. The Portuguese arrived in 1541. As hoped, they reinforced Ethiopian armies and defeated Gran. Historian Adrian Hastings summarizes the significance of the Portuguese aid:

> There can be little reasonable doubt that without Portuguese help the Christian kingdom of Ethiopia would have ceased to exist by the year 1540. It would have gone the way of Nubia. Christians had rallied to help Christians in the hour of their greatest need and [King] Galawdewos was very genuinely grateful. That did not make the Portuguese any easier to live with afterwards.[10]

Now with a comfortable foothold in Ethiopia and responsible for Ethiopia's Christian preservation against the Islamic advance, the Portuguese proceeded to usurp the religious establishment of Ethiopia. Western Catholics fractured the existing church and caused internal divisions that exist to this day. Jesuit priests attempted to correct the perceived errors of the indigenous, Jewish practices of the Ethiopian Christians and to bring them into conformity with Rome. In response the *negus* (king) of Ethiopia, King Claudius, wrote his *Confession of Faith* to the papacy to defend Ethiopian Christian practices. The opening of the confession relays the king's commitment to Ethiopia's venerable history, which did not include acceptance of the Council of Chalcedon in 451 (notice its absence in the quote):

> We go along the path of King Christ, plain, true, and we do not deviate, neither right nor left, from the doctrine of our fathers, the Twelve Apostles, and of Paul, the fount of wisdom, and of the 72 disciples, and of the 318 Orthodox [bishops] who assembled at Nicaea, and of the 150 at Constantinople, and of the 200 at Ephesus. Thus I preach and thus I teach, I Claudius, King of Ethiopia.[11]

---

[10]Adrian Hastings, *The Church in Africa 1450–1950* (Oxford: Clarendon, 1996), 139.
[11]Claudius, quoted in Klaus Koschorke, Frieder Ludwig, Mariano Delgado and Roland Spliesgart, *A History of Christianity in Asia, Africa and Latin America, 1450-1990: A Documentary Sourcebook*, ed. Klaus Koschorke, Frieder Ludwig and Mariano Delgado (Grand Rapids: Eerdmans, 2007), 158.

Despite his apology for Ethiopian orthodoxy, the Catholic Church effectively seized control of the Ethiopian Orthodox Tewahedo Church. The pope appointed the Spanish Jesuit Andre de Oviedo as the *abuna* (or leading ecclesiastical figure) of the Ethiopian church even though the Alexandrian patriarch had been selecting the holder of this office for more than a millennium. For the next several decades the Catholic Jesuits clashed with the Ethiopian rulers and the general populace. In many ways the Ethiopian Christian practices of dance, observance of two sabbaths and annual rebaptism scandalized the Jesuits, who sought to bring the Ethiopians into submission to the Latin rite.

A second Jesuit mission to Ethiopia and Eritrea began in 1603. The Spaniard Jesuit Pedro Páez converted King Za Dengel and King Susenyos I to Catholicism from Ethiopian Orthodoxy. Unlike his predecessor, however, Páez earned the respect and trust of many Ethiopians. Catholicism prevailed throughout the land. The situation changed drastically, however, after Páez's death. The Jesuit Portuguese Afonso Mendes claimed the office of *abuna* of Ethiopia from 1622 to 1634. Despite a reign of twelve years, he made the Catholic Church completely odious in the sight of Ethiopians. Scandalously, Abuna Mendes demanded rebaptism of the laity, reordination of the clergy and reconsecration of the churches. He outlawed circumcision, imposed the Latin rite of the liturgy and changed Ethiopia's Christian calendar. Not surprisingly, civil war ensued. King Susenyos I, who was a mere pawn on Mendes' chess board, abdicated and died shortly thereafter. At the king's death the people rejoiced and sang:

> At length the sheep of Ethiopia freed
> From the bad lions of the west
> Securely in their pastures feed.
> St Mark and Cyril's doctrine [Miaphysitism] have overcome
> The follies of the Church of Rome.[12]

The king's son Fasilides became *negus*. He deposed Mendes and expelled the Jesuits from Ethiopia. He also burned all Latin theological writings. The existing hundreds of thousands of Ethiopian Catholics faced three options: conversion to Ethiopian Orthodoxy, emigration/exile or death. Fasilides banned European Christian missionaries for two centuries.

---

[12]Hastings, *Church in Africa 1450–1950*, 156.

> ## TRAIL MARKER
> ## Becoming Catholic
>
> What happened in Ethiopia in the 1500s and 1600s happened in Asia. Even though Christianity had existed in Ethiopia for hundreds of years and claimed a respectable tradition, the Catholic Church viewed all non-Catholic forms of Christianity as deviant and in need of conforming with its rituals and its presiding bishop, the pope. Foreign occupation and disdain for the local religious culture naturally bred resentment, and civil war ensued in Ethiopia in the 1600s.

Theological controversy, however, did not disappear with the Jesuits. "The overwhelming majority of the Ethiopian Church was never divided on the issue of Salvation, but only on the understanding of Christ's person."[13] Remnants of the Latin-Ethiopian debacle remained, which reached deep into the Christological disputes of the early church. The debate, based on Acts 10:38, concerned the relation between Christ's humanity and divinity—an issue that had long divided Christianity: "God anointed Jesus of Nazareth with the Holy Spirit and with power." Put simply, if Christ the Word had only one nature after the incarnation, what was anointed? Two lines of thinking emerged, each reflecting the two major schools of monasticism. The House of Ewostatewos asserted that the anointing pointed to the divinization of Christ's humanity. In other words, this passage recorded the point at which Jesus the human became divine. The House of Takla Haymanot, by contrast, held that this anointing referred only to the way in which Jesus became the Messiah. In other words, this passage recorded the point at which Christ became the second Adam. The House of Takla Haymanot asserted that the union of Christ's human and divine natures had occurred at the incarnation. King Fasilides presided over a series of synods to arbitrate this debate and eventually affirmed the Ewostathian position. For the next couple of centuries, however, unity eluded the Ethiopian empire as subsequent kings disagreed about this decision.

---

[13]Sundkler and Steed, *A History of the Church in Africa*, 78.

During the next several decades the Ethiopian state expanded and succeeded in converting many new people to Christianity. By this time Europeans lived in different parts of Ethiopia. In the 1830s the restriction from two centuries earlier regarding Europeans eased. Protestants and Catholic missionaries from Europe, who had clashed with King Tewodros II, worked well with the new *negus* of Ethiopia, King Menelik II. Menelik II encouraged missionary work and reestablished Ethiopia as a Christian nation. Throughout the twentieth century nationalism mounted among the Ethiopian people, just as in many other African countries. Weary of the centuries-long rule of Alexandria (and for a time Rome) over the Ethiopian Church, Ethiopians finally received independence from the Coptic Church in the middle of the twentieth century. Nevertheless, the so-called Derg Era, when communism overtook Ethiopia in the later part of the 1900s, led to not only political but also religious disorder. Christianity was struck a blow but endured. While no longer the state religion today, the Ethiopian Orthodox Church is still the largest single religion in the country, with Islam accounting for about a third of the population.

NORTHERN AFRICA

Of all regions in Africa, Islam is most dominant in Northern Africa. Although Christians comprised the overwhelming majority of this region for centuries, the arrival of Arab Muslims beginning in the seventh century led to the steady decline of Christianity. The transition from a Christian majority to a Muslim one occurred gradually yet continuously over the course of centuries. Beginning in the nineteenth century France and Italy occupied and colonized the Maghreb while Great Britain did so in Egypt and Sudan. With European colonization came Christian missions. Unlike Christianity's presence in this region before the rise of Islam in the seventh century, however, the stigma of European colonialism marked the church in Northern Africa. As in Asia, the Middle East and sub-Saharan Africa, many Northern Africans considered Christianity a foreign and Western religion.

At the same time, religion played little role in Europe's invasion and occupation of Northern Africa in the latter part of the nineteenth and early twentieth centuries. This explains in part why Christianity did not (re-)embed itself in Northern African culture. European colonization created the political infrastructure for European missionaries to work in Northern Africa, but it did not necessarily foster indigenous Christian churches with any consistency. With decolonization in the twentieth century after World War II, many European churches and missionaries departed. Those who remained constitute a small percentage of the Northern African population. The vast majority of these Christians are Catholic and Orthodox. Simultaneously, European and North American Protestants of all varieties have penetrated Northern Africa since the nineteenth century—the Egyptian Presbyterian Church serving as the largest of the Protestant bodies.

War has affected Northern Africa for decades. Continued political and military unrest cause Christians, who on average hail from the middle class and receive good educations, to emigrate to the West. What's more, because each of the countries in Northern Africa forbids conversion from Islam (to Christianity), some of those who convert to Christianity emigrate due to fear of persecution or punishment. This exodus of Christians out of Muslim countries in Northern Africa continues at a regular pace and causes concern to the remaining Christian communities in these Muslim-dominated lands.

Egypt. The Coptic Orthodox Church traces its heritage to the missionary efforts of St. Mark in the first decades after the death and resurrection of Christ. Mark reportedly established the patriarchate of Alexandria before he died for the faith. The Coptic Church not only claims to be the oldest church in all of Africa but also the most authentic body of Christians on the continent. Percentages of Coptic Christians vary widely, but their numbers appear to be shrinking due to emigration, persecution and conversions to Islam. At the same time, the Coptic Orthodox Church has suffered ongoing challenges for more than a millennium and has survived intact.

The Ottoman Empire overthrew the Mamluk Dynasty the same year Martin Luther famously nailed the Ninety-five Theses on the Wittenberg Church door in Saxon Germany. By this time the church constituted around 10 percent of the Egyptian population.[14] Although a few Copts served in the Ottoman Empire, most Copts lived in rural communities and no longer influenced Egyptian culture as they had done centuries before.[15] Due to the move

---

[14]Charles Frazee, *Christian Churches of the Eastern Mediterranean* (Placentia, CA: CreateSpace, 2011), 135.
[15]Asterios Argyriou, "Christianity in the First Ottoman Era (1516–1650)," in *Christianity: A History in the Middle East*, ed. Habib Badr (Lebanon: Middle East Council of Churches, 2005), 605.

of the capital in the Fatimid Dynasty, the patriarch or pope of Alexandria lived in Cairo along with a retinue of Coptic leaders. The millet system, whereby Christian communities lived freely in their own neighborhoods under Islamic rule, gave the patriarch a close connection with his parishioners during the transition from one Islamic dynasty to another.

Although the Coptic Orthodox Church is the mother church of Egypt, there have been other traditions as well. The Eastern Orthodox (or Melkite) presence in Egypt existed, but marginally. Many of the Eastern Orthodox patriarchs of Alexandria lived in Constantinople rather than in Cairo. In addition to the Copts and Eastern Orthodox, Roman Catholic missionaries made attempts at establishing a presence in Egypt, mostly by leveraging the existing Coptic community and seeking leadership of it. The Catholics and Copts entered negotiations with each other as early as the thirteenth century regarding a formal union. However, nothing long-lasting took effect. Meanwhile, a steady stream of Copts living in Rome who converted to Catholicism continued. Finally, Pope Leo XII (1823–1829) consecrated a Catholic Copt as bishop, and later that century the papacy established its first dioceses in Egypt with Latin bishops presiding over the people.

European invasion and occupation of Egypt began in earnest at the end of the eighteenth century. The intrepid French leader Napoleon Bonaparte entered Egypt in 1798. The British ousted the French shortly thereafter and restored Egypt as a province of the Ottoman Empire. At this time, the government eased restrictions against Coptic Christians by abolishing the extra tax imposed on them for centuries and by attempting to incorporate them into the national life of Egypt. Egypt became a British Protectorate in 1882. Its governing presence gave space for the resurgence of Coptic influence in Egypt and abroad. The Cairo-born Copt Habib Girgis founded the Sunday School Movement in the Coptic Orthodox Church in the early twentieth century to provide lay education to children and adults. This movement invigorated the Coptic Church.

Apart from the Catholic and Coptic Church in Egypt, changes were underway among the other Christian traditions. The Melkite church in Egypt declared itself autocephalous in 1899, breaking its jurisdictional ties with the patriarchate of Constantinople. British occupation of Egypt brought with it the Anglican Church and other Protestant denominations. The

Egyptian Presbyterian Church (also known as the Evangelical Church of Egypt), which began under the auspices of the United Presbyterian Church of North America in 1854, has grown to become the largest Protestant denomination in all of Northern Africa. In addition to offering theological education and training for clergy, this church also oversees many clinics, hospitals, schools and social service agencies.

TRAIL MARKER
The Melkites

The Coptic Orthodox Church has a checkered history with the Eastern Orthodox Churches. The Copts called Eastern Orthodox Christians Melkites, suggesting that they cared more about being aligned with the king than with God. By declaring itself autocephalous in 1899, the Melkite Church in Egypt became independent and no longer under the authority of the patriarch of Constantinople. Somewhat confusingly, there are now four claimants to the patriarchate of Alexandria—one from the Coptic Orthodox Church, one from the Greek Orthodox Church, one from the Coptic Catholic Church and one from the Melkite Greek Catholic Church.

The British left Egypt following World War II. In a swell of nationalism Egypt became an independent country in 1953. But there has not been long-term peace. Some extremist Muslim organizations such as the Muslim Brotherhood have led assaults against the Coptic Church because these organizations link Islam with Egyptian patriotism (and therefore Christianity with subversion). President Anwar Sadat placed Patriarch Shenouda III under arrest and exiled him to a desert monastery before he returned under the dictatorship of Hosni Mubarak. There has been ongoing political unrest and uncertainty, which resulted in further persecution and violence against Coptic Christians and churches. Like many other countries in the Middle East, thousands of Copts continue to emigrate. Sizeable populations of Coptic Christians now exist in Europe, Oceania and in Northern America.

SOUTHERN AFRICA

Compared to Northern Africa, Southern Africa might as well be part of a different continent. With a couple of exceptions, Christianity potentially entered every country in Northern Africa by the first century, where it became the dominant religion. Beginning in the seventh century, however, Islam began replacing Christianity as the primary religion. Today, Christianity in Northern Africa survives marginally. The religious history of Southern Africa, by contrast, is the reverse. The original inhabitants of Southern Africa practiced indigenous religions for millennia before Christianity was established from the seventeenth century onward. Although each of the countries in Southern Africa has a different history and is composed of different people groups from different religious backgrounds, they each are majority Christian nations mostly colonized by the English. As in other regions there have been great clashes between Europeans and Africans, which have led to ongoing problems.

South Africa. The Dutch East India Company settled in Cape Colony in current-day South Africa in 1652. This settlement aimed to supply Dutch ships on their way to Asia. Before long the dominant African group, the Khoikhoi, experienced conflicts with the Dutch. The Dutch, later called Afrikaners or Boers, established a local church for the settlers. Although it did not generally reach out to the Africans, some of the Khoikhoi converted to Christianity. Over the next several decades many European Protestants added to the number of European settlers: French Huguenots, Scottish Presbyterians, British Anglicans, German Lutherans and German Moravians.

Moravian missionary George Schmidt arrived in South Africa in 1737 at the age of twenty-six. He began his work a hundred miles east of Cape Town by evangelizing the Khoikhoi (or the Hottentots, as the Europeans called them). The Dutch, however, opposed Schmidt and created problems for him. Some of the Dutch even considered the Khoikhoi subhuman and without a soul. The Dutch prohibited Schmidt's missionary work in 1748, and Schmidt left South Africa a failed missionary.

The British took control of the Cape in 1795 (and then again in 1806). The Dutch clashed with the British, just as they had done with the Khoikhoi and local African groups. Back in England, the British Parliament abolished the slave trade in 1807 and slavery in 1836, which led the Boers to further resent their overlords. The words of a local Boer woman illustrate their frustration:

It is not so much [the slaves being freed] which drove us to such lengths, as their being placed on equal foot with Christians, contrary to the laws of God, and the natural distinctions of race and color, so that it was intolerable for any decent Christian to bow down beneath such a yoke; wherefore we rather withdrew in order to preserve our doctrines in purity.[16]

Withdrew they did. In same the decade the British abolished slavery, thousands of Boers or Afrikaners (mostly of Dutch origin, though the term encompassed farmers from French and German Calvinist stock) made the so-called Great Trek out of the British-ruled Cape and into supposed virgin territory. Like the Puritans in New England, these Calvinist Trekboers interpreted their exodus into the wilderness in biblical fashion: God had chosen them to flee Egypt and possess a rich new land to farm and establish as a Christian society. The problem was, of course, that African tribal groups already lived on this land—and they were not willing to give it to the Boers or any foreigners. The discovery of diamonds in this area only accelerated the immigration of Europeans, which subsequently increased conflict among the different African tribes.

The Afrikaners and British continued to fight with each other during the First Boer and Second Boer Wars. In 1910 the British Parliament created the Union of South Africa with shared British and Afrikaner governance. Not surprisingly, indigenous Africans played little part. Over the next several decades the Afrikaners concentrated their power. In 1948 the Afrikaners-dominated Nationalist party enacted a policy of racial segregation called *apartheid* ("state of being apart" in Afrikaans). Between 1948 and 1994 this system classified people according to race and segregated them accordingly. Black Africans, who made up about 80 percent of the population, were stripped of basic rights such as citizenship, educational opportunities and access to adequate medical care. The Dutch Reformed Church in South Africa gave biblical and theological justification for this system of separation. The international Reformed community, however, criticized this policy. Nonetheless, the Dutch Reformed Church in South Africa stood its ground, defying censures leveled against it by the worldwide Christian community. Indignant, this church asserted that it

---

[16]Quoted in Paul Spickard and Kevin Cragg, *A Global History of Christians: How Everyday Believers Experienced Their World* (Grand Rapids: Baker, 1994), 312.

constantly tested [its views of apartheid] against the demands of Holy Scripture [and found the system of apartheid to] fulfill our apostolic calling to be the Church of Jesus Christ giving due consideration to our experience within the unique South African ethnic situation.[17]

Both domestic and foreign pressures against the system of apartheid eventually led the Afrikaners to relinquish control of the government. The formerly imprisoned Nelson Mandela became the president of South Africa in 1994, and he appointed the Anglican bishop Desmond Tutu to lead the Truth and Reconciliation Commission. This commission sought to produce reconciliation and guide the nation as it began the long road toward recovery from centuries of racism, segregation, marginalization, injustice and violence. As elsewhere in Africa and the world, Pentecostalism fuels the growth of South African Christianity today. African Initiated Churches make up a little less than half of all churches. Although the government remains secular, the population at large continues to support new Christian churches, particularly Pentecostal ones, which are becoming the new mainstream of sub-Saharan African Christianity. At the same time resurgence in African identity following Mandela's rise to the presidency has led to the growth of native African religions. In the future there will likely be growth in both non-Christian native religion as well as a more globally minded Pentecostal tradition.

WESTERN AFRICA

Like Central and Eastern Africa, Islam and Christianity are the major religious purveyors in Western Africa. There, the two groups generally divide along a jagged beltline around the tenth parallel. Beginning with Islam, Muslim merchants and missionaries entered Western Africa beginning in the tenth and eleventh centuries. Over time Islam became embedded into Western African culture and came to dominate in the regions directly south of the Sahara Desert. The Muslim Songhai Empire ruled over large parts of Western Africa. Its later capital, Timbuktu (in modern Mali), became a center of Islamic culture and learning. It was a flourishing center of Islam. Given the great Islamic heritage, it is not surprising that the majority of the populations in Burkina Faso, Gambia, Guinea, Guinea-Bissau, Ivory Coast, Mali, Mauritania,

---

[17]Quoted in Koschorke et al., *History of Christianity*, 265.

Niger, Senegal and Sierra Leone practice Islam. As elsewhere in Africa, Catholicism and Protestantism are often associated with Western colonialism.

Just as was the case in other parts of Africa, Christianity sailed into Western Africa in the fifteenth century. The Portuguese landed on the uninhabited islands of Cape Verde in 1456 and envisioned these isles as launching pads for the expansion of Catholic Christianity in the region. The Portuguese formed a church on the islands among the settlers and slaves. From this base they entered current-day countries such as Benin and the Democratic Republic of the Congo. In Benin, Spanish Jesuits baptized one of the kings. Before long Portuguese forts were located across the Western African coast. With the exception of the kingdom of Kongo, however, the Portuguese refrained from establishing colonies in the African interior. Theirs was a shoestring kingdom that lacked sufficient manpower from Portugal to settle beyond the coasts of the lands they colonized. What's more, tensions often flared between the traders and the missionaries due to different priorities. They were simply not safe in the interior.

The Dutch, Danish and English largely followed the model set by the Portuguese. They established colonies along the coast and became masters in the slave trade, which only came to an official end in Western Africa in the early twentieth century.[18] These Europeans erected churches and practiced their faiths. However, they failed to fully engage and evangelize the Africans outside of their colonies. Protestant missions emerged in full force in the nineteenth century in Western Africa. In Nigeria, which is the the largest of the Western African nations, Christianity and Islam vie for religious supremacy. These two powerful religions meet face to face in the so-called Middle Belt, "a two-hundred-mile-wide strip of fertile grassland" that runs along the tenth parallel.[19] Muslims populate the majority of the northwestern part of the country, while Christians comprise the majority of the southeast. Although Nigeria formed in 1960, civil war marked the early years of the country due to rivalry among tribal groups. Today, clashes between Christians and Muslims continue to plague the country, especially in the Middle Belt. In this way Nigeria symbolizes much of the conflict in Western Africa among Christians on the

---

[18]Sundkler and Steed, *History of the Church in Africa*, 78.
[19]Eliza Griswold, *The Tenth Parallel: Dispatches from the Fault Line Between Christianity and Islam* (New York: Macmillan, 2010), 18.

one hand and Muslims on the other. Although religion contributes to this conflict, economic, ethnic and political factors exacerbate the situation.

Liberia and Sierra Leone. Christian abolitionist societies and a desire to repopulate Africa link the religious heritages of the neighboring countries of Liberia and Sierra Leone. In the late eighteenth and early nineteenth centuries Westerners paved the way for former African slaves from Great Britain, Canada and the United States to resettle in these areas. The first settlers arrived in Liberia in 1822. The group consisted of African American Christian and non-Christian former slaves, many of whom later embraced the Christian religion. Liberia became an independent nation in 1847. Prominent leaders signed the Declaration of Independence in Old Providence Baptist Church in the capital. Meanwhile, Protestantism crossed into Sierra Leone beginning in 1787. Former slaves from Nova Scotia and Great Britain landed and negotiated with local African tribes for land. These freed, former slaves appropriately named their new base Freetown, while the African American settlers in Liberia intended to name their capital Christopolis before eventually settling for Monrovia.

Many consider Englishman Granville Sharp the founding father of Sierra Leone due to his tireless efforts in abolishing the slave trade and in encouraging former slaves to settle freely in Sierra Leone. Many give the same distinction to Lott Carey in Liberia. A former slave from Virginia, Cary moved to Liberia along with a large contention of coworkers and families in 1821 as one of the first black missionaries to Africa. Lott served the African Baptist Mission Society as a doctor, governor and soldier. Carey said, "I wish to go to a country where I shall be estimated by my merits not by my complexion; and I feel bound to labor for my suffering race."[20] Besides Sharp and Carey, many other important Christian leaders immigrated to Africa, both Western and African.

Christianity played a pivotal role in the formation of both Liberia and Sierra Leone. African American, Baptist, Catholic, Episcopalian and Presbyterian churches all thrived during the repopulation of African slaves, though Islam continues to make inroads into these countries. After the British made the slave trade illegal in all of its jurisdictions, the British patrolled the seas and repopulated many enslaved Africans into places like Sierra Leone. Perhaps the most famous resident of Freetown, Sierra Leone, in its early days was Samuel

---

[20]Lott Carey, quoted in Sundkler and Steed, *A History of the Church in Africa*, 122.

Crowther. Originally sold in the slave trade, Crowther converted to Christianity in 1825. In 1864, the same year Abraham Lincoln was reelected president of the United States, Crowther was ordained to the bishopric in Canterbury Cathedral in England, making him the first Anglican African bishop. Another significant local Christian thinker was the author, educator and diplomat Edward Wilmot Blyden. An African born in the West Indies, Blyden criticized the posture Western missionaries took toward African culture and customs. He taught in both Liberia and Sierra Leone during his career; progressively for his time, he argued that Islam was more compatible with Africans since Islam respected indigenous African culture more so than Christianity did. In a lecture to the American Colonization Society in 1880, he prophetically declared,

> Africa may yet prove to be the spiritual conservatory of the world. Just as in past times, Egypt proved the stronghold of Christianity after Jerusalem fell, and just as the noblest and greatest of the Fathers of the Christian Church came out of Egypt, so it may be, when the civilized nations, in consequence of their wonderful material development, have had their spiritual perceptions darkened and their spiritual susceptibilities blunted through the agency of a capturing and absorbing materialism, it may be, that they may have to resort to Africa to recover some of the simpler elements of faith.[21]

Although the resettled populations of both Liberia and Sierra Leone largely embraced Christianity, indigenous peoples such as the Grebo and Kru in Liberia also adopted the Christian religion. Among the Grebo peoples, William Wadé Harris, a friend of Blyden's, stands out as its most famous Christian evangelist. Harris evangelized Liberia and Sierra Leone in addition to Ghana and the Ivory Coast. He preached with greater success than any other former Christian missionary. From 1913 to 1914 Harris toured the Ivory Coast and preached the gospel from a decidedly African perspective. This magnetic evangelist affirmed the core of Western Protestant theology but differed culturally by allowing polygamy and adopting other African practices. Harris had received a vision from the archangel Gabriel in 1910 while in jail, which altered his life and set him on the path he became famous for. In this vision Gabriel

---

[21]Edward Wilmot Blyden, quoted in Ogbu Kalu, "West African Christianity: Padres, Pastors, Prophets, and Pentecostals," in *Introducing World Christianity*, ed. Charles Farhadian (Oxford: Wiley-Blackwell, 2012), 46.

instructed Harris to "give up Western style clothing and shoes."[22] In his obe-
dience, and dressed as a Muslim evangelist, Harris "wore a white gown and
black bands, and carried a gourd, a cross, a Bible and a bowl for baptizing."[23]
He was an incredibly powerful preacher. In a little more than a year, between
1913 and 1914, he reportedly converted and baptized more than one hundred
thousand Africans. Out of fear that he would provoke a rebellion, the French
arrested and deported him to Liberia. His evangelistic work, however, endured and has led to the formation of countless "Harrist" churches that thrive
to this day across Western Africa.

Although Harris and his followers did not foment a rebellion as the French
suspected, war and civil unrest have plagued both Liberia and Sierra Leone.
Following a military coup and subsequent civil war, Liberia became a secular
state in 1980. The civil war in Sierra Leone lasted from 1991 to 2002, but the
damaging effects of war persist. Although both Liberia and Sierra Leone grant
freedom of religion to their citizens, there is religious tension between Christians and Muslims. In brief, most Liberians practice Christianity while most
Sierra Leoneans practice Islam. African traditional religions vie for the hearts
of those who do not embrace Christianity or Islam, though Africans commonly cleave to remnants of each of these religions even when they largely
practice one of the others. In Liberia scholars expect Christianity to increase
and Islam and traditional religions to decrease; in Sierra Leone, by contrast,
Christianity and Islam are both expected to grow.

LOOKING TO AFRICA FOR CHRISTIAN GUIDANCE

Following European decolonization of Africa in the middle of the twentieth
century, the number of Christians on this continent has increased at an unprecedented rate. The Africanization of Christianity (whereby Christianity
exists legitimately as an independent and African expression of world Christianity), high birth rates and the Pentecostal movement account for Christianity's growth in this part of the world where close to one billion people call
home. Meanwhile, the remnants of Christianity as a "white man's religion,"
whether an accurate description or not, will continue for some time. This is

---

[22]Quoted in Sundkler and Steed, *History of the Church in Africa*, 198.
[23]Kevin Ward, "Africa," in *A World History of Christianity*, ed. Adrian Hastings (Grand Rapids:
Eerdmans, 1999), 222.

particularly the case among African Muslims, who associate Christianity with European colonization. Like a stain that will not wash away, European complicity in the slave trade blights the witness of Christianity in Africa. As Mark Shaw writes in relation to Africans at the height of the slave trade, "For many Africans who had contacts with Europeans it appeared that Christians evangelized the people one day and sold them into slavery the next." By the early nineteenth century, in fact, Rome had conceded that "the greatest hindrance of missions is the slave trade, operated by the Christians of Angola. It renders our religion odious to the Africans who keep in mind their chains instead of seeing the freedom brought them in Christ."[24]

But it was not just the slave trade that made European religion odious in the sight of Africans. The Rwandan genocide, when more than a million Rwandese men, women and children were brutally killed over the course of just one hundred days, has been traced to European discriminatory practices from colonial times. Even though almost 90 percent of the Rwandan population was Christian in 1994, it has been argued that the discriminatory practices of the European colonizers in Rwanda toward the Hutus and the Tutsi created a culture of systemic racism and violence between these two groups.[25]

Though European missionaries evangelized Africa for centuries, they never fully regarded indigenous cultures and practices on equal footing with Western ones. As in any setting Western missionaries did not always recognize their own cultures and practices as distinct from the gospel. The translation of the Bible into local languages and African oversight of the African church have greatly contributed to Christianity's expansion in the past several decades. The rise of global Pentecostalism is also playing an important role in the growth of African Christianity. Unlike European missionaries, African Christians emphasize healing, wealth, prophecy and spiritual power. They fully affirm certain African customs and practices and reject others they perceive as contradicting the tenets of Christianity. In the future scholars anticipate further growth of Christianity in Africa, where it

---

[24]Shaw, *Kingdom of God in Africa*, 124.
[25]See Emmanuel Kolini and Peter Holmes, *Christ Walks Where Evil Reigned: Responding to the Rwandan Genocide* (Colorado Springs: Authentic, 2008), 25-39; Timothy Longman, *Christianity and Genocide in Rwanda* (Cambridge: Cambridge University Press, 2011), 4, 10.

could one day boast the largest number of Christians in the world. Although other nations will certainly influence its development, African Christianity will grow as a truly African phenomenon rather than a European colonial experiment. Meanwhile, European Christianity will decline and may one day "resort to [Mother] Africa," as Edward Blyden famously prophesied in 1880, for spiritual guidance as from a wayward child. Indeed, as world Christian historian Andrew Walls wrote, "we may need to look at Africa . . . in order to understand Christianity itself."[26]

---

[26]Andrew Walls, *The Cross-Cultural Process in Christian History* (Maryknoll, NY: Orbis, 2002), 119.

twelve

ASIA

*One of the bitter ironies of Asian Christianity is that though born in . . .
Asia, it returned to its birthplace as a foreign religion, or worse, the religion
of the colonizers, and is still being widely regarded as such by many Asians.*

PETER PHAN, *"INTRODUCTION:
ASIAN CHRISTIANITY/CHRISTIANITIES"*

CHRISTIANITY, THE "FOREIGN" NATIVE RELIGION

Asia is the religious mother of the world. It has given birth to each major world
religion: Baha'i, Buddhism, Christianity, Confucianism, Daoism, Hinduism,
Jainism, Judaism, Islam and Sikhism. With such a varied religious progeny it
is not surprising that sibling rivalry has historically crowded out Christianity,
a mere adolescent in relation to older religious brothers and sisters. With a few
exceptions, Asian Christianity is a minority religion. This is certainly ironic
given that Christianity was born in Asia, as were the other major world religions. Nevertheless, Christianity has had to fight for its right to even claim
recognition as a religion native to Asia. That's because a confluence of historic
factors practically extinguished the fires of Christianity; and when the flames
reappeared in the sixteenth century, it was Westerners who were fanning them.
Maybe Christianity is not Asian after all.

But this flies in the face of what we now know to be true, namely, that "the
church began in Asia."[1] Before Westerners began planting their "foreign" religion

---

[1] Samuel Moffett, *A History of Christianity in Asia*, vol. 2, *1500 to 1900* (Maryknoll, NY: Orbis, 2005), xiii.

on Asian soil, Asian Christians had been worshiping Jesus Christ since the first century. In fact, the Church of the East, a body of believers native to Asia, was at one time the largest Christian institution in the world. Collectively, this body exercised jurisdiction over Christian communities from the Mediterranean to the East China Sea. Headquartered in Iraq, the Church of the East was recognized by Islamic states as the head of the church over all of Asia. Due to a variety of circumstances, however, the Church of the East has substantially diminished. Many of those who have survived have emigrated out of Asia and into the West, the supposed birthplace of Christianity. Today, in fact, the headquarters of the Church of the East are in Chicago, thousands of miles from its Asian roots.

In many ways the Church of the East encapsulates the different eras of Asian Christianity. The first period endured from the first to the seventh centuries. At this time various communities practiced Christianity in Western and Southern Asia. Moreover, signs indicate the church's growth in Central and Eastern Asia, especially after Christianity arose in China in the seventh century. The emergence and expansion of the different Islamic empires in the second period, however, led to the eventual decline of Christianity across Asia. Although Christians initially fared well under Arab rule and under certain Mongolian kingdoms, they did not flourish under other kingdoms and declined after the Black Death of the fourteenth century. When the third period emerged, from the fifteenth to the nineteenth centuries, "Asian Christianity" was, without too much embellishment, an oxymoron. Certainly, Christians existed in certain regions around the Middle East, but their numbers had been drastically reduced since the first period and early second period.

The Westerners who inaugurated the third era of missions often evangelized communities ignorant of Christianity's impressive history in Asia. It did not take long, in fact, before tensions arose between Western Christian missionaries and existing Eastern Christians from the first period of Asian Christianity. This led to the further fragmentation and, in the eyes of some Asians, "dismemberment" of Christian churches from the first period in favor of the recent, Western-initiated period of Christianity.[2]

---

[2]Jean Corbon, "The Churches of the Middle East," in *Christian Communities in the Arab Middle East*, ed. Andrea Pacini (Oxford: Clarendon, 1998), 97.

CHAPTER OVERVIEW

In this chapter we will discuss the last five or six hundred years of Christianity in Asia, the largest region on the planet. Unlike our overview of Christianity in Asia in chapter one, where we discussed how Christianity was born in Asia and was quickly spread by Asians to other Asians, we will be forced in this chapter to look at Christianity as a foreign religion. As you read about Christianity in Asia during this time, try to envision living in a world where Christianity is not only foreign but also small. It's not always easy to determine why Christianity "succeeds" in certain Asian regions while not in others, but there is no getting around the fact that Christianity faces many challenges as it seeks to return to its native Asian roots.

CENTRAL ASIA

We will begin our exploration of Christianity in Central Asia. This region includes the five "stan" countries that formed after the collapse of the Soviet Union (USSR) in 1991: Kazakhstan, Kyrgyzstan, Tajikistan, Turkmenistan and Uzbekistan. The term *stan* means "place of." Thus, Kazakhstan is regarded as the "place of the Kazahks," and Uzbekistan is the "place of the Uzbeks." Although the borders have fluctuated over the centuries in Central Asia, the name of each modern country corresponds to its majority ethnic population. Religiously, each of these countries is predominantly Sunni Muslim. However, Christianity was formerly widespread in this region due to the Silk Road running through it. The form of Christianity that existed in these Central Asian countries was Syrian based—just as in the Southern Asian countries of India, Iran and Iraq.

Unlike nearby Armenia and Georgia, however, where Christianity experienced great duress during the Turkic and Mongol empires but prevailed due to its alliances with other Christian groups and a strong national identity, the indigenous churches in Central Asia did not endure in the same way. As a general rule today, Armenians and Russians living in Central Asia belong to the Armenian Apostolic Church and the Russian Orthodox Church, respectively. However, many recent Protestant missionaries have targeted Central Asia in an attempt to reach the people living there irrespective of ethnic identity and their ties to Orthodox communities. These Protestant missionaries will likely face an uphill battle given that the ethnic identity of

Central Asian people groups—whether Kyrgyzs, Kazakhs, Tajiks, Turks or Uzbeks—is historically tied to Islam, just as Armenians and Georgians are to Orthodox Christianity.

Kazakhstan. The Russian Orthodox Church is the major Christian tradition in Central Asia, including Kazakhstan. Orthodox Christians, mostly Russian, now make up a respectable percentage of the population in Kazakhstan and Kyrgyzstan. Ever since the fall of Constantinople in 1453, the Russian Church considered itself the inheritor, curator and carrier of the (Eastern) Orthodox faith. From as early as the sixteenth century, the Russian Empire steadily increased its reign over neighboring regions like Kazakhstan. From 1500 to 1900, in fact, Russia "acquired approximately 50 square miles a day."[3] This Russian intrusion over parts of Central Asia was not completely unwelcomed. The Kazahks requested the aid and presence of Russians to offset the mounting nomadic tribes in the nineteenth century, leading to a further expansion of Russian Orthodoxy. The Russians built churches and constructed schools. By 1871 the patriarchate of Moscow (the head of the Russian Orthodox Church) had created the diocese of Turkestan to shepherd the hundreds of Orthodox churches in the region. By the end of the nineteenth century, Catholics from Germany, Poland and Ukraine also began contributing to the religious diversity of Kazakhstan by moving there.

When the communist regime took over Russia in 1917, Christianity entered a season of intense persecution. Before then the Russian tsars had generally supported Christianity. The creation of the USSR in 1922, however, greatly limited not just the presence but even the survival of Christianity until the USSR's demise. The government closed churches and marginalized, banished and killed many of the clergy. At the dissolution of the USSR, each of the countries in Central Asia gained independence. Restrictions on religion eased, but the church still faced many challenges. The newly created Kazakhstan granted citizens freedom of religion. This act not only saw the readmission of many lapsed Orthodox back into the fold but also the addition of Protestant missionaries from a variety of denominations, including Baptists, Mennonites and Seventh-day Adventists. Unlike the Russian Orthodox Church, which has managed to coexist with Sunni Islam for centuries, the new Protestant

---

[3]Peter B. Golden, *Central Asia in World History* (Oxford: Oxford University Press, 2011), 108.

churches have been less successful legitimating themselves in the eyes of the Muslim elite. A growing secularism in Kazakhstan will also continue to compete with the message of Protestant churches across the country.

EASTERN ASIA

Moving from Central Asia to the east, I might suggest that Christianity has had a peculiar history in Eastern Asia. In China, for instance, Christianity resembles the fabled phoenix, which dies and reemerges from its own ashes. Christianity died two or three times in China before rising from its ashes and becoming an independent and indigenous church in the twentieth century. Though the Catholic mission outdates the Protestant one by several hundred years, Protestants have greatly bypassed the number of Catholic Christians. China's former territories of Mongolia and Taiwan have followed a different course. East Syrian Christianity entered Mongolia in the seventh century, and it also dominated in the thirteenth century when the Mongols ruled over much of Asia. However, Christianity disappeared there and Mongolians eventually adopted Islam. Christianity in China only revived in any numbers in the nineteenth century, but it is now experiencing a veritable explosion of growth, leading some scholars to predict that China may well be the country with the largest amount of Christians in the world over the course of the next couple of decades. As for Taiwan, European missionaries did not arrive until the seventeenth century. There, Christian missionaries played crucial roles in the establishment of hospitals, schools and social service organizations, but it has struggled to maintain its religious exclusivity in the midst of the competing and syncretistic religions of animism, Buddhism, Confucianism and Daoism.

In the Korean peninsula, straddled precariously between the powerful empires of China and Japan, the story of Christianity is a bittersweet one. The sweetness comes from the incredible success that Christianity has experienced in South Korea. There Christianity has thoroughly integrated itself into the Korean culture, and South Korea sends out more Christian missionaries than any other nation in the world, save the United States. Along with the sweetness, however, comes bitterness. Still reeling from more than thirty years of Japanese occupation, foreign powers cut the Korean nation in half, forming South Korea and North Korea in 1953. The communist orientation of North Korea has not only driven the North Korean nation into widespread poverty but has also brought about a spiritual famine. Although it contained the largest percentage of Christians before it was divided from the south, North Korea is now less than 2 percent Christian, despite the fact the Korean revivals in the early 1900s took place in the north rather than in the south. In South Korea it's possible that Protestant Christianity, particularly in its Presbyterian form, has reached a plateau even though Protestantism has found a way to meld into Korean culture the way Buddhism and Confucianism did centuries ago.

Japan. Catholic missionaries first entered Japan in the sixteenth century. The Jesuit Francis Xavier arrived on the southern island of Kyushu, aided by a Japanese convert named Yajiro (his baptismal name was Paul of the Holy Faith). The Jesuit Alessandro Valignano later oversaw the Japanese mission, contributing to what scholars have called the "Christian Century" of Japan, a moment of hope for Japanese Christianity lasting from 1549 to 1650. Although the church numbered a respectable 150,000 in 1582, and would gain 300,000 adherents by 1650, the tide was beginning to turn against Christianity. A *daimyo* (a powerful feudal lord) from the warrior class named Toyotomi Hideyoshi was uniting a divided Japan in the 1580s and moving Japan toward an increasingly anti-Western and anti-Christian posture.

In 1587 Hideyoshi ordered the removal of Western missionaries, the confiscation of mission property and the recantation of Japanese converts. Hideyoshi did not consistently enforce his edict, but he persecuted certain Christians. For the next several decades missionaries spread Christianity across the Japanese islands, leading to the conversion of some in the upper classes of society. But a change occurred in 1597. That year Hideyoshi, apparently under the impression that European missionaries were seeking to overtake Japan (and certainly aware that several *daimyos* had converted), crucified twenty-six Christians in Nagasaki, leaving their bloodied corpses (having been pierced with lances) on the crosses for almost a year.[4]

The most intense persecution of the church in Japan came in the seventeenth century. By this time, unfortunately, the church was fragmented due to squabbles among missionaries, who had come from different Catholic orders. The arrival of the first Protestants in 1600 only added to this fragmentation. During the Tokugawa period the Japanese governors wiped out Christianity.

---

[4]Moffett, *History of Christianity in Asia*, 2:85.

In 1614 they resurrected the former edict against Christians. The religions of Buddhism, Confucianism and the native Shinto triumphed. In 1622 Japanese leaders slowly roasted to death on stakes twenty-three Christians and beheaded their wives and children in Nagasaki.[5] Between 1627 and 1636, five thousand to six thousand Christians suffered martyrdom.[6] Within a strong culture of shame and honor, town leaders shamed villagers by publicly forcing them to step on an image of Christ (called a *fumie*), thereby all but ending their association with the Christian religion. Although many apostatized (including tormented European missionaries), many opted for martyrdom. This persecution uprooted Christianity. Only a few hidden Christians (*Kakure Kirishitans*) remained—severed from the sacraments and priests and forced to forge their own theological course in the centuries to come.

TRAIL MARKER
Japan's Hidden Christians

Although Christianity initially showed signs of potential in Japan, Japanese leaders regarded it as foreign and threatening, and they were intent on wiping it out. The Kakure Kirishitans still exist today in small numbers as a remnant of the Catholic Japanese Christians who went underground during intense persecution in the 1600s.

In 1868 the two-centuries-long Japanese policy of isolation thawed. As the shogunate period ended, Japan was transitioning from a feudal to a capitalist economy under the leadership of Emperor Meiji. Although the former edict against Christianity lasted until 1873, Christian missionaries from the Catholic, Orthodox and Protestant traditions had been living in Japan since 1859. These Protestant missionaries were Episcopalians, Free Baptists, (Dutch) Reformed and Presbyterians. After years of missionary work the first Japanese man converted to Protestantism in 1864. Around the same time the first Orthodox

---

[5]Ibid., 2:90.
[6]Mark Mullins, "Japan," in *Christianities in Asia*, ed. Peter Phan (Oxford: Wiley-Blackwell, 2011), 200.

missionary in Japan, coming from the Russian Orthodox Church, landed on
the island of Hokkaido in 1861 and baptized his first Japanese converts in 1868.
By the time of his death in 1912, he had established an Orthodox community
of more than thirty thousand.

Christianity's reappearance in Japan appeared to be a good omen, especially given that many converts hailed from the upper middle class. However,
Christianity lost momentum as nationalism intensified and enthusiasm for
Western culture weakened. Christianity also struggled as Buddhism, Shinto
and civil obligations were in the process of forming the religious mold of
modern Japan. Christianity found itself on the losing end of Japan's national
unification and military expansion. Further devastation rocked the Catholic
Church as the US government bombed Nagasaki, the center of Japanese
Catholicism, in 1945, destroying the Urakami Cathedral and about 8,500
Christians.[7] In his funeral address for the victims in Nagasaki, a city where
Christianity had suffered so much grief, the Catholic doctor Takashi Nagai
wrote the following:

> Our church of Nagasaki kept the faith during four hundred years of perse-
> cution when religion was proscribed and the blood of martyrs flowed freely.
> During the war this same church never ceased to pray day and night for a
> lasting peace. Was it not, then, the one unblemished lamb that had to be
> offered on the altar of God? Thanks to the sacrifice of this lamb many mil-
> lions who would otherwise have fallen victim to the rages of war have been
> saved. Eight thousand people, together with their priests, burning with
> pure smoke, entered into eternal life.[8]

Although postwar Japan has allowed for freedom of religion, Christianity
faces an uphill battle against new religious movements, Buddhism, Shintoism
and especially secularism. The low birth rate and an aging population have
accelerated the decline of Christianity in Japan, though Christian missions to
Japan continue unabated.

South Korea. Unwittingly, Japan has contributed to Christianity's success
in Korea. Modern Korean Christianity begins when the Japanese took many
Koreans captive in the 1600s, some of whom converted to Christianity and

---

[7]Three days before, on August 6, the US government unleashed an atomic bomb on Hiroshima,
killing more than 100,000 in the aftermath. On August 15, the Japanese surrendered.
[8]Mullins, "Japan," 202.

established a church in Japan. Another chapter was written during the Japanese occupation of Korea from 1910 to 1945. Nothing has the potential of uniting a people like subjection to a foreign power, and in the early part of the twentieth century the Korean people's resentment of foreign domination coalesced with the Protestant church's refusal to bow down to Japan's gods. In this way Japan and South Korea serve as the yin and yang of Christianity in Eastern Asia.

It is clear from archaeological relics that East Syrian Christians resided in South Korea by at least the eighth or ninth centuries, but not enough evidence exists to reconstruct the status of Christianity at that time. Until more evidence surfaces, the story of Korean Christianity must begin in Beijing with a Korean prince and heir apparent named So-hyun. The Manchurian court in China had taken So-hyun as a hostage in 1644. While in Beijing he became friends with the Jesuit Adam Ball, who was the first European to meet with the Chinese emperor. Upon So-hyun's release to Korea, he brought with him several Chinese Catholics as well as openness to Western ideas and religion. Likely murdered, the young prince died shortly after returning to court before he could assume leadership of the Choseon Dynasty, the reigning dynasty in Korea from 1392 to 1897.

Interest in Western ideas and religion, however, outlived So-hyun. In 1784 a young scholar named Lee Seung-hun, or Peter Lee, went to Beijing on a diplomatic mission with his father, an important minister in the Choseon Dynasty. While in Beijing, Lee met with a former Jesuit missionary and received permission from his father to be baptized. Thus in 1784 Lee become the first baptized Catholic from Korea. Upon his return Peter Lee met with his scholarly friends of the *yangban* (the ruling class), and they established a lay Catholic community, illicitly administering the sacraments of baptism, the Eucharist and ordination. The Choseon Dynasty swiftly persecuted this group, and Lee and another leader apostatized under mounting pressure. From 1784 to 1794 the Choseon Dynasty martyred more than four hundred Korean Christians. Why did the Choseon Dynasty persecute its leading citizens just for adopting Christianity? It's likely that Christianity led this fledgling group to reject the Confucian virtue of ancestor veneration, which was the religious fabric that held together the Choseon Dynasty. The Catholic Church generally opposed *jesa*, the rite of ancestor veneration.

Although the first convert, Peter Lee, had apostatized, the Korean church continued to grow. The bishop of Beijing sent James Chou, a Chinese priest, to Korea, and he celebrated the first sanctioned Eucharist on Easter Sunday 1795. After five intense years of ministry, in which Korean leaders made hundreds of martyrs and forced exiles among the ten thousand believers at that time, Father Chou was beheaded in 1801. For the rest of the century Christians experienced ongoing persecution. In 1839 Korean leaders beheaded its first two Western missionaries as well as its first ordained Korean priest, Andrew Kim Taegon. Kim, whose father was martyred, had been ordained in Shanghai in 1844. The most intense period of persecution lasted from 1866 to 1867. The Choseon Dynasty wiped out a quarter of the Christian population. One of the foreign priests, before execution, stated, "I came to this country to save souls. I shall die with joy."[9]

The persecution of the Korean church in the nineteenth century ended when the government signed trade agreements with Western nations in the 1880s. As in other parts of Eastern Asia, openness to foreign trade opened the door to Protestant missions. The first Protestant missions to Korea are traced to 1784, exactly a century after the first Korean Catholic was baptized. Many Northern American missionaries arrived, and the first Protestants established churches in 1887. The Choseon Dynasty welcomed the missionaries since Korea sought an alliance against its encroaching neighbors. These missionaries made historic contributions in education and medicine. Presbyterianism and Methodism served as the backbone of the early Korean Protestant movement.

The twentieth century proved pivotal for Korean Christianity. In 1900 Russian Orthodox missionaries entered Korea and established Orthodoxy alongside the older Catholic and Protestant missions. The Russians erected St. Nicholas Orthodox Cathedral in 1903 and ordained the first Korean Orthodox priest in 1912. Now more than ten Orthodox parishes exist in South Korea. As for Protestantism, the Pyongyang Revival in 1907 invigorated the indigenous Protestant movement. The most prominent leader of this revival was Gil Sunjoo, the first ordained Korean Presbyterian. Gil laid what is today the cornerstone of Korean Protestantism: early morning or dawn prayer

---

[9]Moffett, *History of Christianity in Asia*, 2:316.

(where Protestants attend church every morning), united vocal prayer (shouting out to God in unison with others) and abstinence from alcohol. The March First Movement in 1919 linked Korean nationalism (and opposition to Japanese occupation) with Protestantism, which greatly fueled the growth of the Protestant movement.

In 1935 Japan imposed Shinto rituals on Korea. The Catholics and Methodists complied. They viewed the ritual as a civic rather than a religious act. The Presbyterians, by contrast, rejected the ritual under the belief that it amounted to idolatry. Many gave their lives. After the Japanese lost in World War II and left Korea in 1945, the church in Korea continued to divide. Presbyterianism splintered, and today it consists of more than 150 denominations in a country the size of Ohio.[10] After foreign powers divided Korea into two separate nations in 1953, Christians in current-day North Korea, where the majority of Christians used to live and where widespread revival broke out, moved to the newly formed South Korea, making Korean Christianity lopsided. Today, Christianity is the largest organized religion in South Korea, with Buddhism following. However, the church is greatly divided. Scandal has plagued Protestantism, reversing the image it formerly wielded as a moral and social good. Catholicism and Orthodoxy, however, are on the rise, though the Orthodox Church only contains, at best, a few thousand believers (see table 12.1). In North Korea, decades of communist rule have starved out Christianity, with no signs of reversal until communism is removed.

Table 12.1. Numbers of Christians in South Korea

Year	Catholics	Protestants	Orthodox
1774	4,000	0	0
1883	23,035	0	0
1890	17,577	265	0
1900	42,441	18,081	0
1910	74,517	167,352	Less than a dozen
2000	3,700,000	9,000,000	Less than 1,000

Sources: Samuel Moffett, *A History of Christianity in Asia*, vol. 2, *1500–1900* (Maryknoll, NY: Orbis, 2005), 545, 553; Andrew Kim, "South Korea," in *Christianities in Asia*, ed. Peter Phan (Oxford: Wiley-Blackwell, 2011), 217.

---

[10]Todd Johnson and Cindy Wu, *Our Global Families: Christians Embracing Common Identity in a Changing World* (Grand Rapids: Baker Academic, 2015), xii.

SOUTHEASTERN ASIA

Apart from East Timor and the Philippines the percentage of Christians living in Southeastern Asia is quite small. However, it was not Asians from the Church of the East in the early centuries of the church who transported Christianity—like every other region of Asia—but European Catholics in the sixteenth century who did so. By and large the missionary history of this region shares many commonalities. Feuding Western European merchants and missionaries began importing a variety of Christian traditions into the land beginning in the sixteenth century. Specifically, the Portuguese, Spanish and French introduced Catholicism in the sixteenth and seventeenth centuries; the Dutch and Germans introduced Protestantism in the nineteenth century; and Northern Americans introduced Pentecostalism (as well as mainline Protestantism earlier) in the twentieth century. Despite the theological variety, Christianity clashed with the centuries-long religions of animism, Buddhism, folk religion, Confucianism, Hinduism and Islam, even though the Southeastern Asian religious-cultural mentality has historically been a pluralistic one.

The Philippines. Missions to the Philippines began in the sixteenth century. As mentioned in chapter eight, the papacy granted Portugal, the first truly maritime European power, political and religious jurisdiction over the East (and Spain in the West) in the Treaty of Tordesillas. This is why so many countries in Africa and Asia are Catholic. However, the Spanish, not the Portuguese, eventually came to colonize what would become their most successful colony in the East, the Philippines. The capital of the Philippines, Manila, served as the center of Catholicism in Asia.

Spanish conquest is traced back to the arrival of the famed Portuguese explorer Ferdinand Magellan, who died in battle shortly after converting one of the local rulers to Christianity. In 1565 another expedition arrived, this time carrying monks of the (Catholic) Augustinian order whose missionary labors bore much fruit. From 1565 to 1821 the Viceroyalty of New Spain governed the Philippines. Dominicans, Franciscans, Jesuits and secular priests established schools and hospitals, and converted the masses to Catholicism. Because these Catholic groups constantly bickered, the Spanish crown divided the missionary work among the different orders according to so-called spheres of influence. Though they worked on different islands and with different strategies, in only a matter of decades the Spanish had conquered and centralized the islands, created *reducciones* (towns in the popular Spanish style) and thoroughly Christianized the different ethnic groups. The Filipino Christianity that developed melded together indigenous culture with Spanish Catholicism, which today constitutes more than 90 percent of the Filipino population.

The Protestant missionaries began arriving in the later part of the nineteenth century at a time when the Filipino nationalist movement was on the rise. Before then the Catholic Church had banned Protestant missions. At the end of the Spanish-American War in 1898, however, the Spanish ceded the Philippines to the Unites States, boosting the Protestant presence in the country. Thereafter Baptists, Congregationalists, Episcopalians, Methodists, Seventh-day Adventists, Presbyterians and other rival Protestant denominations poured into the country. These Protestant denominations, however, only competed on a very small scale with the existing Roman Catholic churches. At the same time the confluence of Filipino nationalism and independence, Protestant missions, and American rule and anti-Catholicism (including anticolonialism) coalesced to form the Philippine Independent Church. Although it forms a relatively small percentage of the Filipino population, the Philippine Independent Church remains the second-largest denomination in the Philippines. Today, however, as many other parts of the world, the Pentecostal tradition is blurring the lines between Protestant and Catholic churches, and the Pentecostal movement is making inroads into the existing Filipino churches.

Southern Asia. Unlike in Southeastern Asia, Christianity boasts an ancient history in Southern Asia. It's very possible that the Church of the East founded churches in Iran, Iraq and India during the first century, with evangelization of modern Afghanistan and Pakistan following apace. Over time, however, Christianity declined in this region in all areas other than in India. Although there were pocket of Christians, they did not play a prominent role in society. Today, Christianity represents less than 1 percent of the total population of the majority of countries in Southern Asia. The small groups of Christians who live in these countries are roughly evenly divided among the Catholic and Protestant traditions. India and Sri Lanka contain the largest percentages of Christians, but these percentages are still quite low in proportion to their overall sizes. The countries with the lowest percentage of Christians all live in Muslim-majority countries, where laws severely restrict Christianity. In the Maldives, for instance, citizens who convert to Christianity lose their citizenship, while the punishment for an Afghan to convert from Islam to Christianity is death.

India. In Southern Asia, Christianity has been most consistently present in India. A longstanding tradition maintains that the apostle Thomas introduced Christianity to India in the first century. Whether or not that is true, it is clear that Christianity developed there very early, and the Church of the East has maintained a reputable presence in India for centuries. The St. Thomas Christians, those tracing their lineage to the apostle Thomas in the first century or to Thomas of Cana in the fourth century, were incorporated into the Church of the East by the fourth century. The first Catholic bishop of India was the Dominican Jordanus Catalini, whom Pope John XXII appointed as bishop in 1328. In addition to India, Bishop Catalini's jurisdiction included Afghanistan, Bangladesh, Myanmar and Sri Lanka. It was not until the sixteenth century, however, that European Catholics made their greatest impact on India. The Portuguese explorer Vasco da Gama arrived in India in 1498, carrying a letter from the Portuguese king to Prester John, a legendary Christian king whom Europeans believed existed and with whom they hoped to form an alliance against the Muslims. The Portuguese established a Catholic presence in Goa on the western coast in 1507. From there they went to work in India and across Asia, and Roman Catholicism constitutes the single largest Christian tradition in India.

Not uncharacteristically, the European Catholics and indigenous Indian Christians clashed. Due to the initial challenges they encountered when attempting to convert non-Christian locals, the Catholic Christians turned to converting existing Indian Christians. This practice bred resentment among the St. Thomas Christians, who believed their worship was purer than the Catholics since they did not venerate Mary or use images. Before long the Catholics imposed their theology and ecclesiology on the Indian Syrians and forced them to accept the Latin rite, causing a contingent of the Indian Christians to unite with Rome just as others in the church rejected the Catholic union. (Those that united with Rome were maligned as Uniate churches, which are otherwise known as Eastern Catholic Churches today.)

Due to the realignment of the Indian Church after the Catholic Europeans arrived, a complicated division led to three distinct bodies: the Chaldean Catholic Church, the Church of the East and the Roman Catholic Church.

(Over time this division has proliferated to the point of being difficult to map out.) The Chaldean Catholic Church emerged in 1553, and the first patriarch or bishop was John Sulaka. He had traveled to Rome, accepted the Catholic creed and received papal ordination in 1553. He was murdered two years later. The religious body he formed was now under the jurisdiction of the pope and was thus considered a Uniate church. The Church of the East, which had been the dominant expression of Christianity for more than a millennium, rejected both the newly formed Chaldean Catholic Church and the Roman Catholic Church.

TRAIL MARKER
St. Thomas Christians

Here are two things to keep in mind in this section. First, Indian Christians were called St. Thomas Christians because they traced their origins to St. Thomas in the first century or to Thomas of Cana in the fourth century. This group was folded into the Church of the East at an early period. Second, since the arrival of Catholic Europeans in the Late Middle Ages, St. Thomas Christians have undergone many church splits.

The Roman Catholic archbishop of Goa, Aleixo de Menezes, convened the Synod of Dyamper in 1599 to address the religious unrest. In order to form a majority, Menezes hastily ordained one hundred priests. He came down forcefully against the Church of the East. The synod condemned the theological architects of the Church of the East from centuries past, mandated the use of the Latin rite and the acceptance of Catholic theology, instituted celibacy among Indian priests (which meant that they had to divorce their wives in order to remain priests). What's more, the synod recognized the primacy of the pope and removed Indian Catholics from the patriarchy of the Chaldean Catholic. The synod also burned all the centuries-old Christian manuscripts from the Church of the East.[11] Further

---

[11]Christoph Baumer, *The Church of the East: An Illustrated History of Assyrian Christianity* (London: I. B. Tauris, 2006), 239.

divisions and fragmentation characterized Indian Christianity, which continue to this day. The arrival of Protestants beginning in the eighteenth century only exacerbated this conflict. Although European Protestant merchants had lived in India for more than a century, the first Protestant missionaries—German Lutherans—arrived in 1706. An indigenous Lutheran church formed quickly, and the first Indian pastor was ordained in 1733.

Over time Indian Christianity developed a new identity. Whereas East Syrian Christianity had exercised a virtual monopoly over the Indian churches for more than a millennium, now Christianity in India was completely diffuse. Not only were there divisions among Catholics but also among a variety of Protestant and Orthodox bodies. The caste system of India also contributed to division. Although Indians had historically recognized the St. Thomas Christians as comprising a separate caste in Hinduism, the onslaught of Christian missionaries and the subsequent conversion of local Indians from different castes caused tension. The following eighteenth-century letter from one of the German Lutheran missionary pioneers alludes to this tension in regard to the potential ordination of a man from the lowest rank of the caste system, a Dalit:

> We desired to ordain [this man of the Dalit caste] priest, which we could if his work were confined to the pariahs [the people of this lowest of caste ranks]. But the Christians of higher caste avoid coming into contact with such people. We take great pains to lessen these prejudices among Christians: but to a certain degree they must be taken into consideration. But we should hesitate to have the Lord's Supper administered by him lest it diminish the regard of Christians of higher caste for that sacrament itself.[12]

Not surprisingly, the Lutherans did not ordain this man given his low caste and the concomitant difficulties it would cause in the execution of his pastoral duties. The Roman Catholics proceeded in the same way: they only ordained Brahmins, those of the highest caste, as priests. The church hierarchy believed that the ordination of an Indian Christian from a low caste would not only endanger the reputation of the Christian religion but also produce countless pastoral challenges given that members of Indian society from different castes did not traditionally touch, eat together or associate. Many subsequent Christian missionaries, such as the Baptists, however, rejected this practice.

---

[12]Elizabeth Koepping, "India, Pakistan, Bangladesh, Burma/Myanmar," in Phan, *Christianities in Asia,* 20.

The most famous Protestant missionary to India was the English Baptist William Carey. Carey, the father of modern Protestant missions, was a missionary in India for forty years until his death. He served in West Bengal, just as the world-famous Catholic nun Mother Teresa did a century later among the poorest individuals in Calcutta, the capital of the state of West Bengal. Like other Protestant missionaries, Carey invested his energy in learning the local languages and translating the Bible. Over time the Protestant movement proliferated and Indians from all castes joined the different Christian denominations. Soon after the death of Carey the British gained control of India for a century. After a century of rule the British Empire, whom the Hindu Mahatma Gandhi peacefully pressured, departed from India. The British also divided the country into Hindu (India) and Muslim (Pakistan) states. The Punjab became the dominant region of Sikhs, squeezed in between India and Pakistan. This division, however, has not proceeded peacefully. There is sometimes violent aggression among the different religious groups.

Today, Christianity in India is growing at a fast pace. This is especially true among Pentecostal churches and in the south of the country. Yet the sheer diversity of Indian churches means that individual churches will grow at different rates. The Catholic and Orthodox churches have had great success in gaining acceptance among the majority Hindu population due to their ancient roots and separate identity. But the same cannot be said for Protestant churches, which garner a wide variety of public responses. Because of the stigma associated with leaving one's role in society as a Hindu, many—though certainly not all—Protestant churches contain high percentages of Dalits and Indians of a low caste. Many Hindus regard Protestantism's focus on evangelism and proselytization—which is not characteristic of Hinduism or of the St. Thomas Christians—as ill-conceived and in opposition to their Indian worldview. At the same time, many other Protestant and Pentecostal churches are experiencing great successes, with members from all layers of Hindu society in attendance and in leadership.

WESTERN ASIA

The last region of Asia that we will explore is the one with the most ancient roots, Western Asia, which is made up in large part of the Middle East. As in many Asian countries, Islam is the majority religion in this region. As we well know by now, however, Christianity was actually the dominant religion in Western Asia for centuries before it gradually diminished under Islamic rule. Although many churches have formed in recent memory due to Catholic and Protestant missionary efforts, the historic Orthodox Church has managed to maintain a strong presence in many Western Asian nations, including the three countries where it continues to constitute the majority of the population: Armenia, Cyprus and Georgia. (It also has sizeable number in Lebanon among the Maronite Christians, an autonomous Orthodox community with roots in the early church.) Meanwhile, many of the countries in Western Asia are caught up in great political and religious conflicts that do not appear to be ending anytime soon. Although there are Christians in each of the Muslim-majority countries, there is a mass exodus taking place in many of them since they continue to find themselves targets of discrimination and violence.

Israel and Palestine. One region that continues to witness a decreasing Christian population is the so-called Holy Land, a small area that usually refers to Israel and Palestine. This is surely ironic given the history of the region and the fact that any traveler to Israel and Palestine is struck by the vast array of foreign Christians on pilgrimage. Not only do Christian pilgrims from every language and tradition travel to the Holy Land each year but many ancient churches share space with other historic denominations. At the Church of the Holy Sepulchre, for instance, the traditional site of Jesus' death and resurrection in the Old City of Jerusalem, churches from Coptic, Ethiopian, Greek and Syrian, among other traditions, maintain services. This list of churches reflects both the diversity and the great history of the Christian traditions represented in the region. At the same time, the little-known fact that Muslims (and not Christians) have possessed the key to the Church of the Holy Sepulchre—the most iconic church of the Christian faith—for nearly two centuries illustrates that Christianity is both a minority religion in its place of birth as well as a deeply divided one.

Christians in Israel and Palestine have lived under foreign rule for centuries. This began in the seventh century, and over the centuries different Islamic governments controlled the region until Western Christian Crusaders carved out a temporary kingdom in the Holy Land from 1097 to 1291. But it did not take long for the Muslims to reassume control of the region from the thirteenth to the twentieth centuries. From 1519 to 1917 the Ottoman Empire ruled over Israel and Palestine. During this time Christians lived under the millet system, whereby they lived in religious freedom as a protected class under Islamic law. The highest-ranking figure of each Christian community performed a variety of functions for the Ottomans, including collecting taxes. Despite their protected status, Christians paid high tax rates, causing many to eventually convert to Islam to be relieved of this financial burden.

At the collapse of the Ottoman Empire after World War I in 1922, the British assumed rule over the Holy Land for three decades. Following World War II, ongoing conversations about a country for the Jewish people to inhabit came to fruition. The United Nations partitioned the land of Palestine in 1947, and the State of Israel announced its independence in 1948. Israel then expanded its borders during the Six-Day War of 1967. Regrettably, Arabs living in the Holy Land—including, of course, Arab Christians—immediately experienced violence and seizure of property.

As a result of Israeli occupation, many Palestinian Christians have emigrated in search of better living conditions and greater opportunities for their families. The depletion of Arab Christians in Israel and Palestine has been prominent. In 1948, for instance, Christians accounted for a little more than 15 percent of the population of Israel and Palestine; today, that number is around 1 percent.[13] In Jerusalem alone the number of Palestinian Christians living there has drastically reduced from thirty-one thousand in 1947 to less than ten thousand today.[14] And in the historic Christian city of Bethlehem, home to the Church of the Nativity, the Christian population has decreased from 75 percent in 1947 to 33 percent today.[15] Several Palestinian Christian leaders have publicized this trend and have founded an organization called Kairos Palestine to inform the global church of its current crisis.[16] Contrary to public speculation, these Christians do not attribute Christian emigration to Islam but to the policies of the state of Israel. The document "A Moment of Truth" says,

---

[13]Richard Wagner, *Dying in the Land of Promise: Palestine and Palestinian Christianity from Pentecost to 2000* (London: Melisende, 2003), 209.

[14]Betty Jane Bailey and J. Martin Bailey, *Who Are the Christians in the Middle East?* (Grand Rapids: Eerdmans, 2003), 156.

[15]Andrea Pacini, "Socio-Political and Community Dynamics of Arab Christians in Jordan, Israel, and the Autonomous Palestinian Territories," in *Christian Communities in the Arab Middle East: The Challenge of the Future*, ed. Andrea Pacini (Oxford: Clarendon, 1998), 282.

[16]See Kairos Palestine's homepage at www.kairospalestine.ps.

In this historic document, we Palestinian Christians declare that the military occupation of our land is a sin against God and humanity, and that any theology that legitimizes the occupation is far from Christian teachings because true Christian theology is a theology of love and solidarity with the oppressed.[17]

Despite the prominence of this organization in certain circles, most Christians on pilgrimage to the Holy Land are unaware that Christianity is evaporating in the region where the Holy Spirit was first poured down on the church. Meanwhile, pilgrimages to holy sites among Christians from around the world continue unabated, leading some local Christians to wonder whether historic churches will be devoid of the living Christians the churches were first constructed for.

A RELIGION RETURNING TO ITS ROOTS

In the end the complexity and diversity of Christianity in the Holy Land reflects that of Asian Christianity in general. Asia, the mother of Christianity, has witnessed its fair share of theological divisions and political strife. Despite its early and expansive history in this region, Christianity continues to be a minority religion among major religions like Islam, Buddhism and Hinduism, which many regard as more Asian than Christianity. Although the Asian church is growing more "Asian" each decade, centuries of association of this religion with Western imperialism persist. Only time will tell when or if the religion of Jesus Christ, who, after all, was born in Asia, died in Asia, and was raised again to life in Asia, will successfully embed itself in the hearts and minds of Asians just as the religions of Buddha, Confucius and Lao Tzu have.

---

[17]"A Moment of Truth," Kairos Palestine, www.kairospalestine.ps/content/kairos-document.

WORLD CHRISTIANITY BLOWING WHERE IT WILLS

The wind blows where it chooses, and you hear the sound of it,
but you do not know where it comes from or where it goes.

GOSPEL OF JOHN 3:8 (NRSV)

THE WIND BLOWS WHERE IT WISHES

The history of the worldwide Christian movement resembles the wind. It blows where it wishes and we can hear its sound and see its effects, but we cannot contain it and we do not know where it is going. We have witnessed how the divine wind empowered the earliest believers in Western Asia and scattered them across the known world—eastward to Syria, Iraq and Iran; southward to Arabia and Africa; westward to Cyprus, Italy, Greece and the Balkans; and northward to Armenia, Georgia and Turkey. The Christian movement gained momentum as it passed through Asia and Africa during the first millennium before crisscrossing Europe for several centuries. From Europe, Christianity began to impact Africa and Asia anew, and it completely shaped the American peoples. In the past two hundred years Christianity has transformed Oceania into one of the most Christianized regions in the entire world. And today the worldwide Christian movement is growing once more across parts of Africa, Asia and Latin America.

With only mild embellishment, scholars of yesteryear wrote the history of Christianity with Europe and Northern America as the primary backdrop. References to Christianity in Africa, Asia, Latin America and Oceania were stories on the fringe of a greater narrative that God was writing on the "real" pages of history—in the West. That day has passed. For not only does that kind of narration ignore countless individuals and communities who devoutly lived out their Christian faith—sometimes in incredibly difficult circumstances—but it also turns a blind eye to the historical record, which clearly demonstrates that Christianity has always been a worldwide Christian movement. As world historian Lamin Sanneh argues, the Christian message does not rightfully belong to any one culture or people, but has been translated into all languages and cultures and is therefore the rightful possession of *all* people. This thought has been echoed recently by many other historians: "It is becoming clearer that Christianity never was, and never will be, simply a Western faith; it has always interacted with culture in nuanced and culturally sophisticated ways as it migrated from the Middle East to Africa, Asia, Europe, and beyond."[1]

Christianity does not belong to Europe or America, or to Asia or Africa or Oceania any more than the wind can be captured, claimed and bottled. The wind continues to blow today, just as it did in the past. We can hear the sound of it and witness how it transforms peoples and cultures. But we do not know how long the wind will remain with us and where it will go next.

---

[1]Dyron Daughrity, *The Changing Face of World Christianity: The Global History of a Borderless Religion* (New York: Peter Lang, 2010), 227.

UNITED NATIONS
GEOSCHEME FOR NATIONS

For this book I have adopted the United Nations geoscheme for nations to demarcate the different world regions. In each section and chapter of the book you may refer to this list for clarity on which modern countries are referred to in each world region. As stated in the introduction, my aim generally has been to narrate the history of Christianity in each of the subregions for each chapter.

ASIA

- **Central:** Kazakhstan, Kyrgyzstan, Tajikistan, Turkmenistan, Uzbekistan
- **Eastern:** China, Japan, Mongolia, North Korea, South Korea
- **Southern:** Afghanistan, Bangladesh, Bhutan, India, Iran, Maldives, Nepal, Pakistan, Sri Lanka
- **Southeastern:** Brunei, Myanmar, Cambodia, Indonesia, Laos, Malaysia, Philippines, Singapore, Thailand, East Timor, Vietnam
- **Western:** Armenia, Azerbaijan, Bahrain, Cyprus, Georgia, Iraq, Israel, Jordan, Kuwait, Lebanon, Oman, Palestine, Qatar, Saudi Arabia, Syria, Turkey, United Arab Emirates, Yemen

AFRICA

- **Eastern:** Burundi, Comoros, Djibouti, Eritrea, Ethiopia, Kenya, Madagascar, Malawi, Mauritius, Mayotte, Mozambique, Reunion, Rwanda, Seychelles, Somalia, South Sudan, Tanzania, Uganda, Zambia, Zimbabwe

- **Central:** Angola, Cameroon, Central African Republic, Chad, Democratic Republic of the Congo, Equatorial Guinea, Gabon, Republic of the Congo, São Tomé and Principe
- **Northern:** Algeria, Egypt, Libya, Morocco, Sudan, Tunisia, Western Sahara
- **Southern:** Botswana, Lesotho, Namibia, South Africa, Swaziland
- **Western:** Benin, Burkina Faso, Cape Verde, Ivory Coast, The Gambia, Ghana, Guinea, Guinea-Bissau, Liberia, Mali, Mauritania, Niger, Nigeria, Senegal, Sierra Leone, Togo

Europe

- **Eastern:** Belarus, Bulgaria, Czech Republic, Hungary, Moldova, Poland, Romania, Russia, Slovakia, Ukraine
- **Northern:** Denmark, Estonia, Finland, Iceland, Ireland, Latvia, Lithuania, Norway, Sweden, United Kingdom
- **Southern:** Albania, Andorra, Bosnia and Herzegovina, Croatia, Greece, Italy, Malta, Montenegro, Portugal, Macedonia, Serbia, Slovenia, Spain, Vatican City
- **Western:** Austria, Belgium, France, Germany, Liechtenstein, Luxembourg, Monaco, Netherlands, Switzerland

Northern America

- Bermuda, Canada, Greenland, United States of America

Latin America

- **Caribbean:** Aruba, Bahamas, Barbados, British Virgin Islands, Cuba, Dominican Republic, Haiti, Jamaica, Puerto Rico, Trinidad and Tobago, US Virgin Islands
- **Central America:** Belize, Costa Rica, El Salvador, Guatemala, Honduras, Mexico, Nicaragua, Panama
- **South America:** Argentina, Bolivia, Brazil, Chile, Colombia, Ecuador, Falkland Islands, French Guinea, (British) Guinea, Paraguay, Peru, Suriname (Dutch Guyana), Uruguay, Venezuela

OCEANIA

- **Australia:** Australia and New Zealand
- **Melanesia:** Fiji, New Caledonia, Papua New Guinea, Solomon Islands, Vanuatu
- **Micronesia:** Guam, Kiribati, Marshall Islands, Micronesia, Nauru, Northern Mariana Islands, Palau
- **Polynesia:** American Samoa, Cook Islands, French Polynesia, Niue, Pitcairn Islands, Samoa, Tokelau, Tonga, Tuvalu, Wallis and Futuna

GLOSSARY

Aksum(ite). Aksum was the capital of the Aksumite Empire, a kingdom ruling over Ethiopia (and at times, surrounding nations) from roughly AD 100 to 1000. Originally Jewish in religion, Christianity became the state religion in the fourth century. It was Miaphysite in theology and therefore part of the Oriental Orthodox Church. According to some, the Ark of the Covenant is currently located in a church in Axum, the ancient capital of the Aksumite Empire in the northern part of Ethiopia today.

Arian(ism). Arius was a fourth-century priest from modern Libya who taught that Jesus was God's first creation and thus not of the same substance as God the Father. Arius and his theology, called Arianism, were condemned at the First Ecumenical Council in 325. Nevertheless, Arianism prevailed for several decades more, and the Germanic peoples initially adopted Arian Christianity before later converting to Catholicism.

Asia Minor. "Small Asia" in Greek, this was the ancient region corresponding to most of modern Turkey, specifically the western portion of Turkey. It was a thoroughly Christianized region before the emergence and expansion of Islam.

autocephaly, autocephalous. "Self-headed" in Greek, churches that were autocephalous did not report to any higher-ranking churches (specifically, to their bishops). The Church of the East, for instance, became autocephalous by the fifth century.

Byzantine (Empire). Named after the ancient city of Byzantium (or Byzantion), the Byzantine Empire was the East Roman Empire. Scholars commonly date this empire from 330, the year Constantine consecrated the city of Constantinople (its capital), to 1453, the year that city was overtaken by the (Muslim) Ottoman Turks. From 1204 to 1261, the Byzantine Empire was ruled by Latin Christians. Residents of Constantinople called themselves Romans and spoke Greek.

Caliph. "Successor" in Arabic, the caliph or *calipha* was the head of Islamic world. The term had both a political and religious overtone.

Catholic Church. The church forming out of the (West) Roman Empire, which eventually wielded great authority over much of Europe. The head of the Catholic Church is the bishop of Rome—the pope, the first of whom is believed to be the apostle Peter.

Chalcedonian(ism), non-Chalcedonian(ism). Referring to the theology codified at the Council of Chalcedon in 451, namely, that Christ was one person with two inseparable and nonmingled human and divine natures. The Byzantines and Catholics held to Chalcedonian theology; the Church of the East and the Oriental Orthodox Church were considered non-Chalcedonians since they rejected the definition of Christ's union as defined by the Council of Chalcedon.

Church of the East. A Syriac-based church founded in the first century (and active today). This was the most geographically widespread church body during the early and medieval periods, almost principally confined to Asia. They are also called East Syrians. They were unfairly dismissed as "Nestorians" in generations past and recently rehabilitated as a crucial body of the worldwide church by scholars. They were condemned by the Eastern Orthodox at the Council of Chalcedon (451).

consubstantial, homoousios. "With the substance" in Latin, this term asserts that Christ is of the same substance as God the Father. It is based on the Greek term *homoousios*, which means "same substance" in Greek. Though in existence before, these terms came to prominence in the early christological disputes of the fourth century.

dhimmi, dhimmitude. Coming from the word "protected person" in Arabic, a dhimmi was a protected group under Islamic law. For our purposes Christians were dhimmis. By law Muslim governments were supposed to protect them from harm. Dhimmis paid higher taxes than Muslims and lived in separate neighborhoods, but were otherwise free to worship given that they did not break any Islamic laws. Scholars invented the word *dhimmitude* to refer to the structure of being a dhimmi.

diophysite, dyophysitism. "Two natures" in Greek, the term was principally used during the Christological disputes. Diophysites believed that Christ had two natures—one fully human and one fully divine. Technically, both Byzantine and East Syrian Christians were diophysites, though these two strenuously disagreed with each other. Usually the term is put in contrast to miaphysitism.

Donatism. Coming from the name Donatus, an influential bishop in this movement, Donatists were Christians in the Roman Empire (specifically Northern Europe and Southern Europe) who separated from the Catholic Church. Donatists believed that Catholics had lost their purity since they too liberally allowed backsliders and apostates during times of persecution to return to the church.

East Syrian(s). The adjective for those in the Church of the East. East Syrians (diophysites) are to be contrasted with West Syrians (miaphysites).

Eastern Orthodox(y). The common way to refer to the type of Christianity that coalesced during the Byzantine Empire. It was the state religion of the Byzantine Empire, with the bishop of Constantinople regarded as its head. They were (and are) widely dispersed across Eastern Europe, (eastern) Southern Europe and Western Asia.

Franks. A Germanic people that transformed the (West) Roman Empire. During the Middle Ages the Franks ruled over much of Southern and Western Europe, and Charlemagne was the most famous ruler. West Francia is mostly France today, while East Francia is mostly Germany.

Germanic. Referring to the people groups speaking a Germanic-based language in the (West) Roman Empire. The Germanic peoples were largely Arian before converting to Catholic Christianity and assimilating into the Roman Empire.

Gnostic(ism). Coming from the word *knowledge* in Greek, Gnostic Christians were collectively condemned by mainstream Christians in the early church on account of their theology, which has come down to us primarily in the Nag Hammadi Library, unearthed in the 1940s. They affirmed secret knowledge and preferred to see Christ on earth as a divine being trapped in a human shell and thus denied his full humanity.

Jacobite. Named after the sixth-century bishop of Edessa, Jacob Baradaeus, "Jacobites" was a pejorative way to refer to miaphysite Christians.

Maghreb. "West" in Arabic, the Maghreb was the region Muslims used to describe what we call today northwest Africa, from Libya to Morocco.

Manichaean(ism). Named after its third-century founder, Mani, Manichaeanism was a religion of Iranian origin. It was a large and very influential religion that spread across Asia, Northern Africa and Europe. There were Manichaean Churches, though they did not survive the Middle Ages.

Melkite. "The king's men" in Syriac, this term was a pejorative way for non-Chalcedonian Christians to refer to Eastern Orthodox Christians who were not living in the Byzantine Empire.

miaphysitism, monophysitism. Miaphysitism means "one nature" in Greek, while monophysitism has the sense of "[only] one nature." In the past, Jacobite or Oriental Orthodox Christians were called monophysite under the notion that all such Christians believed that Christ only had one nature—the divine. Today, scholars opt for the more neutral term *miaphysitism*, implying that such Christians believed that Christ had one human and divine nature.

Montanism. Named after its second-century founder Montanus, Montanism was a Christian church that stressed the ongoing work of the Holy Spirit, equality of sexes in leadership and rigorous spiritual practices. Called "the New Prophecy," this church tradition was stamped out during the sixth century by the Byzantine Empire.

Nestorian(ism). Named after the fifth-century bishop of Constantinople, Nestorius, Nestorianism was the common way to refer to East Syrians, that is, the Church of the East. It's now an outdated term since it has been proven that the theology of the Church of the East was not based on Nestorius; nor, in fact, was Nestorius himself really a "Nestorian"—a term that came to refer to someone who so divided Christ's human and divine natures that he was two persons.

Nubia(n). In the ancient world a region along the Nile River in what is now mostly Sudan. The Nubians embraced Christianity as their state religion in the sixth century. As miaphysite Christians, we group them under the Oriental Orthodox Church; they were under the ecclesial head of the patriarch, or pope, of Alexandria.

Oriental Orthodox(y). An Orthodox group of Christianity believing that Christ the Word had one human and divine nature. Hence they were miaphysites. They were condemned at the Council of Ephesus (431) by the Eastern Orthodox Church. They were widely represented among the Copts (in Egypt), Nubians (in the Sudan), Aksumites (in Ethiopia), Jacobites (in West Syria), Arabians (in the Arabian Peninsula) and the Armenians (in Armenia).

Orthodox(y). Meaning something like "right praise" in Greek, the term has two major meanings. The first, and more general in tone (and in lowercase), is a way to refer to someone understood to be correct in theology. When capitalized, it refers to the ancient body of Christians who were part of one of three Orthodox bodies: the Eastern Orthodox (seen as the only "orthodox" Orthodox body for centuries), the Church of the East, and the Oriental Orthodox Church.

Pentecostal(ism). Deriving from the word *Pentecost*, Pentecostalism is the fastest-growing segment of Christianity in the world today, with well more than 500 million Christians. Pentecostalism emerged during the first decade of the twentieth century across the world. Although the term *Pentecostal* is often distinguished from *charismatic*, I do not make that distinction in the book. Pentecostalism emerged out of Protestantism; it emphasizes the continuation of the spiritual gifts during New Testament times, for instance, speaking in tongues and divine healing.

Slav(ic). The Slavs are a people group prevalent in Eastern Europe and (eastern) Southern Europe. From the ninth century onward many Slavs converted to Eastern Orthodoxy. Yugoslavia (discussed in chap. 7) was a recent (but unsuccessful) attempt to unite some of the various Slavic peoples under one rule.

West Syrian. A common adjective used to describe Christians from the Oriental Orthodox Church.

NAME AND SUBJECT INDEX

Finding the Textbook You Need

The IVP Academic Textbook Selector
is an online tool for instantly finding the IVP books
suitable for over 250 courses across 24 disciplines.

www.ivpress.com/academic/